THE BEST SHORT STORIES OF PHILADELPHIA

Quinn D. Eli, Guest Editor
Matthew M. Perez, Editor

Copyright © 2021 by Toho Publishing

All rights reserved. Published by Toho Publishing LLC, Philadelphia, in 2021.

No part of this work may be reproduced or transmitted in any form or by any means, electronic or mechanical, including photocopying and recording, or by any information storage or retrieval system without the proper written permission of the copyright owner unless such copying is expressly permitted by federal copyright law. Toho Publishing is not authorized to grant permission for further uses of copyrighted selections reprinted in this book without the permission of their owners. Permission must be obtained from the individual copyright owners, the authors, herein.

FIRST EDITION

Cover design by Andrés Cruciani
Cover art, *A Silent Storm Approaches*, by Alexandra Marie Morehead
Original layout design by Ana Mitchell
Layout by Matthew M. Perez

Guest editor: Quinn D. Eli
Editor: Matthew M. Perez

ISBN 978-1-954093-10-2 (paperback)

"Getting Out" is published by permission of the *Madison Review*.

Versions of some of these stories first appeared in the following publications, to whose editors grateful acknowledgment is made: *Hotel Amerika*, *Kweli Journal*, and *Wilderness House Literary Review*.

www.tohopub.com

To the people of Philadelphia

Contents

ix   Foreword by Quinn D. Eli

FIRSTS

3   Jamari
     Christine Kendall

6   Getting Out
     Bill Hemmig

13   Billy Jack
     Julie Odell

22   Nobody Makes It Big in Philly
     Pietra Dunmore

25   Zane Anderson, MFT, PsyD
     Louise Bierig

29   Fortune's Wish
     K. B. Carle

33   The Shape of Stealing
     Tracey Levine

41   Boxes
     Skylar Althouse

50   Crabs
     Sam Gridley

Contents

57	Green Suede Shoes	
	Liz Waldie	
68	The Sitting Tree	
	Constance Garcia-Barrio	

COMMUNITY

79	Philly Scam, or Paying It Forward	
	Oni Lasana	
84	Praying for a Miracle, Praying for Absolution	
	Shannon Frost Greenstein	
91	The Weight of It	
	Thalia Geiger	
100	Manayunk	
	Peter Cunniffe	
109	Amalgam	
	Selene Lacayo	
118	Obligation	
	Herman Beavers	
122	Charlie Parker Has a Voicemail	
	Sophia DuRose	
131	Graves & Glory	
	Jeannine Cook	
140	Road Show	
	Liz Kerr	
147	Mysteries of the Street	
	Ann de Forest	
154	Pests	
	Sofia Rabaté	
159	Mr. Friend	
	Jeffrey S. Markovitz	

Contents

172   Chuck Taylors
      Robin Jarrett

177   Turnabout
      Will Clattenburg

180   Balayage
      Debra Leigh Scott

192   Take a Joke, Leave a Joke
      Neil R. Wells

202   Penny Ante
      Roland Williams

212   Driving
      Joshua Isard

218   Cadillac
      Chuck Corson

225   Hope Is Dawning for Peace in the Congo
      Anndee Hochman

RELATIONSHIPS

237   Millie Floating
      David Biddle

247   An Old-Fashioned Story
      Andie Tursi

257   Three Yellow Lights
      Corianna Jackson

265   I Was Always a Mad Comet, but You Have Fixed Me
      Stephanie King

270   Chill
      Amy Beth Sisson

276   How to Walk across the Beach: A Simple 66-Step Guide
      Nicholas Puntel

Contents

280   The Wingman: A Philadelphia Story
Melissa Strong

286   Lilith and Adam
Kathleen Murphey

294   Red Flags
Jamila Beale

300   Bliss
Merry Jones

Please note: several of the stories in this collection contain depictions of sexual violence.

Foreword

Not everyone is cut out for cities. The loveless pace and indiscriminate noise. The graying clouds and crowded streets. All my life I've categorized humans according to their viewpoint on living in cities—those who embrace it versus those who avoid it—and my sympathies lean always toward those who take on the challenge, navigate the pavement, and rush head-on into city living, with arms and hearts wide open. If nothing else, it tends to make us resilient. Forces us at every moment to take stock of our surroundings. So even if we eventually leave the city—chasing some elusive dream to the countryside or the oceanside or, God help us, the suburbs—at least we know we gave the city a chance and lived to tell the tale.

This book you're holding is a chronicle of those tales, a compendium of stories and reflections on what it means to live in, around, near, or adjacent to the City of Brotherly Love, if not geographically, then spiritually. The authors represent some of the best Philadelphia has to offer, and their gifts—and insights—are as vast as they are prodigious.

In these pages, you will find a fairly comprehensive map of human experience: childhoods disrupted by unexpected events, love affairs torn asunder, passionate encounters among strangers, class wars and racial strife, and neighbors coming to the rescue of neighbors. There is a disquieting but ultimately familiar intimacy to these stories, a reminder that no matter your neighborhood, your tribe, your language, we are all of us heart, blood, and bone under the skin.

Foreword

Lurking here, too, is a synthesis of Philadelphia's history, traditions, and uniquely blended culture. I don't mean cheesesteaks and *Rocky*, or Rizzo and Street, or paeans to the birthplace of the Three-Fifths Compromise. Rather, I mean that our diverse neighborhoods and citizens exist side by side, engaged in an unruly, ongoing discussion about what it means to be human and free and self-determining in the very location that such conversations were first codified in this strange experiment of a nation.

This tradition—this debate—about how to live in peace, build community, and find love, grace, and fellowship is one that Philadelphians carry on each day, often at loud volume, from Kensington to Manayunk, from Olney to Fairmount, from West Philly to Fishtown. You'll see that conversation brought to life in these pages, dramatized in the stories and conflicts of everyday humans, brought together by twisted fate to a Lenape land. And apparently—to paraphrase Luther Vandross, a great and departed Philadelphian—together is where we're meant to be.

In other words, Dear Reader, this isn't simply a collection of the best stories of Philadelphia; more accurately, it's the *best* of Philadelphia as a whole—a hodgepodge of tales of what it means to embrace this city, negotiating its rough and scenic terrain, accompanied on the journey by friends and family and lovers and strangers, all of us pressed in close proximity, striving to be our best selves.

Quinn D. Eli
Philadelphia, March 2021

FIRSTS

Jamari

Christine Kendall

Miss Anderson's scared of Jamari. Our whole class knows that. Well, everybody except Jamari. He doesn't know 'cause he likes school. Jamari likes everything: birds, drawing, and snakes, like the yellow-and-green one we found near the piers in Riverside Park. Jamari says it's a corn snake. He knows 'cause he looks up stuff to show Miss Anderson. He likes her so much, but she doesn't like him back.

I think she's mad, too, 'cause we're twins—Jamel and Jamari Walker. Her face gets all squinched up whenever she says our names. So, after what happened, I asked Mama why she had two eight-year-old boys at the same time. She was standing in front of the refrigerator looking at the picture Jamari made today. It shows a boy pointing up at the sky wearing big, big glasses. Mama didn't answer me, so I asked again.

She said we weren't eight when she had us. I went outside after that and sat down on the stoop. A little bit of water was still trickling under the curb from Mr. Witherspoon washing his car again, and there was quiet church music next door. Some big kids were playing basketball in the street, but I didn't wanna ask if I could go down there. A red bird was up in the elm tree, and Mama came looking for me. She gave me a popsicle and sat down real close. She smelled sweet, like Johnson's baby powder.

"Twins are double luck, Jamel." She tickled me under my arm, and it made the popsicle crash up against my front teeth. "Double love and—"

"Double dirty," I said. I stretched out my T-shirt, so she could see the raspberry popsicle stains that were already all down my front.

Mama laughed and then she didn't look so tired. She looked like Sunday morning's pancakes, light brown and airy. Her curly hair was like the syrup that drips over the sides. The red bird chirped, and Mama looked up into the treetops.

"How many cardinals do you think there are in Harlem?" she said.

"I don't know." I wrapped my twisted-up napkin around the popsicle stick. "That's a Jamari kinda question."

Mama looked off down the street. "How was it at school without your brother?" she said. Her voice sounded different. It sounded like it did after she finished talking to the principal about Miss Anderson. I said school was okay 'cause I didn't want to make her mad again. I didn't want to see her get so mad and then sad and then cry like she did when I told her Jamari got handcuffed by the school resource officer, so I didn't say how Miss Anderson wouldn't look at me the whole day. "He didn't do anything wrong, you know. There's nothing wrong with asking questions."

I knew that already; she told us that before. Mama should tell Miss Anderson. She's the one who doesn't know. She turns red every time Jamari asks one of his million questions. He jumps up and down kinda like a rocket until he gets an answer. And even after he gets one answer, sometimes he keeps asking more and more questions 'cause he's just thinking real hard. I think his head is exploding 'cause he's so smart. Somebody should tell Miss Anderson not to be afraid. Jamari saves up questions for her 'cause she's the teacher.

Mama stood up and dusted off the back of her skirt. "Let's go find your brother," she said.

"He's drawing a picture for Miss Anderson."

"A picture?" Her head jerked back real hard, and she touched her skirt again. "A picture of what, Jamel? She called the police on my child."

Mama turned around so fast I was afraid she was gonna lose her balance and fall down the stoop. She snatched the door open, tore down the hallway, and ran into our apartment like a tornado. I followed her in.

"Jamari, come out here right now," I could hear her saying. Mama ran into our bedroom, but he wasn't there. "Jamari," she called again. She sounded like she did when I got lost at Great Adventure.

We went into the kitchen, and I saw the scissors drawer hanging open. Then I heard Jamari humming out on the back steps. We went outside and there he was. He was down on his knees with a long, long, long piece of brown shopping bag. That's how he makes his drawing paper, by cutting the handles and the bottoms off, but this time he did way more. He'd taped all the bags Mama keeps under the sink together into one piece. It was falling down the steps, and it showed a row of big brownstones, Mr. Witherspoon's car, the yellow curtains on the church lady's window next door, just our whole block with all our birds all over it—cardinals, blue jays, and hawks like we see over by the river.

Mama slumped against the screen door and put her hand over her heart. "That's beautiful, Jamari. What are you going to do with it?"

"I'm gonna give it to Miss Anderson," he said. "She told the cops there aren't any birds in Harlem."

Christine Kendall's short fiction has been published in numerous literary journals. "Jamari" was previously published in the Kweli Journal. *She is the author of the middle-grade novels* Riding Chance *(Scholastic, 2016) and* The True Definition of Neva Beane *(Scholastic, 2020). She resides in Philadelphia, where she cocurates and hosts the award-winning prose reading series* Creative at the Cannery.

Getting Out

Bill Hemmig

They declared their partnership over last month, Corbett moved out on Saturday, and now it's Monday, and John is alone in the house, getting ready for work. He's gotten dressed and is standing in the center of the en suite master bath. He fixes his eyes and ears on the toilet. Its lid is down and it is not running. His eyes move to the wall switches near the shower. One controls the twin heat lamps and one controls the exhaust fan. But there's too much light in the room. The ceiling light is still on and it can't be and so none of this can start yet. He goes to the double switch by the bathroom doorway and turns off the ceiling light. Now it can start.

He reestablishes himself in the center of the room. He is able, has been for a long time now, thanks to the coaching of his therapist, to check everything off the list without having to touch it all. In addition to enabling me to get out of the house faster in the morning, this has enabled me—or rather, this enabled me, simple past tense—to complete signing off on the bathroom with diminished commentary from Corbett.

He fixes his eyes and ears on the toilet. The lid is down and it is not running. His eyes move to the wall switches near the shower. Both are in the off position. He finds himself across the room, touching the switches. They are not warm and they are in the off position. Of course they are, stop it, you're past touching everything, stop it or you'll have to tell Maureen that you backslid after all this time, it's because Corbett isn't watching. He steps away from the switches.

For eighteen years Corbett's worked—no, Corbett worked—from home, and every weekday he'd just be getting out of bed as I was getting ready to get out of the house and go to work. It took several years for the checklist to fully take hold, but once it had I thought it was just coincidence at first, but then I realized, no, he's choreographed the beginning of his day in order to follow me through the checklist.

"The toilet's not running," he'd say.

"It's August. No one's had the heat lamps on since March," he'd say.

I found Maureen, and she coached me eventually to reduce it to only visual checkpoints. And not to get distracted.

Which he now is. Distraction means starting over. It has to be a clean sweep once all the lights are off, toilet, heat lamp switch, exhaust fan switch, so on.

Visual checkpoints only.

He stands in the center of the room. Eyes and ears on the toilet, fixed on it long enough to form an acknowledgment. The lid is down and the toilet is not running. To the wall switches near the shower. Heat lamp switch off. Exhaust fan switch off. He backs up two steps and looks up. Heat lamps off, the ceiling fan is still, the ceiling light is out.

"Yes, everything is off," Corbett would sigh from the bed or just beyond the bathroom doorway. The bathroom door is open when the toilet is not in use. That's always how it is.

He is on his toes, arm stretched upward, three fingers against the motor housing of the ceiling fan. It is not warm. Of course it's not warm, it wasn't on this morning.

He pulls his hand away. This is not good. I have to get out.

This is, was, such a part of why the relationship had to end. He must have believed he was encouraging me to stop, and yes, I see where he would find it personally frustrating, but how could he not see that he was making me feel stupid and helpless? So finally I found Maureen and she coached me to reduce it to a series of visual checkpoints. That made it less obvious. And me less vulnerable to him.

"Yes, the ceiling fan is off. It's the dead of winter. Nobody uses it."

And the fear of hearing that was enough to send me on to the next checkpoint.

Back to the center of the room. Toilet lid down. Toilet not running. Wall switches near the shower. Heat lamp switch off. Exhaust fan switch off. Back up, back up, stop. He looks up. The heat lamps are off. The ceiling fan is still. The ceiling light is off. He turns toward the doorway. There's a rhythm to this when it runs smoothly, like clockwork. Clocks are so wonderfully complicated, all those dozens of gears and wheels and springs and pins behind the face and the hands and the hours and minutes, and they all need to be clean and work perfectly together, and that's why I have the shop in town full of lovely old clocks and I fix and clean them and make them run. And when it's all working perfectly, you don't know any of it is there, you don't see the gears and wheels and springs and pins, you just see time passing, like Corbett back there observing only a clean, smooth series of visual checkpoints and still sometimes—"Trust me, dear, the bathroom light's been out for ten minutes." I never respond—responded (must work on adjusting my tenses)—because that would (a) constitute a confession and (b) prolong the distraction he'd just supplied me.

Crap.

He doesn't check the time because that's not part of Getting Off the Second Floor and it doesn't matter. He knows it's getting late, later than usual. The clocks in the kitchen—the oven, the microwave, the toaster oven—are still to come. He'll find out then. Corbett has moved out. He reestablishes himself in the center of the room.

Toilet lid down. Toilet not running. Wall switches near the shower. Heat lamp switch off. Exhaust fan switch off. Back up, back up, stop. He looks up. Heat lamps are off. Ceiling fan is still. Ceiling light is off. He turns toward the doorway and fixes on the switches for the ceiling light and ceiling fan. Switch for ceiling light is in the off position. Switch for ceiling fan is in the off position. He leaves the bathroom and walks the length of the bedroom. The bedroom ceiling light is out. The switch for the bedroom ceiling light is by the door. The switch for the bedroom ceiling light is in the off position.

The bedroom door is always open. He leaves the bedroom. Like clockwork.

Heading toward the stairs and then down, I'm reminded again that I never need to checklist everything—anything, nothing at all—in the hall, the guest room, the guest bathroom, Corbett's office, the stairs.

Nor do I need to check off anything in the front hall or the living room or the dining room. He goes to the front hall closet and pulls out his coat and scarf and puts them on. Why can I glide by or through all these other spaces without making checklists of them? He goes to the hall table with its drawer and takes up his wallet, cell phone, and keys. I do make a mental note of the lack of checklists as I pass by or through each, as I've just been doing, but that is not the same. After all, every part of the house contains the gears, wheels, springs, and pins that make it run. He stuffs everything into his coat pockets and then goes to the kitchen.

Before today Corbett would have pulled on his bathrobe and slippers as I was occupied in the coat closet and come down to the kitchen to make himself a pot of coffee. He would be standing at the island right now or at the stove.

He begins his sweep of the kitchen. Tugging on the knob to the back door will make a sound that will attract derision, and so he can see in the space between the door and the jamb that the dead bolt is in place.

"Are you afraid that if the back door is unlocked someone will come in and steal me?"

Corbett is not here. Corbett has moved out.

So wait. Does, did, Corbett follow me only through the rooms that I had checklisted? Or did I checklist only the rooms that Corbett uses—used—at this time of day?

He reaches out and tugs on the doorknob. The door is in fact locked. Stop. No backsliding. You'll have to tell Maureen.

His eyes return to the space between the door and the jamb.

I don't know what my role is here without him.

Visual checkpoints only. Must get out. The toaster oven is next to the back door. The microwave is above it. Both are plugged into the double wall socket beside the toaster oven. Both have digital clocks that aren't really clocks at all, they're just little computers that tell you the time. Which is eight forty in the first case and eight thirty-nine in the second. If they were real clocks, it would be possible to get them perfectly in sync, but they are not real clocks as the microwave clock goes over to eight forty. Visual checkpoints only. Both machines are turned off, and of course there are no sparks shooting out of the wall sockets around the plugs. He finds three fingers and a thumb lightly squeezing the plug to the microwave. The plug is not warm.

"It's all right, dear, the appliances aren't overheating while turned off."

Corbett is not here.

His hand drifts down to the plug to the toaster oven. The plug is not warm.

Stop. Of course the plugs aren't warm. Visual checkpoints only.

It is now eight forty-one and eight forty. It's a fifteen-minute drive into town. If I get out of here in the next four or five minutes like a normal person, I'll get the shop open in time, and I do know enough not to schedule customers for nine, but I have what's-his-name coming in at nine fifteen with his Seth Thomas for cleaning. Visual checkpoints only.

Visual checkpoints mean somewhat less derision and humiliation.

So let's say Corbett has not moved out. Let's say he's standing by the stove boiling water for coffee or across at the island spooning coffee into the press pot while the water heats up.

"Seriously, dear, I'm not going anywhere. I'll make sure the kitchen doesn't explode in your absence."

For the moment, toaster oven and microwave are in agreement at eight forty-two. His eyes make a deliberate sweep of buttons and dials and plugs. Both machines are turned off and the plugs are calm. On to the refrigerator. Visual check that the doors are completely closed, which they are. Now to the sink, in the corner under the window. Three checkpoints in a vertical stack, bottom to top.

"After you're gone I'm going to wash up after breakfast. After which for my own amusement I will stop up the sink and run water until the whole place floods. I promise to clean up before you get home."

Vertical stack, bottom to top. Drain filter: in the open position. Faucet: no water is dripping. Window: lock in the locked position. He turns away from the sink. The stove is ahead on his left and the island ahead on his right. He approaches. The not-a-real-clock on the stove tells him that it's eight forty-four, which is ludicrous if it was just eight forty-two behind him thirty seconds ago. I'll have to fix that but not now, now I must glance very quickly at each of the dials that light the burners except the one that Corbett is using to boil water for coffee and make sure that the rest are in the off position except that Corbett is not here.

His hand goes to each one of the dials that light the burners, and it jiggles each one gently and acknowledges one and two and three and four and five and six and also, yes, the center dial that controls the oven, that each is in fact in the off position.

Corbett is not boiling water for coffee.

The kitchen ceiling light is on. It stays on when I get out of the house because Corbett is still in the kitchen.

Corbett is not in the kitchen.

Corbett is not here.

When I get out of the house, it will be empty.

Is it possible to miss someone's worst qualities most of all?

The ceiling light will need to be turned off, and then I will need to acknowledge that it is off and then that the switch is in the off position. The not-a-real-clock on the stove needs to be reset.

There may also be lights on in the living room. The dining room. The fireplace flue might be open. The light in the front hall.

Maybe the back door is unlocked.

The gears and wheels and springs and pins have stopped and the house is broken.

He walks around the island, where there is no press pot. He returns to the back door and tugs on the knob.

Bill Hemmig's novella, Brethren Hollow, *was recently published by Read Furiously, which also published one of his short stories in* The World Takes: Life in the Garden State, *an anthology of writings about New Jersey. He was also recently published in* Philadelphia Stories. *He holds a degree from the University of Pennsylvania and lives in Bucks County. "Getting Out" originally appeared in the* Madison Review.

Billy Jack

Julie Odell

"Billy Jack!" my father shouted. "Lucy, it's Billy Jack!"

I was in the kitchen grilling cheddar and tomato sandwiches with spicy brown mustard, my father's favorite. I cut them on the diagonal and flipped them onto plates.

My father leaned back in his recliner. I handed him his plate and sat cross-legged on the couch. "Is this the original?"

"No. *The Trial of*. But he's still tough."

"I don't know," I said. "He kicks more in the original." I bit into my sandwich, and the hot mustard flooded my sinuses.

My father ate his sandwich in huge, brutish bites. He wiped his mouth with his napkin, crumbled it, and dropped it over the side of his chair. He was a Neanderthal with his food, hurtling toward it like he was starving, devouring it and leaving the ruins of his meals wherever he wanted. Lately everything he did disgusted me, every bad habit amplified.

I watched my father watch *Billy Jack*. His arm hung over the edge of the recliner, and he clenched and unclenched his fist. He'd boxed when he was younger, still lifted weights in the basement, but he ate too much and was fat. I looked back at the TV. Billy Jack was talking to the cops.

We'd seen this movie three times already. I used to think I'd never get sick of it, wondered who liked it more, me or my father, but today it just seemed stupid, basically a cartoon.

* * *

Todd Alstead started on the bus. He sat behind me and chanted my name under his breath. "Lucy, Loooseee." I never turned around.

He was a junior. He smoked pot and wore black Rush T-shirts and scuffed work boots with the laces open at the ankles. At school he stood in the hallway outside the gym with the other stoners, slouched against the wall with their thumbs hooked in the belt loops of their jeans. They lazily mocked the rest of us, the good kids. I noticed them, especially Todd with his long, tight thighs. But I was a clean-scrubbed freshman and thought his attention on me was boredom at best.

He started coming to the tennis courts after school where I played challenge matches day after day for ranking on the girls' team. He sat in the passenger seat of his friend Scott's Ford Bronco, way up high on monster truck wheels. He made me sweat large ugly half-moons under the arms of my pink tennis team T-shirt, and I tugged at the back of my shorts.

Once when I turned to fetch a stray ball, Todd thrust his head out the window. "Wanna party with me, Lucy?" He didn't yell. He said it in a normal voice like he really meant it.

I hated the challenge matches. I longed to just rally without keeping score. I wanted to hit the ball squarely, feel the solid ping of my racquet vibrating up through my arm, through my torso. But the coach made us compete every day, and I had to pull my seed from seventeen to fifteen to stay on the team. I was getting headaches at the base of my skull.

Todd clearly sensed my anxiety. "Hey, Lucy," he shouted once in the middle of my serve, "show me the way, baby."

I wanted to think he liked me, understood that my goody-goody clothes were my mother's choice, not mine, and that inside my bland exterior was a girl who might be wild. But he was too much: too sexy and too dangerous. He just wanted to make me squirm. His attention felt more like rejection than if he'd never paid attention to me at all, and it filled me with a new kind of anger I'd never felt before.

I was losing at tennis. When I got the nerve for a quick comeback, the best I could do was turn to the Bronco and yell,

"Get the hell out of my life, Todd Alstead. I hate you!" Todd and Scott laughed, and I felt worse. The Bronco remained at the courts.

* * *

Friday night my family returned from a concert at the junior high where my little brother played second violin in the orchestra. It had rained while we were out, and as we turned up the driveway and the car's headlights moved across the wet lawn, I could see that something wasn't right. The yard was lumpy, dark.

My father backed up and maneuvered the car so the headlights played right on the house. "What the—" my mother gasped. Large swaths of mud had been flung to the second-floor windows.

"Somebody spun their tires," my father said. "Some goddamned son of a bitch backed their vehicle onto the fucking lawn and spun their goddamned tires all over the grass."

He pulled the car up the driveway and jumped out of the driver's seat. "Who the hell would do this?" he said, jacked up as he stepped back and forth over the tracks like a detective.

I got out of the car and followed him. "I know!" I offered, thrilled. "It's Scott Brubaker's Bronco. Him and Todd Alstead."

A frantic desire for vengeance coursed through me as I told my father about Todd and the tennis courts. I made Todd's taunts sound menacing, even threatening. "Dad, he's such a . . . goddamned shit. I'm going to get kicked off the team if he doesn't stop."

* * *

I lay across my bed doing algebra a few nights later when my father knocked on my door. "Hey, Lucy," he said. "I've been thinking. It's time to give a little what-for to that asshole Alstead."

I sat up. "What?"

"Okay," my father said, putting his hands up, ready to lay it out. "I'm not going to hurt him. I'm going to scare him. I'll go to his house, maybe throw rocks at his window or something. Get him outside for a little, you know, a little man-to-man."

"Why don't you just go to the door? You could talk to his dad."

My father shook his head. "No. That's a weak move. I want a *private* conversation with him."

My mind went blank for a second, and then I felt that same loathing I'd felt when we were watching *Billy Jack*. What the hell kind of crazy scheme had he cooked up down there on the recliner, where he spent half his life watching how many vigilante movies? I stared at him, at his bright, sweaty face, eyes ablaze. I wanted to throw my algebra book at his head.

But maybe it would work. Why not use my father's lunacy to my advantage and let him mess with Alstead? He deserved it. I felt a little jolt of excitement.

But then I wondered whether it really was Todd and Scott who tore up the lawn. It could have been anyone, really, random vandalism. Still, did it matter? "Yeah," I said. "Go ahead, Dad."

My father's face went slack. "I was thinking maybe you'd like to come with me," he said.

Was he kidding? I was ten minutes away from washing my face and putting on pajamas. But he looked so sad. "Fine," I said. His face lit up again. "But I'm staying in the car." I left my algebra book open and didn't bother to put on any shoes.

My mother was curled neatly in the corner of the couch, reading a book under the yellow glow of a lamp. "Hey guys," she said with a smile. "Where are you two headed?"

"Ice cream," my father said.

I admired the deftness of his lie. "Want some?" I asked, the ready accomplice.

My mother shook her head as I knew she would; she rarely ate sweets.

My father wore a black T-shirt and black sweatpants. He

looked fit in the outfit; the black hid his belly and he looked tough. Ready.

The glowing dash inside the car threw a greenish cast across my father's face as we drove. Todd's house was in Greenwood, the next development over, and I wondered if he ever thought about how easy it would be to come to *my* bedroom window in the night. But that was ridiculous. I wasn't his lust object; I was his joke. He wouldn't be coming to my room or to my house. But here I was, going to his.

My father cut the engine a few houses away, and we coasted to the curb. "Hey, Lucy," he said, "this is gonna be fun." He pulled up a leg of his sweatpants, and I saw the handle of my mother's best knife coming out of his sock.

"Jeez, Dad," I said, and thought of my father with his huge, muscular arm curled around Todd's skinny neck. I felt my father's pleasure in pretending he was Charles Bronson or Clint Eastwood, a lone vigilante with a long, sharp knife under Todd's pimply chin. I knew my father dreamed of moments like that.

But then I began to really doubt Todd and Scott had torn up the lawn. This was crazy. "I don't think you need the knife, Dad," I said. "I think if you just threw rocks at his window or whatever, that would be enough."

"Oh, come on, Lucy—that little shit is messing with you."

"Fine," I said. "Do what you want."

"What do you care what I do to him anyway?" he asked. "Unless you like this punk. Unless this is the sort of attention you go for."

I shook my head.

"Huh, Lucy Goose," my father said, leering at me now across the console. "Do you think I'm going too far? Is that it? I thought you knew how to play this game."

I could smell his aftershave. I also smelled liquor on his breath, coming off his skin. Why hadn't I noticed it before?

"Lucy Goose," I repeated. It was a ridiculous nickname, and my father was a ridiculous man. "Fuck you, Dad."

My jaw tightened as I looked up at him. His face was blank, stunned. I had startled him. I opened the car door and ran. My father waited for a minute, then started the car back up. The tires squealed as he made a U-turn in the street. I listened as he away drove away, and then I heard nothing.

I stood alone in the silent night, and the whole vigilante scheme seemed like a dream. This was probably as far as my father had intended to take it, shake me up a little bit, just pretend he was going after Alstead. But then I'd changed the game.

Fuck you, Dad. I'd really said it. Jesus.

But now, this character he was playing, this maniac, had turned his attention away from Alstead and was now focused on me. The knife and the arm around the throat—now they were mine. My father didn't go home. He parked the car somewhere else and now he was after me, silent, stealthy.

I ran the empty streets of Greenwood. I knew he was out there, hiding in yards, ducking behind cars, following me. I felt him everywhere, a giant black leopard. He wore black soft shoes that didn't make a sound as he sprinted across driveways.

This was real, more real than my life had ever felt. I was terrified, but also strangely elated. This was better than a movie.

The houses in Greenwood were sweet, set back in their lawns and hugged by soft shrubs. Lights glowed warmly in their windows, owners tucked inside, nestled on couches, numbed by television. That's what most people really wanted around here, wasn't it, to be left in peace to watch their shows. But not me, not my father.

The pavement was wet and rough as I ran in my bare feet. I felt sure that if I kept running, the skin on my toes would scrape and scrape until the blood flowed and my toes were bare bone.

I stopped. There were no cars on the street, no one walking. But the stillness was a betrayal because I knew my father was out there, and I knew eventually he would catch me. I could go to Todd's. I could throw rocks at his window myself. He'd come down, and I could tell him about my father out there like a rabid dog. We could get to the Bronco and drive away.

But Todd wouldn't help me. He'd find my father and they'd join forces. My father would like Todd. They were cut from the same cloth.

I could hear my heart beating hard in my ears, and as I caught my breath, I could feel my T-shirt soaked, hot, prickly. A dog barked somewhere, and it snapped me back into reality. I was being ridiculous. My father didn't want to kill me. He just wanted to scare me, rattle my chain for cussing at him, for the casual contempt with which I'd been treating him lately. Any other father would ground me, but that was too boring for my dad. He was having a blast right now, sneaking around pretending he was a wild rogue avenger, a cinematic hero.

I felt the jagged fear in me drain away and, along with it, some excitement. I could walk slowly now, easing my tender feet. When I got home, my father would be waiting for me. We wouldn't say a thing to my mother; in fact, we wouldn't mention it to each other. It would remain unspoken, our secret, like our secret need to have the world a little bit stranger, a little more exciting than it really was.

I rounded the corner of Hillcrest Drive, moving back into our development. I listened to the zap of the Coopers' bug light as I heard soft thuds on the pavement. My father was jogging up behind me.

"Lucy, Jesus Christ, I've been looking everywhere for you." His hair was soaked with sweat.

"What do you want?" I asked.

"I wanted you to help me scare Todd, that's all." He bent down and took the knife out of his sock and held it close to his face. His eyes shimmered under the streetlight. He regarded the blade for a moment and then tossed it into the Gibsons' yard with a high, graceful arc and the point stuck in the grass.

"Dad," I said finally, my voice sounding adult in my ears, "I don't think Todd did it."

"What?"

"The lawn. I don't think him and Scott Brubaker tore up the lawn."

My father looked at me hard. "Do you like this guy or something? Is that what this is about?"

"No," I said, keeping my voice even. "I don't. He's a jerk."

"He is and he isn't," my father replied, pulling a flask out of the pocket of his sweatpants. He unscrewed the lid. "I've seen him around. He's skinny, sure, but he looks like he can take care of himself." He held the flask to his mouth and took a long draw.

We stood right there in the street. I wondered if anyone in any of the snug little houses could see us. I hoped so.

My father stepped in the grass. "Give me a kick," he said.

"What?"

"Come on, throw me a kick like Billy Jack."

"No," I said, moving onto the Gibsons' grass. Then I lurched forward and grabbed the flask from my father and put it to my mouth. The liquor was strong and hot as it went down. I took another long swallow and recapped the flask, dropping it in the grass. Then I spun in a circle and tried to throw my leg in the air, tried to kick my father. He stepped back and my kick missed him.

"Try again."

I tried a few more kicks, tried to get my leg higher.

Finally I nicked his hip. He grabbed my ankle in the air and pulled, and I landed on the small of my back, knocking the wind out of me.

My father laughed. "Come on, get up. Come on, come on." He reached behind me and got the flask off the grass.

"Get away from me," I said from where I lay. The pain was searing. "Fucker," I added.

My father ignored it. And then I saw it—we were in a new place now, a place where I could cuss and drink his booze. A place where we were fellows in our strangeness, stuck in this stultifying life.

He leaned over and pulled me up. "Shake it off," he said, "shake it off." His voice was heavy with bourbon.

"I think my tailbone is broken."

"No, it's not. You just got the wind knocked out is all."

I moaned dramatically, even though the pain was lessening. "I hate you, Dad." I didn't know why I said it. I didn't mean it. At that moment, I loved my father as I never had before.

My father laughed and rolled his eyes.

"I hate you too, Lucy Goose. Let's have a hate fest." He walked a circle around me, arms flapping like a chicken. "Hate fest, hate fest," he squawked.

"Moron," I said.

"Kick me again," he said. "Come on, I deserve it. Kick me good."

I whirled around and got him in the stomach this time. He fake-stumbled away.

"Ooh, Lucy, you got me." He grabbed my arm as though for support. Suddenly he got me in a headlock and pulled me down on the ground. I fell into his shoulder.

We lay like that in the grass for a minute, my head resting on his arm. The booze had gone to my head, making the soft lights around me twinkle. I could smell my father's sweat beneath the alcohol. I knew he was drunk, and so was I.

"You're all right," he said. "I'm glad you know how to kid around."

"Yeah, kid, kid," I said boldly, right there beside him. "Kid with my motherfucking dad."

An English professor at the Community College of Philadelphia, Julie Odell has published short stories widely. She's drawn to the ugly, the unmentionable, and strives to lay bare what both binds and compels us. Philadelphia is her home now for several decades, and through her work and her passions, she feels in lockstep with its beat.

Nobody Makes It Big in Philly

Pietra Dunmore

Elizabeth did the best she could to make ends meet. There were times she'd pay the light bill and times the lights went out. Sometimes we had a place to stay, other times we had to flee in exodus. Those times, I could never bring more than I could carry. We'd get to the apartment of some new artist boyfriend of hers that I had to call "uncle" so-and-so, and he was gonna take care of us, but it never lasted for more than a few months. We always outstayed our welcome.

I always assumed my father was one of the many artists she had lived with. I had no pictures or physical description, just the drunken ramblings of my mother yelling in an ear-piercing tone that I "looked like that motherfucker". I remember going through a phase where I studied every brown-skinned man on the street and wondered if he was my father. His name did not appear on my birth certificate, so all I could do was wonder.

When I was around eight, she settled with Fingers, a pianist and singer. She followed him from gig to gig, usually stumbling home in the early twilight hours. A tap at my feet would signal their return, and I'd awake to see his tall, dark figure standing over the bed. All I could see were his eyes in the moonlight and the red-orange of his cigarette dangling from those curving dark-colored lips. I was forced to sleep on the couch in the living room.

I used to share the same bed with my mother, sleeping on her right side, while her night guest lay to her left. Until one evening, Fingers got mad and shouted, "When is he gonna get a bed of his own?" Ever since then, I was forced to sleep on the lumpy old couch in the living room. I hated laying there alone in the dark while he enjoyed the comfort and warmth of the bed and my mother's affections. Watching from the crack in the door as their bodies merged in the moonlight, I'd see how he held my mother, and how she looked at him. Fingers would call her "Baby", and he'd sing to her.

In the morning, I'd have to tiptoe past their sleeping half-naked bodies, with the fragrance of cigarettes, liquor, and sex stinging my young nose. Forging my way to the bathroom and stepping on their carelessly flicked cigarette butts, together with empty bottles of Night Train lining the threadbare carpet. This became a part of my morning routine. Fingers would usually stir a little when I closed the door after having used the bathroom. He'd rub his eyes, smile dryly, and say something like, "Hey little man." I'd scowl at him and walk back to the couch, wishing he'd leave so I could sleep comfortably.

When Fingers slipped out the front door in the morning before mom could prepare breakfast, I could hear her quietly sobbing in the bathroom. When she finally made her appearance in the living room, she'd push a bowl of cereal towards me.

As Fingers and Elizabeth's relationship progressed, there would be weeks Elizabeth wouldn't come home and I'd be left alone to fend for myself with nothing but liquor bottles in the apartment. Eventually I found my solace in those bottles. I'd sit in the living room and drink until I passed out, my little body numb to the reality of neglect. While alone, I began to channel my thoughts into a black and white marbled composition book, waxing poetic about the things that didn't make any sense to me, about not knowing my father, about how poorly Fingers treated Elizabeth, and how I wished for a place to call a permanent home.

By the end of the year, Fingers stayed with us. I stayed as far away from home as possible. I passed the hours after school in the library, meandering through the art section, falling in love with the surrealism of Dali, the artful graffiti of Basquiat, and the collage of Romare Bearden. I began to see my world of abandoned buildings and liquor stores in geometric patterns. I began drawing and sketching this world in a spiral pad, seeing the images before the pen ever touched the paper. I consumed the writings of Richard Wright and listened to the sounds of Gil Scott Heron and The Last Poets. I was in the library until they kicked me out.

Elizabeth and Fingers were up nights talking about moving to New York. Fingers said he was tired of taking the Chinatown bus.

"Nobody ever made it big in Philly," he told my mother.

A few weeks later, my mother told me that we were moving. I didn't bat an eye. I got up from the couch and started the familiar ritual of shoving my clothes into my duffel bag. Moving in with Fingers would be just another of our many relocations.

"What kind of dump he taking us to?" I asked.

"Baby, there ain't no place for you where we going." I walked down the stairs with my duffel bag and waited for Fingers to start up his Monte Carlo.

I hopped in the back, not sure where I was going. Fingers looked at me through the rearview mirror for a while. I wasn't about to give him the satisfaction of seeing me cry or asking my mother to pick me over her lover. Elizabeth sat in the passenger's seat and remained silent as the car went down Grays Ferry Avenue.

Pietra Dunmore writes short stories, creative nonfiction, and poetry. Her writing has appeared in Philadelphia Stories, Santa Fe Writers Project, Hippocampus Magazine, For Women Who Roar, *and the* Journal of New Jersey Poets. *Pietra is a graduate of Drexel University and received her MFA in creative writing and an MA in publishing from Rosemont College. Her work can be found online at pietradunmore.net.*

Zane Anderson, MFT, PsyD

Louise Bierig

Every month Zane had an off day.

Whenever he had a quiet moment to think, he tried to figure out what triggered these days. Most of them were caused by his three-year-old son, Micah, throwing a tantrum right after lunch and making it close to impossible for Zane to get him to day care and then to get himself to work on time. Zane liked to brew his own café au lait with Café du Monde coffee, a reminder of his student days in New Orleans, but most days Zane only had the energy to pick up some rotten coffee from Starbucks.

In December, right before lunch, his three-year-old son, Micah, puked on Zane's new pink shirt. He would have to change, but even worse, now that Micah was sick, Zane wouldn't be able to take him to day care, making it tough for Zane to get himself to work.

He called Hannah and left a message. After forty-five minutes of pacing and hoping Micah wouldn't puke again and trying to formulate backup plans so he could get to work on time, Hannah finally called back. No, she could not come home early. She had a meeting in five minutes.

Zane sighed and hung up. It was times like these when he missed his mother most acutely. She had lived an hour away, but when she was alive, she would zip down the turnpike to help him.

Zane thought of asking his father for help and laughed a bitter laugh. Last spring, when Zane's older son, Shad, was playing baseball, Zane's dad didn't attend a single game. A professor emeritus, his father was busy writing a book on General Lee and tending his gentleman's farm, which consisted of a few acres of blueberries and twenty beehives. Zane knew that if it wasn't history and farming, it would be some other thing, some other topic that kept his father from interacting with him and his sons.

His mother used to say, "He's just not a people person."

Zane suspected that it was more than that. His father had a personality disorder of some type, or even some mild Asperger's, but Zane shied away from diagnosing his relatives. Instead, he told himself there was something not quite right in the emotional development of his father's brain. Yes, his father *felt* emotions, but the expression of them was so difficult as to preclude maintaining relationships.

Zane ran down the list of sitters.

"No way," Veronica said. "Last week a baby barfed in my face, then I got sick. I'm not risking it."

Zane kept calling, getting voicemails and nos. Finally, he noticed his friend Emily's car in her driveway when she was normally at work and called her.

"How you feeling over there?" he asked. "I haven't seen you all week."

Typically, when he came home from work, he found Hannah and Emily in the backyard, their children playing on their shared play set.

"We've all had this horrible stomach thing," Emily said. "I'm finally back on my feet."

"Sorry to hear that."

"Thanks. And you?"

"Micah's sick, and I'm trying to figure out how to get in to work."

"Throwing up?"

"Yep."

"Bet he got that from Brian."

"Yeah, probably." Zane felt guilty asking her to watch a

sick kid, but maybe Micah was done puking, and she'd had the illness already herself. Besides, he took both her kids every time school called a snow day, so she could go to work. "How would you feel about taking him for three hours until Hannah gets home?"

"Sure. We'll come over there, so you don't have to bring him out."

"Thank you," Zane said, overwhelmed with relief.

Of course, when Emily and Brian arrived, Micah clung to Zane, who was now wearing his least favorite pin-striped shirt, and it was another ten minutes before Emily could get the boy distracted, and Zane could escape.

* * *

He walked into his office at exactly one o'clock, the time of his first appointment. Of course it was the day he saw Shelly and Terry. Zane's bad days seemed to coincide with Shelly's menstrual cycle. When he walked past her in the waiting room, he could see the stitch in her brow. This was a sign that she had a menstrual migraine and would take half of what he said the wrong way and then text him saying the therapy was destructive to her psyche.

This day Zane started off on the wrong foot. He felt discombobulated, wearing his pin-striped shirt when he had wanted to wear the pink one. Shelly was complaining how Terry put the Thanksgiving turkey in the oven at five hundred degrees, then disappeared. When she woke up at nine a.m., her sensitive nose told her that the turkey was already overcooked.

To illustrate the point that we needed to accept our lives as they were (the way he'd accepted Micah's illness and moved on—thanks in great part to Emily), Zane said, "Sometimes the turkey might just burn. That's okay. It's just a turkey."

Shelly sprang to her feet, her pointer and middle fingers pressed against her temple. "Do you know how much a turkey costs? Have you ever even cooked a turkey? Is that your family motto? *Just let the turkey burn.* You really think you're some kind of Zen, don't you?"

Terry reached for his wife, around the edge of the giant couch. "Honey, sit down."

"No, I will *not* sit down. That must be the Anderson family motto: Just let the turkey burn. Do you want that to be our family motto too?"

* * *

Long after he got home, Zane could still hear Shelly's words.

It was true that Zane had never cooked a turkey. His mother had hosted the holiday meals. This year, their first year without her, he had bought a Whole Foods Thanksgiving dinner to take up to his dad's, but it tasted store bought and not full of his mother's loving care. Christmas was a month away, and Zane knew he was going to have to learn how to prepare holiday dinners for his family.

Micah continued puking every hour, and Zane was in constant motion, washing one load of laundry after another. Climbing up and down the basement steps, he muttered to himself, "Just let the fucking turkey burn. That's the Anderson family motto."

Louise Bierig grew up in the northwestern corner of Pennsylvania and now lives in the southeastern corner. She has published her short stories and essays in Philadelphia Stories, Peregrine Journal, Philadelphia Inquirer, *and the* Swarthmorean. *She leads the Lansdowne Writers' Workshop, in Lansdowne, Pennsylvania, a few miles outside Philadelphia.*

Fortune's Wish

K. B. Carle

Nandi glances over multiplication problems and unfinished graphs while turning to chapter 24. Tucked in her textbook's seam is a cootie catcher with worn edges, its surface split into four color-coded squares: red, blue, green, and yellow.

During recess, she shows the cootie catcher to her best friend, Ese, who swipes the paper toy and brings it to life, small hands flapping its mouth. Shasta—a cautious girl who chews on her collar when nervous, bored, or tired—reaches for Nandi's textbook instead.

"Look." Nandi rests her chin on Shasta's shoulder. The names of the textbook's previous owners are all listed in Sharpie, some with heart-dotted *i*'s, some underlined three or four times, some barely there. "All girls."

"Who cares?" Ese says.

And because Ese doesn't care, Nandi suddenly doesn't care either. "Let's play."

"I'll go first."

Nandi sits in front of Ese while Shasta traces each name. Nandi picks the color blue, the numbers two, eight, and four.

"What's it say?" Nandi leans forward, her nails digging into her bare knees. Even Shasta looks up from the textbook to watch Ese peel back the triangle flap revealing Nandi's fortune.

"You will marry at nineteen."

"That's it?" But Nandi can tell Ese's upset.

Ese is never quiet.

Shasta closes the textbook and looks at the fortune. She chews on the collar of her uniform and then withdraws it, the spit soaking through. Her blue eyes meet Nandi's.

"What?"

You will marry appears on Nandi's triangle fortune, followed by 19, written in someone else's handwriting. The words, *you will marry*, appear over and over again. *You will marry, you will marry, you will marry*, until they blend into one.

Ese bounces back from her momentary silence, claiming that Nandi is just unlucky. This is also why Shasta is left in charge of telling Ese her fortune.

"You will have many children."

Nandi holds Ese's hand, witnessing her best friend's face crumble, an eyelash falling on her cheek.

Ese doesn't like children.

Shasta continues the game, opens a triangle flap to reveal her fortune. "I'll become an old maid, forever alone."

All three read Shasta's triangle together, chanting *forever alone*, the words sinking to the cootie catcher's center.

"This can't be right." Ese throws the cootie catcher across the room. "These fortunes are lame."

"Are they?" Nandi surprises herself. She has never questioned Ese.

"Did you know that the cootie catcher was originally called the 'salt cellar'?" Shasta whispers into the wet spot of her collar. "It was meant to be a container that—"

"Nobody cares!" Nandi says louder than she means to. When Shasta burrows her face behind her damp collar, Nandi bites her tongue.

Ese rolls her eyes at Shasta before turning her attention to Nandi. "You *want* to get married?"

"You don't?" Nandi says.

Ese thinks about this. "Maybe. I don't know."

"Maybe she'll be nice." Nandi smiles, thoughts of what her future wife might look like causing her palms to sweat.

"Maybe *she* will be a *he*." Ese pinches Nandi's elbow.

"We should put it back," Shasta murmurs, retrieving the cootie catcher from underneath a classmate's desk.

"We should throw it away," Nandi adds, despite opening her textbook to chapter 24.

"We should burn it." Ese moves away from Nandi and Shasta, who returns the cootie catcher to its crease.

"What do you think the others got?"

Shasta holds herself, her question left to linger between the three of them. Nandi looks to Ese for an answer but receives a shrug and averted eyes. This was supposed to be fun, Nandi thinks, approaching Ese with the same caution she approaches Shasta after school when they practice kissing while waiting for the bus. She plucks the fallen eyelash from Ese's cheek.

"We can make things right with a wish."

"All of us?" Shasta asks.

Ese takes her eyelash back. "Yes, and whoever has the worst fortune, their wish will come true."

They close their eyes, each making a wish. One girl wishes to have her fortune erased. Another wishes to make a slight edit to hers. One pleads for the fortune of another.

They go to the window and Shasta unlocks the latch. Nandi presses her palms against the glass and forces the window open. Ese ensures her finger is outside, dangling just over the sill, and blows. All three girls watch the eyelash carry their wishes into the distance, to someone who might grant them.

"What now?" Nandi checks the clock: five more minutes until recess is over.

"Now"—Ese opens the textbook to the page where the previous owners are listed—"we add our names to the book."

Nandi hesitates. *What if writing our names spoils our wishes?* she thinks. But Shasta has already retrieved a Sharpie from her desk.

Ese steals it and writes her name first, putting two dots for eyes inside the lowercase *e*'s center.

Shasta writes her name in perfect cursive, causing Ese to

scoff and shake the desk, which gives Shasta's *t* an extra-long tail.

They both look to Nandi.

"Why?"

"Because they did it." Ese tilts her head to the list of names. "There must be something to writing your name down in the book."

Shasta takes Nandi's hand in hers, slips the Sharpie into her palm. "Trust us, Nandi."

Shasta's hands are so warm, Nandi allows herself to stay in their grasp for a while.

"Come on." Ese taps her foot.

Nandi adds her name, no heart over the *i*, no flourishes, just *Nandi* in her stilted handwriting.

"Now to get rid of the book." Nandi turns back to chapter 24, runs her finger along the edge of the cootie catcher still tucked within the seam.

Ese and Shasta nod, their hands on Nandi's shoulders.

Nandi slams the book closed and takes it to the Lost & Found. She wraps it in an old sweater and buries it beneath a deflated football, some tattered workbooks, and muddy cleats.

K. B. Carle is the associate editor at Fractured Lit *and editor at* FlashBack Fiction. *Her stories have appeared in* Passages North, Porcupine Literary, APIARY Magazine, Jellyfish Review, *and* The Offing. *Her story "Soba" (Black Warrior Review) was one of the winners of Sundress Publications' 2020 Best of the Net Anthology. She can be found on Twitter @kbcarle.*

The Shape of Stealing

Tracey Levine

My superstitions started at the 7-Eleven. I was thirteen, and my best friend Darlene and I used to linger outside by the payphone, where we could still see the front steps of my house. The phone would ring occasionally, and we'd pick it up, usually close to sundown, and someone would ask in a gruff voice for a John, a Sue, sometimes something more exciting like Cous or Buzz—and we'd take turns, smiling and giddy, politely telling these people that they weren't there. The line would close immediately, and one of us would slam the receiver back in its place, feeling some sense of accomplishment.

Of course, we went inside sometimes. I always had some allowance money that I'd share. I used to talk about the people that walked by us, imagining what they did, but Darlene hated when I did that. She had an aunt in Arizona who sent her books about Native American vision quests and about people who could channel the dead, although I never saw those books.

One evening after we'd had a session by the dumpster, some employee came out, a new guy, and threw a bag over our heads. He wasn't wearing the 7-Eleven polo but a tight white T-shirt and a weathered pair of jeans. He asked us what we were doing, and when we had no reasonable answer, he invited us back into the store. My mom fed me enough stories of men looking normal enough in khaki trench coats. I'd never seen anyone wearing a khaki trench coat at the 7-Eleven. When Darlene hopped up from the curb and joined him immediately, this guy that had about ten years on us, I followed but at a distance. He wanted to show us behind the scenes at the store. And I wanted to see it.

His name was John, and he was cool and wanted to talk to us. Darlene started to tell him about the books that she read, but he said that he didn't mess with that sort of thing, but he wasn't Catholic either. He asked us what kinds of music we listened to as he led us to a door by the refrigerated aisle. I mentioned some of my mother's albums that she'd recently bought on CD that I considered somewhat more acceptable than the rest. He said that he'd tell us what to listen to. Darlene peered into the room behind all of the cases first and hesitated while a cold fog circled her face. I was uncharacteristically eager then because it seemed she was always first those days, so I pushed her aside and went in.

Inside it was colder, darker than I expected, lined with a system of motorized shelves that held the milk and all of the other drinks. At the end of the corridor there was what looked like a velvet curtain, but it couldn't have been. My best friend eventually came in when John encouraged her by saying that very few people got the chance to see how the place ran.

He was the new manager, and his store was going to be the best. I turned to look through the cases that were cut off of the store by glass doors. I could see right around the bottles and cartons and into the store, like I was spying. John mentioned that we could see out, but they couldn't see in. He gave us a few cartons to stock, a few bottles. John said it was a good job that he'd been trying to get for a while, and then he suddenly skipped to the far end where the curtain was and pulled it back. He revealed a checkerboard of screens, all showcasing different parts of the store and parking lot in grainy green images that moved slower than real life. We watched a woman pump gas in slo-mo. Then there was someone at the counter, and John told us to stay where we were, until the store was empty again, or everyone would want the tour.

We went back almost every night John was working, to see him, to have the tour again, to look at the cameras, to peer through the glass and see the customers in front of the drinks. John admitted that he was often tempted to push his hand through and grab onto someone, to gently slide a finger onto an arm to see if they'd notice. But he'd just been given a dollar raise, and being manager was important to him.

We'd often sit on the counter while he leaned by the cash register and ask him questions. I wanted to know about being a manager, and if he had to memorize all of that stuff. There had to be a system, some paperwork, but John said that he knew everything that was in his store and everything about his store. Darlene wanted to know if he had a girlfriend. He did, but she worked as much as he did and wanted to go to school. He wouldn't go to school. Darlene asked him how much money he made, and he said that it was enough for him to buy his girlfriend and himself brand-new leather jackets.

Darlene started smiling at John too much, and he smiled back, but in a coy way. The only time he touched us was to pat our shoulders on our way home around eight or nine o'clock when the outside of the store got busy with older kids. We nodded at our friend, trusted, and took some beef jerky and semi-stale pretzels with us occasionally as gifts.

At the opposite corner one night, in the near dark, Darlene told me I was a terrible person for saying that I never wanted to work at the 7-Eleven. She went home in a huff, and I thought to call her, but instead I sat in my room a few minutes later and dialed the pay phone. I never told her that I'd written down the number, that sometimes I'd call and just listen, just breathe and wait, and sometimes people would really start yelling at me. That night I called and asked for John many times, and each time someone hung up on me.

The first time I heard of a Ouija board was from John. He wouldn't let me go back and look at the cameras that night. I liked knowing that I could see people and that they'd never know I'd seen them. If somebody stole something, if they were good at it, the image was so grainy anyone would miss it, but John told us that he was so good at deciphering the images that he knew what the shape of stealing looked like. It was when there was an intense and very sharp but quick quiver on the screen. He was the only one who could see it, so far. I imagined that I could see it too, but our time in the room behind those cases was limited. I never told him that I knew that I could see it too because he couldn't be the only one. He just couldn't be the only one if it was a real thing.

Darlene called John smart a lot and asked him if he'd do a vision quest with her. I hit her arm when she said that. I thought that she just sounded dumb. But John said that she should do what she wanted when she was eighteen. Leave Philadelphia, go to the desert, find some peyote. I said that none of this was a good idea, and John pointed a finger right in my face. He believed in fate and ghosts, but he said that messing around with that sort of stuff was going to get us in trouble with the devil. I reminded him that he said he wasn't Catholic. He told us that the devil wasn't Catholic either, the devil was the devil. He told Darlene to throw out her books, to never touch a Ouija board or tarot cards or any of it, and to try and take care of people. He gave us candy bar gifts that night and caught my eye on the way out in a way he'd never done before, like I'd hurt his feelings.

I was convinced that we needed a Ouija board, and Darlene was tickled, although she made me swear I wouldn't tell John. I asked my mom, and she took me to the toy store, and we picked one up. When we got home with it, I asked my mom if the devil was Catholic. She told me that the devil didn't exist, and she meant it.

We set up the Ouija board on a chest covered by a stretch of satiny fabric my mom never used for curtains in my basement. My dog sat anticipatorily beside us as we set up to communicate. The basement was damp and barely lit, and therefore appropriate. There was a row of three fish tanks, all empty except for the one with a sole, surviving hamster. My mom blamed the pet store and then me for all of their deaths. They were diseased, and I wasn't as attentive as I should have been. We both pressed our fingers so tightly they could have been flippers and laid them on the viewer. I noticed my dog's half-German-shepherd ears erecting and then quivering, a sign of intrusion, but she also looked like she believed somehow the Ouija board was or would produce food.

Earlier that evening, sitting outside of the 7-Eleven, we tried to make a list of dead people, making sure that John couldn't hear. My grandparents were alive, but there'd been a few neighbors on my block who'd passed. I expressly felt strange trying to contact them. Darlene's grandparents were dead on her mother's side, and she'd never known them but wouldn't mind trying to ask them secrets about her mom. There were dead children from our school, younger than us, who'd had cancer; a girl in the neighborhood had died of an ear infection because her parents were serious Jesus freaks and refused medical care. I came up with the idea that we could try and talk to dead famous people. I suggested Carl Sandberg, the poet I'd written a paper about. He was a good writer. But this was boring to Darlene. She crumpled the blank piece of paper and threw it toward the gas pumps as I carefully uttered the name John Lennon.

In the basement, the rain rattled and the lights flickered, but they always did that. My mom said that we'd have one hell of a lawsuit if the place ever caught fire considering how many electricians proclaimed there was nothing wrong with the wiring. I caught eyes with Darlene and thought to not assure her, not tell her that there was nothing paranormal about the flickering, but I told her the truth.

She asked me to call his name. We had a question written down about the day John Lennon died, which we assumed all spirits wanted to talk about. I intoned his name just like I'd heard actors do in movies. I made it to a second uttering and immediately laughed, and Darlene smacked my shoulder, forcing me to imbalance the viewer, which I hadn't realized I'd been putting so much pressure on. It shot out over the chest, landing on the floor, where my dog almost grabbed it up. Then the lights went out, the rain got louder, and the dog started barking. I asked John Lennon to sing us a song as Darlene grabbed me and held me like I was her mother. I left her and picked up the board, held it up to her and my barking dog, forcing the letters and symbols, the sun and the moon, the yes, no, and goodbye right at them.

When that got weird, I ripped the satin fabric up and covered the board with it. I put it back on the floor. The dog didn't care anymore and stopped barking but went over to the fish tank where the one hamster remained and started sniffing it. Darlene told me that it was my fault because I picked John Lennon, which I didn't understand, and I wanted to cry, but instead a soft but sharp sound, like a muted bicycle pump in use, could be heard. The hamster was gasping for air, and I lifted him out and let his body grow fainter with each gasp in my palms. This was how the others died: from disease and maybe neglect, and not from the ghost of John Lennon. But it didn't make any sense to try and tell Darlene that then. She was crying and I wasn't. I said that we should inscribe the name John Lennon on the hamster's tombstone, but she grabbed the Ouija board and took off.

I knew where Darlene had gone.

I stopped running just in front of the 7-Eleven, where I stood in the rain and watched John take the Ouija board and crack it over his knee. It split in two, almost symmetrically. He held the parts up and was saying something and staring right at me. He looked utterly disturbed as I watched Darlene latch onto his waist like he was her mother. It was like watching a play inside of a light bulb.

I went home after that and went straight to my room, didn't turn on the lights, and sat on the carpet with my back to my dresser, listening to the sound of my breath, and it was so dramatic then, heavy and filled with things I did not understand. I leaned and grabbed the phone from the top of my dresser and dialed the pay phone, feeling with certainty for a few seconds that someone would pick up and that it would have to be Darlene. In her sheepish way, she'd tell me that she was going to help me fix the Ouija board and that we'd summon so many others, or at least try. We had plenty of time. But the phone just kept on ringing, endlessly. When I eventually hung up, it was so quiet in my room that it felt like I was nowhere and that there was nothing.

I walked by that 7-Eleven many times in the months after that night, and I saw John as he leaned like he always did, talking to groups of older kids. I don't think he ever saw me, but I stared like I wanted him to, and every time I was sure he'd turn and see me, I started walking faster. Sometimes I even ran past and felt like a coward.

Darlene never called and never came by after that. And I didn't see her for a very long time until one night I did go into the 7-Eleven and John wasn't there. He worked almost every night, so it was odd. It felt like he was gone. The store even seemed a little grimier, a little dimmer. I bought some beef jerky and held it tight between my fingers as I stood at the register, enjoying the crimson press against the plastic, until I had to pay for it. An older man was behind the counter, and he didn't even look me in the eye.

I sat out in front of the store after that on the curb as I used to do with Darlene, just watching. Not many people walked by, and the pay phone didn't ring at all. I watched mothers pump gas into their minivans. There was a muscle car that grumbled in, and it was interesting how it shook and seemed so powerful, and when a little, middle-aged man climbed out of it in a conservative suit, I really wished I could talk about who he was with Darlene.

I thought of how my mom sent me to camp that summer before I sat there on that curb by myself that night, because I was down, because I hadn't any friends anymore. There was a Ouija board one night, and we asked it very general, boring questions and didn't summon anyone in particular. The bugs outside, the screeches of the woods were pleasantly haunting like they were putting on a show for us, like we couldn't get hurt if we wanted to. The board told us that it was a farmer, that it had lost a wife. It was angry, but it wasn't going to hurt us. It was just lonely. And as all of this was being spelled out, each letter progressing the development of a word through that viewer, I pressed and pushed like you're not supposed to do, but there were so many fingers, and really, we were all liars.

Then I looked up from the curb and saw three girls. They were maybe taller than me, or at least they looked like that from where I sat looking up, their legs in tight jeans, their jackets cropped. The middle girl had black curly hair that had product in it to make it shinier and curlier; it wasn't the hair but the awkward jerk of the shoulder every third step or so that let me know it was Darlene.

They were clomping up the sidewalk in front of the gas station, and it was very possible that she didn't see me, but maybe she did, my shape on that very familiar spot on that curb, just a blip in her evening. She looked so much older than she used to, and it felt like she were made of mist and that the 7-Eleven might have been a dream. I knew I'd still have to live there on that block for many years, but that place would seem from then on as if, forever, I could just walk right through it.

Tracey Levine is a Philadelphia native who lives in Port Richmond and teaches creative writing and film at Arcadia University. Her creative writing work has appeared in Verbal Seduction, Halcyon Review, Corner Club Press, Streetlight Mag, Crack the Spine, *the podcast* Streetlight Voices, *and the anthology* Broken Skyline. *She has a chapbook with The Head and the Hand Press. She is also the cocreator and former cohost of the Philadelphia reading series The Hatchery.*

Boxes

Skylar Althouse

I think I was eleven when my mother sat me down on the living room couch. The day before, I had been playing with my friends, who had already had The Talk, and I felt inferior in my knowledge. After all, I was older than them—what could they know? So I asked my mom some questions, and the next day she decided it was time.

My mother, a clinical scientist, had on her lap her old biology books from college. She flipped open to the pages of the male and female anatomy. I had seen all of this before; the body never scared me. When I was four years old, I had asked my mother what the body looked like on the inside. She tried to explain to me, but I wanted to *see* it. After that, she got me every biology book she could find that was suitable for a little kid. I couldn't read them, of course; I just liked looking at the pictures. For some reason, even when I got older and could read some of them, I just skipped over the parts about the reproductive system, as if those pages had a PG-13 rating on them and to look at them I had to be accompanied by an adult.

"The sperm comes out the penis and then into the uterus to fertilize the egg," my mother said, tracing the penis with her finger. Up to that point, I was fine. It all made sense; everything was scientific and factual. She didn't tell me about love, how it would feel to lie awake thinking about someone, the pulsing in your core when you have your very first kiss. And she definitely didn't mention the outcome of lust, that thing that people do when a kiss isn't enough. My mother never even used the word sex. The penis just happened to end up in the vagina when two people wanted a child, and nothing more was said or done.

"Every month, if a woman's egg isn't fertilized, she bleeds as the uterus sheds her lining. That's why I wear those pads, for my period. When I was a little girl, I would get cramps so bad that I wouldn't be able to move. Maybe you will get them too."

I was never scared of the body before, but I was then. It was changing in ways that I didn't want it to, and I was changing in ways my mother didn't want to see. She didn't tell me how I would get curves that someone would like to trace one day; she didn't say that blossoming into womanhood was a wonderful time. I wasn't taught to appreciate what was happening to my body, to enjoy the new desires and feelings. All I got were warnings.

Don't be a stupid teenager.
Don't have sex. Be a good girl.
Don't get pregnant.
Don't do drugs.
See this girl? She ruined her life because of a stupid boy.
Teenagers are rude and ignorant—don't be like them.
Don't don't don't . . .

I grew up learning to hate the changes, to fear the teenage years, when so many things could go wrong because of raging hormones, making you dirty and only focused on the needs of the flesh. But we couldn't stop it.

I think that was when my mother stopped liking me.

Many people would try to argue with me. "Don't say that. Of course she does. She loves you very much." But I never said anything about love. I knew she loved me. You didn't want something that much and go through all that pain only not to love the product of your efforts. She didn't like me.

She liked the little girl she refused to let grow up. The girl who would sit in front of her mother so she could curl her hair. The girl who would play with dolls and go on adventures in imaginary worlds and only dreamed of a good prince to marry and nothing more. Now I was too scared to tell her what time had done.

"I don't know who you are anymore," she would say to me. "You always used to hug me and kiss me good-bye. You were such a sweet little girl. You would tell me everything."

I didn't know who she was remembering, this girl she knew. The girl I knew had learned how to hide in plain sight. She had learned that only innocent perfection was accepted. So this girl my mother knew was the daughter she had created in her head—that sweet, pure girl who would never be defiled, forever playing tea party with her many dolls. We had packed those dolls in boxes years ago.

* * *

The couple hours alone I had after I got home from school were always my favorite part of the day. I could do what I wanted, watch what I wanted, and relax without the fear of someone being upset with my contentedness. But as those minutes creeped toward four o'clock, my muscles tensed in anticipation, and my ears strained for the sound of a car door.

Have I done anything wrong today?
Is there anything I need to clean?
What should I be doing?

I knew what to expect depending on how hard the car door slammed, whether my mother said hello to me as she walked in, how loud of a sigh she let out when she set her work bag on the counter.

Don't let her catch you watching TV.

I had my first boyfriend at fourteen. For a first boyfriend, Luke was an excellent choice. He was in the top ten of his class and came from a good family. (Our mothers bonded over their mutual fondness for keeping their kids on a tight leash.) And he had a bright future.

In the beginning, the idea delighted my mother. Someone thought her creation was attractive.

Her delight quickly turned to repulsion when she realized what a boy could do to the carefully constructed rules and warnings she had nailed to the boards she'd built around me. She was a mother who never really knew me because she wouldn't let me be known. The first time she glimpsed through the cracks, she didn't like what she saw.

Usually I was careful to delete the messages, but she hadn't gone through my phone in a while. We were sitting on the couch watching a movie, and she was using my phone to look up a fact about whatever was on the TV. I was on edge as soon as she picked it up.

When I heard my phone buzz, I could tell that she was reading something. Soon her fingers were working, and she was reading more and more. My mother got up, straight-backed and stiff, refusing to look at me and throwing my phone back on the couch. Instantly, I felt the loathing and rage rise off her like vapor, tainting the air. My throat seized. My heart slammed against my rib cage. She walked out of the family room in complete silence.

I grabbed my phone. The buzz had been a message from Luke.

You're so sexy

From there, she must have gone back through every heart and kiss, every sweet nothing and word full of want.

I love your body

Can't wait to see you again

I love the feel of your hands

She had looked inside the box and seen me bare and dirty. And she did not like it.

I sat there in the chair, not even hearing the TV or noticing the touch of the blanket against me. Everything was just the intense beating of my heart and the feeling of everything that made me alive slowly draining out of me.

What I did next would determine how long I would get the silent treatment. Should I sit there and accept my guilt? Go to my mother and beg for forgiveness? Or should I just pack my things and leave now? A part of me wanted to be dramatic and rebel. What was I being punished for? Having desires and feelings? Surely she couldn't have expected me to stay a child forever. But beneath it all, I remembered what I had been taught and repeated one word to myself over and over: *bad bad bad bad* . . .

Finally, a new thought flashed through my mind and broke the spell: *I need to tell Luke.*

While I felt as though I was trembling like an earthquake, my hands steadied when I picked up my phone and began typing.

Luke, my mom read through our text messages. She's really upset

Crap do you think she is going to tell my mom?

No, but I think it's best that we don't see each other for a while

Okay, I think you're right

I'm scared

Me too

I put my phone down, turned off the TV, and stared into the darkness of my living room, thinking about what I had done and what I was going to do. I decided to plead.

I slipped down the hall to her bedroom, but she was already in the shower. I sat on her bed, going over what I could say.

The closet doors to my right were entirely mirrors; there was a mirror to the front and left of me. Out of the corner of my eyes, I could see my hunched image in them all. But I couldn't look at myself because I knew I was dirt, an endlessly reflected ugly smudge that I was sure my mother just wanted to wipe away.

I couldn't even get myself to sit fully on the bed. This was my mother's domain. These were her things that I was surrounded by, and at that moment, I was not welcome. I perched on the edge like I might need to escape at any second.

I decided to play the innocence card, to blame those words on my boyfriend, because I thought that's what she wanted to hear. It was the coward's way out, but I had grown up learning to lie: it caused the least damage. My mother didn't want to hear the truth.

I remembered one time when Luke was leaving and she'd heard him say, "Bye, love."

"He's just joking, right?" she had asked me.

"Yes of course," I'd replied without hesitation. I knew the correct answer was that teenagers don't know what love is.

It could have been just minutes, but I felt as if I had been sitting tense on the bed's edge for an hour, dreading the moment my mother would come out of the bathroom. *I didn't mean it, I didn't mean it, I'm sorry sorry sorry . . .*

The door opened, and yellow light and steam burst out. My heart stopped.

"Mommy?"

No response.

I had to press forward. "What's wrong?"

Then finally, when it was clear I was just a speck of dust in the air: "I didn't mean it!" I begged.

Start crying, I thought, but I couldn't find any sorrow in myself. Those tears had dried up and left me like the desert. I was traveling in a foreign land that was empty and filling my mouth with sand. There was no path for me to follow.

"Please listen. I'm sorry." I didn't recognize my voice.

I forced as much regret and guilt into it as I could, but it still came out sounding stale and overused. "I thought that's what he wanted." I knew what I had written, and I knew I had meant everything I'd said to my boyfriend.

I was met with only a cold, unbreakable silence. Still hunched over, I hugged myself and watched my mother ignore me as she got ready for bed. After a few more moments, she spoke.

"I just can't look at you or speak to you right now."

I nodded and got up to go to my bedroom, heavy with the feeling that I had broken something that I could never repair.

* * *

In the almost three years Luke and I dated, we never saw each other's rooms. Our mothers wouldn't let us near them. Finally, that summer, Luke was preparing to go to college. At first, it had been filled with secret meetings during the day, adrenaline coursing through our veins as we wondered if we would get caught, and the feeling of hands on skin that had never been touched before. I was ready to lose my virginity to him, but the time was never right. I would forever regret that I couldn't share that moment with him.

My mother's silence was a wall that had been towering over me for two days. When she was home, she moved around me as if I was an inconveniently placed piece of furniture. Dinners were fast and silent, and I tried to stay out of her way as much as possible. All I could think about was what to say to break that wall down. But I knew it wouldn't fall. I had to wait for my mother to open a door.

Feeling like I was on the edge of a cliff, waiting for someone to push me off, I finally texted him.

I think it's best if we don't see each other for a while.

I was sitting in my chair in my bedroom, when my mother walked in. My room was bright with the afternoon sun and almost comic in how perfectly opposed it was to what I was feeling inside.

"Okay, I am ready to talk," my mother said, staring down at me.

I nodded. I didn't want to say anything for fear it would just upset her more.

She stared expectantly at me, as if I was the one who had been giving her the silent treatment for days. When I still didn't respond, she sighed and said, "Those messages were disgusting and dirty. I'm not stupid. I know this is how teenagers are. I just think sixteen is too young for this." Her voice was getting louder and louder. "Did this start when you were fourteen?"

"No! Of course not! I just thought that's what he wanted," I said, wincing internally at the lie. I may have wanted it more than him. "We didn't do anything—I swear." I knew my mother thought I was a dirty slut, and the funny thing was I was still a virgin. All this pain and I was still a virgin.

"Men are disgusting. They just take and take. If you are uncomfortable with anything, just say no. You don't have to do what he wants."

Even as my mom was saying this, we both knew Luke wasn't the one to blame. We both knew I wasn't uncomfortable with it at all. This was just a way for my mother to start rebuilding that box again, one board at a time.

I finally was able to cry, a few tears of self-pity, for not being careful enough. If I had deleted those messages, my mask wouldn't have been torn off. If I had done a better job of hiding, Luke and I wouldn't have been torn apart so suddenly. He would be going to college soon, and I could feel our ties to each other loosening.

* * *

A few weeks later, my mother and I were back on speaking terms, but I could still see disappointment in her eyes whenever she looked at me. She had noticed that I wasn't hanging out with Luke. "What happened? Did you break up?"

I shrugged, keeping my face in its mask. "I don't know. We haven't been talking."

Her anger flared. "What do you mean?"

I was shocked. I hadn't expected her to react at all. She must have read the confusion on my face saying, *Isn't this what you wanted?*

"I didn't want you to break up!" She was as exasperated as I was now feeling.

I didn't know how to respond, but I knew that no matter how much I loved Luke, I couldn't be with him and keep up my perfect masquerade at the same time. I tried so hard to stay inside my mother's box, and one mistake had brought it crumbling down. While my mother worked to rebuild her box, I worked to put her little girl back together, and I wondered if there would ever be a time when we could both just stop our labor and see that we really hadn't made any progress at all.

Skylar Althouse attends Saint Joseph's University on City Avenue, and she has lived in a suburb of Philly all her life. She loves this creative city. There is always something beautiful to see here, and she is proud to call it her home. She loves to write poetry, and she hopes to one day publish a novel.

Crabs

Sam Gridley

We were fishing off the dock, me and Mom and this guy Dennis she invited for part of the week. It was muggy, with the sun burning our arms. Mom and I wore these big floppy hats to protect our faces, and we laughed about what Grandma always says: "Ladies must be careful of their complexions."

The bay smelled kind of salty fresh one minute and stinky the next. We smelled like sunscreen and sweat and DEET spray. I was trying not to scratch the mosquito bites that drove me bonkers. The people down there say mosquitoes are the official state bird.

We'd rented a cottage on the island a couple times before, Mom and me, but never fished. It was Dennis's idea, and he brought the rods. We had minnows for bait. Dennis put them on the hook for me. I could barely watch. Fish aren't intelligent like dogs or whales, but getting a sharp piece of metal jammed through your guts, that must hurt.

I was first to get a bite. Dennis wrapped his arms around me to help wind the reel. I'm saying to myself, he's OK, right? This isn't creepy with him almost hugging me. He's kind of short but good-looking. Fuzzy blond hair and arm muscles that stretch his T-shirts.

"Woo-hoo!" Mom yelled as the fish came up. "Should I try to catch it in the scoop thing?" Mom's pretty useless at outdoor stuff. She does online marketing for a shoe company—what would she know about fishing? But I think she played extra-dumb for his benefit. He works in ticket sales for the Phillies.

"Yeah, Peg, grab the landing net," said Dennis. She swiped at the wiggling fish and missed a few times before snagging it.

Dennis pulled the net over to show me. "Congratulations!" he said. "It's a flounder." The fish was flat with a big mouth and these two beady eyes squished together on the dark side. The other side was this awful pasty white. "It's too small to keep, though," he said. "We oughta throw it back. Sorry, Livvy." He reached in and grabbed the fish's ugly head with one hand and wiggled out the hook with the other. It splashed in the water and sank out of sight. I couldn't see if it swam off. Something that gruesome, I'm not sure I care if it lived.

Then nothing happened for, like, an hour except Mom also caught a fish too small to keep. The sun was beating down and the mosquitoes biting. I sprayed more DEET. The islands across the bay disappeared in soupy fog. Gulls swooped. I had this huge itchy welt on my neck, and I was tired of standing and feeling all sticky. Over to our left, a big white bird sat stock-still on a post. Mom guessed it was an ibis, and Dennis said egret. "We should get a bird book," Mom said but didn't argue with him. Waves went *plish* against the pilings, and you could see the tide going out.

Then Mom's rod yanked, and she was pulling something up. At first I thought it was a plastic toy, but no, it was a big crab. It had latched onto the minnow and hook with one claw. While it rode high in the air, it was nipping off little bits of the minnow with its free claw and stuffing them in its mouth. *Gross!* Mom let the creature drop on the pier and stared at it.

"Do you guys like fresh crab?" Dennis asked. "This one's a good size."

Mom said her only experience with crabs was when they're made into cakes and served on a bun with tartar sauce on the side.

"Look at him," I said and pointed, "he's still trying to eat the fish!"

Dennis laughed. "He's a greedy bastard, isn't he? We could

pick up some others to go with him, have us a crab feast tonight or tomorrow."

Mom didn't say no, so Dennis tossed him in the ice cooler we'd brought for the fish we weren't catching.

A few minutes later Dennis caught a crab too. More laughs, and this one also got dumped in the cooler.

That night I forgot about the crabs when we went to dinner. I ordered baked flounder. I'd had it before, but I wanted to see what it tasted like after catching one. It was good but basically, you know, fish. With lemon sauce all over, you couldn't tell how nasty it'd looked alive.

After dinner I wanted ice cream. They have this shop on the main street with the best homemade flavors anywhere. My favorite is Marsh Mud, it's like extra-fudge chocolate. Mom said it was too late, the lines were always horrible, we'd get ice cream another day, but actually it *wasn't* late, just eight thirty, so I argued and she got angry and I got angry back. She said this is no way for someone almost twelve years old to behave, throwing a tantrum, and I was furious she accused me like that. *Tantrum?* I don't throw *tantrums*, for fuck's sake, but I do stand up for myself if I'm right. Dennis said nothing, which made me mad at him too. Maybe they both wanted to get back to the cottage to be with each other.

I heard them later. Thin walls. They were trying to be quiet, but I could tell they were doing it. It's fine with me. I know Mom's lonely, and Dennis is by far not the worst. I mean, compared to the one that left the bathroom door open when he peed, Dennis is Prince Charming.

The next day, after canoeing in the morning and beach time in the afternoon, we were hot and tired. My bites had gone from itching to burning, and I wasn't hungry at all. But Dennis said it was time for our feast. "Oh?" said Mom, looking at me. "I was thinking something simple. I'm not sure we have an appetite for—"

"The way I fix crabs, you'll be licking your lips, I promise."

We stopped at a fish store for a dozen crabs to add to the

two in our cooler. They came in a paper bag inside a plastic bag. You could see them wriggling around in the dark in there.

After we all showered and changed, Dennis searched in the cabinets and found a big pot that he filled partway with water and put on the stove to boil. "This seasoning you bought," Mom said, "should I sprinkle it in the water now? How much?"

"No," Dennis said, waving her off. "The Old Bay goes in later."

He was bossy about the meal, telling her the best way to cook the corn on the cob and when to set out the coleslaw and beer and paper towels. I watched when the crabs went in the pot. He knew how to drop them easy, so they didn't splash hot water on us.

They didn't scream. I don't know how soon they were dead, but in boiling water I guess their tiny brains explode or melt or something.

I peeked in each time he lifted the cover to shake in Old Bay. They changed color till they were bright orange. He rinsed them off fast and piled them in two big bowls. Some of their claws were broken off like they'd been struggling inside the pot.

We ate at the picnic table on the screened-in porch. Dennis put a whole crab on Mom's plate and one on mine. "Step up to the plate, ladies!" he announced. Then he instructed Mom, standing over her shoulder and reaching down to point. I wasn't going to try until I saw her do it. He had her snap off the legs and claws, pull this tab thing that opens the middle, break off the shell, but then there was this gooey greenish stuff inside that you're not supposed to eat. She had to clean it out and heap it in a bowl in the middle of the table, getting her hands all gummy.

She was gritting her teeth, but she kept at it. She wiped and wiped on paper towels. Dennis showed her how to tug the meat out with her fingertips, and when she got a taste at last, she said, "Oh . . . that's good, I admit. Better, in fact, than a crab cake. The Old Bay gives it a spiciness. Livvy, you haven't started on yours. Did you watch the way we opened it?"

"I'm just having corn and coleslaw," I said.

"No, no," said Dennis, "I'll prepare it for you." He reached for my plate, and in a minute he had the crab spread open with a bunch of the meat out so I could pick it up with a fork.

Mom worked through the one crab, then started a second. She even used the claw cracker and sucked to get the meat out. It was still really humid, so her face was sweating and she kept trying to push her hair back with her arm because she was smeared up to the wrists with gunk. Meanwhile, Dennis was cracking and chomping and swallowing—I stopped eating to watch his jaw muscles. When he finished each crab, he scooped up the remains and tossed them in the bowl of trash. The entire porch smelled like crab guts.

I did try my crab meat with the fork. Not impressed.

All at once Mom shrieked. "Ohmigod! Ohmigod!"

She was, like, gawking at the middle of her crab. "What?" said Dennis, and he leaned over to look. "Hah!" he laughed. "Whaddaya know."

He lifted out a tiny spiky thing and held it up with his finger and thumb. "Recognize this, Peg?" he said.

"It looks like a skeleton!"

"The minnow you caught him with."

"*Ewww*. Noooooo, don't tell me that."

"Definitely a minnow," he insisted. "Definitely in the crab's stomach."

I felt sick.

He laid it in the middle of the table between us. Mom stared at it. "Amazing," she finally said. "It's almost perfect . . . all those teensy ribs . . . He swallowed the whole *thing*! How did he *do* that? I didn't think his mouth was that big."

"If your appetite's strong enough," Dennis said with a smirk.

Mom went back to picking at her plate. "Maybe I'll find a pearl now," she joked. "Or a gold coin." But she was kind of revolted, I could tell.

I asked Mom if I could have peanut butter and jelly. "I'll make it myself."

"C'mon, that's *kids'* food," Dennis teased. "I thought you were a big girl."

Isn't "big girl" what you say to a four-year-old? I wanted to kick him under the table. Mom just tilted her chin to the side with her eyes on me, like she does when she means, Not now, Livvy. Which is also what you say to a four-year-old.

Dennis pushed himself up. "Want another beer, Peg? Livvy, more coke?" We shook our heads.

When he'd gone in the house, I said, "Are you gonna keep *eating* that?"

"Well, it's not so bad. The actual taste of the flesh is . . . I'd almost say . . . refined." She tried to grin at me while she dragged a string of guck from her teeth. "And Dennis made such a production of cooking them for us."

I scrunched my nose. "I'm a vegetarian now," I said.

Mom snickered. "You know, honey, sometimes you have to push through the icky stuff to get what's worth having."

I watched some little puckery lines around her mouth I'd never noticed before. "No thanks," I said. "I'll pass."

When he came back to the porch chugging a second beer, Dennis laid into the crabs again. The mound of glop built up till he fetched a plastic trash bag and dumped out the bowl. Shells, green goo, bits of leg and claw all mushed together.

Yeah, I'll pass.

That night there was more noise from their bedroom, Mom groaning pretty loud, and this time it bugged me. First I worried about her, then I blocked them out with my earbuds, but I couldn't fall asleep. I was picturing the greedy crab that kept eating while he was on ice in the cooler—and kept digesting till he hit the boiling water.

In the morning Dennis left, heading back to his job. Soon as his car pulled out of the driveway, Mom sank down on the couch, flinging out her arms with a big sigh. "Just the two of us," she said. "Time to relax. God, I'm tired."

We stayed home that morning and read books. At lunchtime when we checked the refrigerator, there was a plate of leftover crabs. I made a disgusted face at her and she made one back at me.

We had peanut butter and jelly. *Kids'* food. And that night we went for ice cream. It was the best day of our vacation.

Sam Gridley is the author of the novels The Shame of What We Are *and* The Big Happiness *and a forthcoming novella,* The Bourgeois Anarchist. *His fiction and satire have appeared in more than sixty magazines and anthologies. He has received fellowships from the Pennsylvania Council on the Arts and a Wallace Stegner Fellowship (Stanford University). He lives in Philadelphia with his wife and neurotic dog and hangs out at the website Gridleyville.blog. His story "Crabs" first appeared in* Wilderness House Literary Review.

Green Suede Shoes

Liz Waldie

Norman was addicted to spying through the windows of St. Agnes's Mortuary and Crematorium, and rightfully so. He'd found the perfect spot for performing the act—a nicely secured bench, nestled away in a patch of brambles at the rear of the complex. The bench stood decaying below a row of frosted windows. Luckily for him, one square of glass above the bench was always open, probably to let in fresh air, which inevitably allowed for his uncanny hobby to commence each day after school.

He'd slip into the olive suede shoes his father had gifted him and shuffle toward the kitchen door. Aunt Mona would eye him skeptically but continue with the persistent motion of whisking whatever batter she'd been conjuring up.

"I'm going out to dig a hole," Norman would promptly say.

"Oh really?" was Aunt Mona's standard reply, along with raised brows. "Where will you be digging this hole?"

The boy would then shrug into his green corduroy jacket. "Not sure yet, but someplace that'll be good for a hole."

"Will you be taking William with you?"

He'd always stop, stare at his aunt for a moment or two, then say something along the lines of "You know, that's not an awful idea," or "Oh, I can't believe I almost forgot!" Then he'd kick off his shoes and dart away, only to poke his head around the corner seconds later. "Do you think he'll run away?" he asked every time without fail.

Aunt Mona would shake her head, and the boy would venture back into the depths of his home to retrieve William the salamander from his spot on the rock in the aquarium.

It was possible that Aunt Mona knew of Norman's hobbies, knew the boy only dug holes on Sundays when the mortuary was closed, but as far as Norman was concerned, she was oblivious, and he was getting away with much more than a boy of eight years should. Aunt Mona had her suspicions. For the two years she'd been his guardian, she'd noticed something about Norman. It was in the way he asked questions about death. He knew of the accident in which his parents passed away and brought it up regularly. There was a fixation there, and Aunt Mona wasn't sure whether she should make him stop. Especially when he went to the mortuary. But he'd had an unusual life, and he was an unusual boy, and from these evolved his unusual hobbies. Who was she to judge the child?

* * *

It was a dreary Wednesday in mid-October when Norman started mapping out the mortuary. After deciding to leave William at home, he gathered up a roll of paper, some assorted pencils, and a wooden ruler.

"What's on the agenda today, Mr. Norman?" Aunt Mona continued to fold vegetables into a sticky dough.

He wrinkled his nose at his prospective dinner. "I'm going to make maps today." Not technically a lie.

"What sort of maps?"

"It's a secret," he said and slipped out the door.

The walk to the mortuary was one of his favorites. He had to walk through a cemetery, but it didn't matter, because it was small, and Norman wasn't bothered by the notion of walking over graves. His mother used to say that whenever Norman got a chill, it was somebody walking over his grave, many years in the future. He liked the idea of giving chills to people in the past. It was as close to time travel as he could get. Sometimes he'd walk over his parents' graves and wonder if they were getting chills years before while tucking him into bed or cooking dinner. After walking through the cemetery, he would come upon an even smaller patch of forest, easily navigated by a rough path, and after the forest came the mortuary.

The place had intrigued him from the first day he happened upon the property. He'd been walking home from school and decided to take a detour, and suddenly he'd been standing before the large stone steps. It was a familiar place. Snow littered the muddy ground. The building cast a shadow over the front yard and horseshoe driveway. A tall man in a long black overcoat stood at the foot of the steps, staring up at two enormous open doors.

"What does that say?" Norman had asked the man, pointing to a large sign beside the doors.

"It says, 'St. Agnes's Mortuary and Crematorium,'" the man responded flatly.

"Oh," Norman said, puzzling over the name. "What's that, exactly?"

"It's where they take dead people, clean them up before burying or burning them to ashes."

Norman liked this man. He didn't beat around the bush or lie. He simply stated what was and didn't seem to care about whether Norman's presumably still-alive parents would be upset that he was learning about death.

"That's very interesting," Norman responded, remembering flashes of flowers and black. "So there are dead bodies in there now?" A current of cold air flowed out of the building.

The man nodded. "Many." He had a young face and scraggly beard. His eyes hollow, cheekbones prominent. His hat matched his coat, and his shoes matched even more.

"I'm Norman." He paused. "Do you live here?"

The man shook his head. "I'm waiting for my wife."

Two men emerged from the building, carrying a large,

black, rectangular box. A coffin, Norman suspected, based on what he could remember from his parents' funeral. The men were odd. One tall and lanky, another short and stout.

The man in the overcoat extended a hand. "Pleasure meeting you, Norman."

Norman shook his gloved hand and watched as he helped the other two men put the coffin into the back of a long car. Then, the two men who presumably worked at the mortuary slid into the front seat. The man whom he had spoken to drove off with them. Norman paused for a moment, puzzled over why the man hadn't waited for his wife, but he shortly realized that the man had.

Something about the peculiarities of this situation intrigued Norman, which drew him back to the place many times after. Sometimes he wondered if the two men who worked there ever caught a glimpse of him standing outside on that bench or if they heard him rustling in the thorn bushes. Maybe they liked his company. Maybe they didn't care. Norman just enjoyed the idea of being sneaky. It made everything more exhilarating, and it also gave him more of an excuse to be quiet. His most articulate words and phrases were best kept in his thoughts, after all.

* * *

Nearly a year later, on the damp October day of Norman's mapmaking, he once again found the mortuary doors wide open, a whole family waiting at the bottom of the steps. The older woman of the group was talking too much, while the others stood in silence. Norman didn't like it when people talked more than they should.

He crouched low and decided to walk through the woods to get to the back of the building, where he stashed away his mapmaking tools and returned ever so silently to the tree line just beside the building to spy on the neatly clad family.

The talkative woman was still talking, and the two

morticians emerged from behind the little white car parked out front, carrying vases of assorted flowers. The family turned without a sound—with the exception of the unusually loud woman. That's when Norman saw her, small against the others. He felt his breath catch and quickly grasped his lucky dime, which had found its permanent home in a crevice of his coat pocket many moons before.

Norman hadn't seen her since maybe six months prior, when she'd scrambled off into the woods to run home for supper. Blood had stained her mustard turtleneck and overalls. Her lips had been cracked and red, and her hair, which had gotten caught in the brambles by the bench, had been a knotted brown mess. It was the first time he'd seen a girl in such a beautiful state, and it was also the last. Today, her overalls were gone and replaced with black. She matched her family. Her hair was pulled neatly into a braid down the center of her back, and he could barely see her lips, but they didn't look as well-worn from a day of playfully screaming into the chilly air. Her name was Julianne.

A gust of wind blew strands of hair out of her braid, but she didn't lift a finger. Norman looked on as the quieter of the two older women tucked the loose hair behind Julianne's ear, then decided to undo the braid and recreate the masterpiece. It was at this moment that Julianne's eyes met his.

Her muddy orbs widened, and she lifted a frail hand, slightly, gesturing for him to stay put. He could just make out the sliver of her hand where the skin was slightly darker, discolored. Her family started toward the car. Norman hesitated. Aunt Mona wouldn't be expecting him for a while, anyway. He had to wait for Julianne to come back. He glanced downward to his own scar. A lovely line, similar to that of Julianne's, creased the center of his palm.

* * *

Six months earlier, Norman and Julianne had been friends for almost one whole day. They'd met behind the mortuary, where Norman caught her sitting in his spot. She'd whirled around when he stepped on a twig.

"Your shoes are kind of funny, don't you think?" she said.

"My dad gave them to me."

"They'll get muddy."

"I don't care."

Silence, staring.

"How old are you?"

"Eight. You're in my spot," Norman stated.

"I'm eight, too. And I'm not sorry." Julianne swung her legs back and forth.

"Why are you here?"

"I just wanted to see what sort of place could make my dad look like he used to."

Norman frowned. "Your dad is dead?"

"No! Why would you say that?"

"I mean—"

"My mom and dad visited here a while ago. When they got home, I heard my dad say, 'They'll make me look the way I used to, with hair and everything.' He's bald now. I wanted to see what kind of place could do that—give him hair again. Sounds like magic."

"I think you went to the wrong place," he said. "That sounds like a barber."

"Maybe," Julianne said, her face reflecting deep thought. "Why are *you* here?"

"I always come here. It's my spot. I like looking in there." He pointed to the window. "It's interesting."

"What's in there?"

"You didn't look?"

"Not yet."

The wind rustled in the pricker bushes, and Julianne's hair flew about, framing her face in an abstract way.

"Dead people."

"What?"

"That's what's in there. Dead people. They come here and get all clean and stuff, and then they go out with the families to get buried."

"Wow." Julianne gazed at the window. "That's . . ."

"Scary?"

"Cool," she responded. She stood up on top of the bench and stared through the little window.

"What do you see?" Norman asked.

She inched to the side so Norman could join her on the bench. It was the same view he'd seen every other time. A long hallway, lined with candelabras, flowers, and stained glass. The carpet was ugly. He sometimes imagined seeing the actual dead bodies, but he knew they must've been kept elsewhere. All he got were coffins. And the occasional sobbing woman. One time he saw a man pass out in the center of the foyer.

"I like your lizard," Julianne said, pointing at William, who had been perched on Norman's shoulder the whole time.

"His name is William, and he's a salamander."

The rest of the day was filled with more spying and running through the woods. At some point, Norman ran home to drop off William, leaving Aunt Mona curious, as she watched her nephew run off happier and more excited than ever. When the sky grew darker, and the sun finally began to fade, Julianne said she had to go.

"Supper's soon. My ma will want me home."

Norman wondered what it'd be like to have a mother who'd want him home for supper. Aunt Mona always waited, never pressed time. "Where do you live?"

She pointed straight back past the mortuary. "It's not far, but it's through there."

"I have an idea." Norman scuttled off and feverishly dug through the dirt.

"What's that?" Julianne asked, eyes widening.

"Pocket knife. In case my enemies find me."

"You have enemies?"

Norman nodded. Red ants and policemen, he thought.

"Why do you need it now?"

"Let's make a blood bond."

"For what?" Julianne licked her chapped lips. A droplet of blood dripped from her bottom lip onto her chin. She wiped it away, leaving a smudge.

Norman shrugged. "To be in a secret pact. So I know you're not my enemy."

Julianne nodded. "That sounds good."

"I'll do you first," Norman said, flicking the knife out of its wooden casing and extending a hand for Julianne. She put her hand in his, and he flipped it palm up, then brought the knife to the skin. "Ready?"

Julianne sucked in a breath and nodded. "Yeah."

"Bite on your sleeve. One, two . . . three!" Norman quickly drew a line with the knife down the center of Julianne's palm. The girl winced but stayed calm. A thin stream of blood flowed down her hand, over her wrist. The cut was deep, but not enough to be serious. She could've just as easily gotten it from thorn bushes.

"Now I do you, right?" she asked.

Norman nodded. He hesitated to give her his knife but realized he'd spent a whole day with her, and nothing had gone wrong. She hadn't thrown him in the prickers. She hadn't let him fall out of the tree in the woods. She hadn't even pushed him into the stream at the base of the hill. He handed over the knife and held out his hand. Julianne didn't hesitate before slicing an almost-perfect replica of her own cut into Norman's palm.

"What now?" Julianne asked.

"We shake."

The two reached out and matched their bleeding hands together.

"I'm Norman," the boy said.

"I'm Julianne."

"You are not my enemy," Norman informed her.

"Good." She ran off.

* * *

Autumn was a muddy season filled with slippery leaves and ugly grubs, and Norman didn't want to wait in the mud under the trees until Julianne came back. He decided it would be reasonable to sit on his bench and begin his maps. The first map came out well. It was easy for him to mimic the outer design of the building, but he had trouble envisioning the inside layout. After a long period of frustrated window peering and then another of imagining with his eyes closed, Julianne finally tapped him on the shoulder.

"What are you doing?"

"I'm making maps."

"Oh."

She wasn't wearing black anymore. She was wearing a green sweater that matched Norman's jacket and shoes and the same bloodstained overalls from the first day they'd met.

"Did somebody die?" Norman asked.

"My dad," Julianne replied. She undid the braid from her hair and allowed the tangled strands to fall about her shoulders. She pulled a piece of chocolate from her pocket and snapped it in half.

"The one with the hair?" Norman took the other half of the chocolate.

"The one with *no* hair." She paused, her eyes visibly watering, but no tears falling. "He was right. He looked like he used to, at the funeral. With hair."

Norman felt a pang of sadness for the girl. But at the same time, he wondered if she would share in his fascination with death and if they could stay friends and explore things together.

"Your dad must've been able to predict the future," he spoke. "He was probably really special."

Julianne nodded. "What kinds of maps are you making?" she asked and wiped her nose with her sleeve.

"Maps of the mortuary." He showed her the first map he'd drawn.

"Looks good."

"Yeah, except I can't draw the inside of the building."

"How come?"

"Because I can only see what's through the window. I don't know what else is in there." He hesitated. "Actually, I guess I know what the hallway looks like." He'd been in there before, and he'd seen other rooms. But they were foggy in his memory.

Julianne's face lit up. "I know what it looks like!"

Norman raised an eyebrow.

"I do! I had to go in there with my family. I could help make your map!" A recent encounter with the other side! It enthralled the boy, but he shook his head.

"I don't know . . ."

"Then let's explore the place together," Julianne blurted.

"What?"

"My family just walked in last time, and I bet if the weird guys who work there find us, they'll remember me."

"That doesn't sound like a good idea." In fact, this idea went against everything Norman believed in. Never trust anyone, keep ideas to yourself, and be as sneaky as possible. Don't jeopardize your spying spot by waltzing into the place you're spying on. But he'd already broken two of those rules by being Julianne's friend. Perhaps it wouldn't hurt to break another.

"Come on." Julianne held out her palm. "I am not your enemy, remember?"

Norman took her hand, and the two walked around the side of the enormous stone building and stood before the wooden doors. The handles were bigger than both of their heads. The children could practically hear each other's hearts racing. Norman tucked his rolls of paper under his free arm.

"Ready?" he asked.

Julianne nodded and placed her hand on the doorknob. As the two friends braced themselves, scarred hands interlocked, Norman looked down at his green suede shoes, thought of his parents, and smiled.

Liz Waldie is a filmmaker, photographer, and writer whose work is inspired by the uncanny. Her childhood was spent with wild-raspberry-stained fingers in a wooded Pennsylvania suburb, where she lived with ghosts, tumbled through grass, and frequently befriended caterpillars. She holds a bachelor of fine arts from the University of the Arts and currently resides in Philadelphia with her partner, her gecko, and her growing plant collection.

The Sitting Tree

Constance Garcia-Barrio

I accelerated on the entrance ramp and shot onto the interstate just ahead of the speeding tractor trailer.

"Praise the Lord!" said Aunt Carrie, glancing back at the rig and wiping her brow.

I hadn't counted on an amen chorus in the back seat, but since Aunt Carrie was there maybe she'd pray us through the speed traps. I didn't plan to lose time. This wasn't a leisure trip, and it wasn't my idea.

This morning my mother had phoned and used a tone that wavered between plea and command. It was like a red flag. It meant trouble.

"Mother Jessie's taken a turn for the worse," she'd said. Mother Jessie, my great-grandmother, was well over a hundred. How well over no one knew. She had been born into slavery, which meant off the record. She had known a world far different from the one I was living in with tailored suits and a business card that read, "J. Ann Johnson, CPA."

"A turn for the worse," I had repeated. At a hundred-odd you don't expect a season of pollen and promise. I felt my mother building up to something, and tension sawed my shoulders.

"I haven't seen Mother Jessie as often as I'd like with my bad heart and all," my mother said. "She might not make it this time. Could you take me down, baby?"

I jerked the phone cord as if to cut off the question. Any answer would be wrong, either for my mother or for me. My temples drummed home the dilemma.

"You there?" my mother said. "I don't like asking you. I know you're busy. I wouldn't do it if there was any other way, Jesella."

Aunt Carrie had invited herself along at the last minute. Now we would get three soap-opera summaries per gallon and reruns of family gossip. A long drive to a short dirt road, pigs, chickens, and a whitewashed house with an aged woman inside.

For the privilege of seeing these things, I'd had to break a date, an important one. He was supposed to come by my place, as usual. The table was set, and the food in the refrigerator. A dip with cheese and chives, steak, herbed brown rice, and crème brûlée I'd made myself. I'd bought a good burgundy to lubricate the conversation. We had a lot to talk about. I'd been waiting two years for him to get a divorce, and I wanted to tell him, gently, that I was getting anxious. I was giving up plenty for him. Other men, job mobility, my child-bearing years. In my inner ledger, I put his investment in our relationship under "Accounts Receivable".

"What in the world are you thinking about, child, that you don't hear me talking to you?" Aunt Carrie thumped the back of the driver's seat. "The sign said, 'Food and Fuel One Mile.' There's nothing I'd rather see right now than a restroom. My back teeth are underwater."

"And I could do with a cold drink," my mother said. "Ever since I got the call this morning, my mouth's been dry."

I sighed and maneuvered to the right. "If you make it quick," I called after them as they ambled toward the McDonald's, "we can beat the rush-hour traffic."

A half hour after we left the service plaza, we hit the traffic jam. The stop-start chewed my nerves, but not my mother's or Aunt Carrie's. It loosened them up, got them talking. Funny. There'd been times when they hadn't spoken to each other for months, but now they talked torrents about down home and their girlhood.

"Do you remember those winter days," my mother said, "the

sweet smell of the apple wood logs in that old black stove, or breaking the ice on watering troughs for the cows to drink?"

In a sidelong glance, I saw a smile flash and then fade from her face.

"I still have three of the quilts Mother Jessie made back then, all of them with parts of clothes from dead kin," my mother added. "She would have us drag out that big sack of old clothes. Then the three of us—we would cut out the good pieces, spread them and fit them together, and quilt from morning till night. The men would mend harnesses and mix feed for the stock, and we would quilt and tell stories."

"I recollect freezing my butt off in that two-seater outhouse," Aunt Carrie said. "Lord Jesus!"

"Ma Lucy used to feel her way to the outhouse—and all over the farm—with her stick, she knew the land so well," my mother said. "Remember how she would sit with her head tilted toward our voices?" Ma Lucy, Mother Jessie's mother, died when Aunt Carrie was barely nine. My mother was sixteen then.

"Such a little old thing, with hair that hung all the way down to her contraption," Aunt Carrie said. "Lord Jesus, the stories she could tell. Overseers with nigger dogs and slaves' secret prayer meetings in the woods."

"When Ma Lucy died, Mother Jessie went and sat in the sitting tree, sat there half the night," my mother said. "It started raining, and Cousin Lewis went out and brought her in."

For a moment they were both quiet, and I welcomed the respite. I could hear horns honking, drivers cussing.

"You and I sat there too," my mother said. She'd told me more than once about her parents dying in an accident and the long train ride down home with the caskets. "Mother Jessie found us wedged together in the tree. She smoothed our hair, wiped our faces, and asked us if we wanted to live with her."

"I don't guess Jesella knows about the sitting tree," Aunt Carrie said.

"No," I snapped, taut with the bumper-to-bumper tension. "That's a privilege I haven't had."

"It's no privilege, child," Aunt Carrie said. "Nobody sits in it for that. The tree has a big old trunk, two, maybe three feet high. Then it divides and makes a crook, so you sit right in it."

"I'll stick to my vibro-recliner."

"At the rate you're going," Aunt Carrie said, "you'll need to."

My mother said nothing but cleared her throat to hush us. Aunt Carrie tried to lighten the mood. "Well," she said, "we Johnson women are padded enough to sit wherever we want. There's plenty to be said for a good ass, and more than a few men have said it to me too."

That touched a nerve. My man had given me a nickname along those lines, one that rated a triple X. Aunt Carrie hadn't only touched a nerve of mine. My mother cleared her throat again and quick-froze the conversation.

Once out of the traffic jam, I made good time. Still, night caught us a couple of hours from the place.

"I hope you remember the way," I told my mother.

"Not from this new road, baby."

"But you do have a phone number?"

She did. I called and asked for directions. I might as well have asked for the Ghost of Christmas Past. I hung up and said, "They don't know the way, and neither do we. And my map doesn't even show their road. I'm not poking around in the dark. We're stopping at a motel."

I wouldn't have won a popularity poll just then, but I wanted comfortable accommodations for the night. I found a decent place at a decent price. "One single room," I said, "and one double." We quickly settled in.

I spent half the night tossing on the bed, wishing I were feeling my man's weight and hugging the pillow as if it were my consolation prize. Toward morning, I drifted off in a dream in which I entered a crowded boardroom to deliver financial statements. As I approached the polished oak table, I saw one of Mother Jessie's quilts draped over it. I hesitated and then put the papers on it. People looked startled. Some applauded. I awoke to the clapping of heavy rain on the leaves of a tree outside my window.

We hit the highway after an early breakfast and bumped onto the dirt road by midmorning. The car kicked up pebbles as we went.

"We're almost home, baby," my mother said.

"You mean you and Aunt Carrie almost are."

"Damn!" Aunt Carrie punched the back of my seat. "Your mother put everything on the line when you asked her so you could get your CPA. But what you got was a m-e-s-s."

"And what you got was half the story."

I recalled my parents' separating, the last of my girlhood swallowed up caring for my brothers because my mother worked late. I cut a look at Aunt Carrie through the rearview mirror and almost missed Mother Jessie's rutted drive. I turned the wheel hard, and the sharp turn threw my mother and Aunt Carrie to one side. At the end of the drive, I stopped the car under a tree, jumped out, and came around toward Aunt Carrie.

"Even after I finished school, things were hard. Remember that year Momma got sick and you and the others said you couldn't help? I worked two jobs, paid Momma's bills, the boys' school, every damn thing." I took a step forward so that I was right in her face. "I'm paid up, Aunt Carrie. I don't owe my mother, I owe you less, and as for this place—"

I ducked, and Aunt Carrie's hand just missed my cheek. My mother grabbed her shoulders, held them.

"I'm glad y'all made it down," called a voice from the porch. A bent old man came down the two weathered wooden steps and shuffled toward us. I recognized Cousin Lewis, Mother Jessie's son.

"Jessie's bad off, poor critter," he said.

We walked to the house and stopped just inside the door.

"Better go on up," Cousin Lewis said. "Maw been holding on just to see you."

I hesitated. The fight, the trip, and the rough night gripped me. "I'll wait here." I stood at the foot of the stairs. Cousin Lewis scratched the white stubble on his nut-brown face. Aunt Carrie scowled and started up the stairs. Then my mother spoke.

"Help me up the stairs, Jesella."

Her heart was bad, but not that bad.

"Help me up, please."

Our eyes locked as I took her arm.

When we reached the top of the steps, I saw a chair outside Mother Jessie's room. I didn't look at my mother, but at the clean white wall in front of me. My mother's gaze pressed against me before she turned and went in alone. A while later Aunt Carrie came out. She was sobbing and wiping her eyes. She stopped in front of me, balled up her handkerchief, crushed it in her fist, and then said, "You've got to go in."

"Aunt Carrie," I said, groping through a maze of unexpected feelings, "I really don't know if I—"

"Lord Jesus, child!" She didn't realize that she was shouting.

The door of Mother Jessie's room opened, and my mother came out. So did a voice. "Jesella," it said.

I got up, stood still.

"Jesella," it repeated, in a high creaky voice. The tone worked its way through knots of doubt, and I went in.

Dark-brown weathered face, hooked nose, gray eyes. Her lips parted. "Come over here, child."

She took her time, looking me over. "Comely," she said. "Let's see the rest of you."

She asked me to lift my skirt. Her gnarled fingers pressed into my knees, thighs, and calves until she knew all there was to know about them.

"You're sound, child. Do you have a man?"

"Yes."

"A good man?"

I said nothing.

She shifted her head on the pillow and looked toward the

window. I followed her gaze and saw that the clouds of the morning rain were lifting.

"I had a man once," she said. "He'd leave fruit on my windowsill in the morning so that I would know to meet him in the woods in the evening. Such evenings! But he married another gal."

Married another gal. The words she used to speak her old hurt stirred me like the clean voice of one instrument making the strings of another hum in sympathy. And that humming swept away everything but her old pain and my present one and brought us face-to-face.

Mother Jessie sighed. I sat down on the floor beside the bed so that I could hear every word and look straight into her face.

"Then I met a man as plain as a post, but he was as good to me as ever he could be. There was hard years farming, and choking fear when the Klan would ride, but we had good times too."

When she stopped to catch her breath, I heard the wheezing in it. "I was still a young woman when he died. Broke my heart."

"But it didn't break your nerve."

Her lips barely lifted at the corners when I said that.

Mother Jessie had run the farm, reared her children and two of her grandchildren, my mother and Aunt Carrie.

We shared the silence, searching each other's faces like painters learning a landscape. I wouldn't miss a thing; nor would she. The gold at my ears and throat, laugh lines starting to etch ironic grooves, and signs of the restless nights, signs of the restless years.

"Jesella," Mother Jessie said, "you've got trouble, child, but you've got strength, too." She rested and then spoke again. "Call your mother and Carrie."

My mother went in, pulled up a chair to the bed, and sat holding Mother Jessie's hand. Aunt Carrie went in and stood by the bed, then sat on it, then stood again and paced, humming one spiritual after another. I could just hear her from where I sat in the hall, my eyes closed, my thoughts whirling.

Late in the afternoon, Aunt Carrie's humming stopped. I didn't need to go in the room. I knew. "And the evening and the morning were her last day," I said to myself.

The trickle down my cheek startled me. It was as if by laying hands on me, Mother Jessie had reached nerve and sinew of some secret inner flesh. In so few words, in so few minutes, I had a kinswoman. And in the next hours, I lost her. On what balance sheet could I figure this arithmetic? Subtract one hundred years of wisdom, take away two eyes, two hands. Place a zero in the column marked time. Damn that night wasted in the motel.

I had to get out of the house for a while. Take a walk, take it in. I trudged along the edge of fields that Mother Jessie used to plow with a mule. I recalled summers long ago when my mother brought us to the farm for a few days. I ate some grapes—not quite ripe—from the arbor and drank well water that tasted of stones. I looked toward the grazing cows, smelled them, and gazed at rows of corn, green and growing, that stretched toward the woods. I picked up earth and pressed its grit and coolness to my powdered cheeks.

Hours later as the family gathered, Aunt Carrie came out looking for me. When she saw me, she stood back in surprise.

"I see, child," she said, "that you've found the sitting tree."

Constance Garcia-Barrio is a lifelong Philadelphian who has had the good fortune to travel a bit. Her maternal grandparents came here from Spotsylvania County, Virginia, in the 1920s. She has a love of Philadelphia's Black history, and she has often written about it.

COMMUNITY

Philly Scam, or Paying It Forward

Oni Lasana

I grew up on Huntingdon Street in North Philly—an original Soul Sista from Cool World Valley, a bona fide concrete-jungle city girl. Even back then, though, I could imagine another life, one outside the city. In the eighth grade, I wrote a prophetic poem about country life called "A Dream".

Fast forward to 1983, many, many years later: I live in the countryside of Chester County, Pennsylvania—across the bypass from the exact farmhouse I depicted in my childhood poem. This dream farmhouse regularly greets me when I enter the busy bypass from my empty-nested, soul-stirring studio and sanctuary.

A queen on Kingsway Drive, my domain sits on a quiet cul-de-sac, woodsy and peaceful, where everyone waves hi but minds their business—until an emergency, like when a tornado hit our house. Then they will show up and be down for the get down like real old-school country neighbors. Tall trees surround our big bucket pool and half acre of riding-lawn-mower backyard. We're not far from rolling hills and Amish farms and up the way from an old steel town in the valley.

Ten years ago, my husband and I lived in a cramped row home in Germantown with our two kids, so all this space we have now is a blessing. I enjoy the bliss of being a wife and mother on a hilltop outside the little steel underground-railroad town of Coatesville, forty minutes from the big city of Philadelphia and about the same to Lancaster.

Our closest connection to the area was the Veterans Hospital around the corner. My brother, Sisco, spent some days or weeks there after he was wounded in Vietnam. One of the many young African American boys sent from Edison High School and the gang wars of North Philly to the gang wars of Vietnam.

Where we live has its drawbacks, for sure. As the mother of three young children, with a husband who often works late, I'm alone a lot with the kids in this unfamiliar place, worrying that a traumatized vet might escape from the VA, sneak into our backyard, and mistake us for the Viet Cong. Even scarier, I worry that I will never see my people from the hood ever again.

Country life is as safe and quiet a place as you can imagine. Rabbits hop off into the bush, deer eat berries from the trees, and stray cats hunt field mice. Far from the city life of police sirens, music blasting from cars, dogs barking, children in the streets, and folks chatting loudly across backyard fences. I absolutely loved my world in North Philly—playing hide-and-go-get-it, chink, handball, and double Dutch, running through fire hydrant sprays, on the way to the Connie Mack Recreation Center. In the sweet city of Philly, in the Valley, I lived a happy, rambunctious childhood. Italian ices, hoagies, steak sammiches, soft pretzels, and chocolate milk—I feasted on the ultimate in corner girl cuisine. I always felt alive and connected to a world of three dimensions and infinite sensations.

One chilly day in November 2016, "daylight losing time" is in effect. At three p.m. I'm on the road to showcase my storytelling offerings at the African American Museum of Philadelphia, scheduled for five p.m. By four, it's dark and rainy, and I'm stuck in red-lighted traffic. And I have to *go* (as in, take a leak). So I take the very next exit at Girard Avenue, the Philly zoo—not my usual pit stop, but nature is calling, and it's no time to do Kegel exercises, sitting in traffic without Depends to depend on! Right, right, left—I swerve into the A Plus gas station and mini market.

As I'm trying to park my Jeep, a distraught black man approaches me as if we are cousins—before I can even open my door! I jump out and wave him off: "Sorry, I can't hear you now, brother. I gotta use the bathroom!"

"OK, I'll catch you later!" he hollers back.

Relieved, I exit the store and see him on the phone talking in a panic to someone. Much more comfortable, and feeling kinda guilty, I make eye contact, though I think it's a little shady that he is still hanging outside the gas station store in the rain, waiting for me, with "Sucker" written all over my face.

It is pouring rain, so I invite him into my car to hear his case. I know I'm taking a chance, but I grew up in the hood, and you'd have to have a gun or knife to scare me. Even then, I'd either talk my way out of death or fight like a cat. Being from North Philly, I wouldn't go down easy.

Pepper spray is also in my door pocket, but so far I feel no urge to dig for it. As a child, I could often "feel" people, and his eyes aren't too crazy or threatening. And he isn't towering over me. He looks innocent enough as he gets into the passenger seat.

"Ma'am, my transmission is shot, and my car broke down. I'm trying to get to Wilmington, Delaware. I have to take a train, but I'm short thirteen dollars. Can you help me out?"

I pause to let his request marinate. Finally, I tell him I'll give him a ride to the train station, since it's on my way. He says he just called a cab, but he's still short the cost of the train ticket. *So he can afford a cab but is short of the ticket . . . Hmmmm . . .* I'm not feeling like arguing, so I give him all the cash I have, a ten and a five.

He sighs. "Oh, miss, thanks. I promise I'll pay it forward."

I give him my business card and joke, "I don't know about paying it forward, but you can pay *me* back." We laugh. I ask him his name. We shake hands. My address isn't on my card, but maybe he'll find me on Facebook or phone me for my address to mail the money.

Yeah right. The bell rings.

He's out of my car, and I creep into traffic. I think to myself, *Dag . . . he's just pulled a fast one on me, hasn't he?* I look back, and he is gone. I can't see in the dark and the rain where he went. Was it into a car? Running down the street to ease his stress? Or to buy food or drugs? The Philly zoo parking garage a block from the gas station is a perfect spot to hit up tourists with a lame story for money.

But why, if he needed money, would he ask for thirteen dollars? Why not five, ten, or twenty dollars? Or just rob me! And to beg for such a small *uneven* amount? Maybe he really was short of the train ticket?

Wonders of wonders, I think. *Is my life in the country turning me into a real-life Stepford wife, complacent and naive?* I'm going to need that fifteen dollars, maybe not tonight but sure enough tomorrow.

Suddenly, I start to feel grateful that I was able to help someone in genuine need—or so I hope. I'm experiencing mixed feelings, for sure, so I tell myself, *Think positive, girl. Yes, you did a good deed for someone else.*

With so much hatred in the world, the day after Trump won, what can you believe if you can't believe in helping others? No matter who is president of Americ*an't*, believe it.

I hit my music—time to chill it away. I press the UP button for Chrisette Michele's "Be OK" and turn away from the jammed slo-pressway onto the inner-city roads, through the park drive to Center City. It feels good I helped him. I've spent more on a pair of shoes or blouse I've never worn.

I didn't write down or remember his name. When I reach the African American Museum, I mention the experience to my friend, and she assures me it was a scam. He scammed me! He probably was drunk or on drugs or in a panic to get high. Or his car was broken down, and he *would* pay my kindness forward.

Maybe. Maybe not.

Either way, I'm still alive, swerving on Lincoln Drive, swagging on 76 with style and fortitude, enjoying all the twists and turns the streets of my hometown give up to the universe.

Oni Lasana was born at Temple University and danced on the Hy Lit show. Her mother owned a boutique on 52nd Street. She is a member of Keepers of the Culture, Philadelphia's Afrocentric storytelling group, and can be found online at www.OniLasana.com.

Praying for a Miracle, Praying for Absolution

Shannon Frost Greenstein

Hail Mary, full of grace, the Lord is with thee . . .
I skip that one.
St. Francis, please, help me . . .
I skip that one, too.
Please, God, don't let him find out . . .
That one piques my interest.

I exhale, a puff of air between pursed lips like a tsunami of wind, the flame blinking out and a meandering ribbon of smoke ascending toward the ceiling. Toward God.

It gets a little darker, colder.

I reach out, pluck the stout, waxy column from its glass prison, and wince as a drop of hot wax falls onto my thumb.

I'm sorry, God, please, please, I'm sorry . . . don't let him find out.

I hold the candle to my nose, inhaling the woman's desperation. She'd had an affair, and her husband was catching on, and she was afraid she was going to lose the children.

Typical.

The late afternoon sun pours through stained glass, piercing me with shards of color that illuminate me from within and shine out from my very skin.

It is deathly quiet in the Cathedral Basilica of Saints Peter and Paul, a few souls kneeling before the altar clutching their rosaries, obedience made incarnate. The sounds of Philadelphia echo outside, but subdued, like even Ubers and angry pedestrians and the pervasive wailing of a rapidly shifting climate dare not intrude on this sanctity.

I examine the candle, now cool, now benign; no trace remains of a panicked young woman, falling back on the security blanket of an all-loving deity, frantic enough to drop two dollars into a wooden box and strike a match, strike it to produce fire and then spread that fire outward, wick burning her wish up to heaven, frantic enough to think any of that would work.

I replace it, exactly the same, but wishless, miracleless. Her prayer was between her and God and, despite that exclusivity, or because of it, now will never be heard. Or answered.

Nietzsche said God is dead. But that's not right. God is there, and he's listening. But sometimes, he just doesn't care. And sometimes, prayers don't always make it up to heaven. And sometimes, there are forces in play down here on earth.

Like me.

Her fingerprints on the candle are smudged now from the oils on my hands, but still her plaintive yearning rings in my ears and around my cerebrum.

Please don't let him find out.

Bored by now, her not knowing God will never hear her prayer, I run my hands across the row of votives, always burning. Always someone wishing. Always someone hoping for a miracle. Always someone in trouble, in need, cold, hungry, sick, dying, lonely, scared. Always voices in the din calling out to God, and always me, trapping them, catching the voices of the troubled, the cold, the hungry, sick, dying, lonely, scared on their way to where they're going and making sure they go no further than me.

Why?

Well, if he doesn't answer my prayers, why should anyone else get an answer to their own? If I have fallen to my knees before God, stood strong against the devil's temptations, screamed in misery to the sky for him to hear me, if I have done all that and *still* heard nothing but silence . . . then why does anyone else deserve a miracle?

Please...
Don't...
Why...
Our Father...

The prayers run under my fingertips, the prints of their owners leaving behind a script I can read clearly, the swan song of unacknowledged dreams.

Our Lady of Guadalupe, Patroness of the Unborn, please take this child into your loving arms at the feet of our Heavenly Father. Please, please, I can't have this baby.

This could be interesting.

I rest my thumb against the candle, barely touching its surface, and feel the weight of this desire course through my limbs and fill my fingers and toes and echo deep within my teeth, where I usually feel the bass line in rock songs and my pulse when I run.

Please, God, I can't. Forgive me, and I'm sorry.

I get a mental picture of her from her fingerprints: a young woman—unmarried, of course, and barely making ends meet. Her clothes are ratty, her car is always breaking down, and she cannot rise above the lifetime of trauma that has kept her so downtrodden.

Deep down, in the part of me that once lost everything while God laughed, I can almost feel empathy for her. I can almost understand her panic and her fear, but that part of me is quiet now, and empathy is dead, just like Nietzsche's God.

I lean forward and blow out the candle, extinguishing the light, extinguishing the warmth, extinguishing the prayer. I can almost hear her sigh as the smoke drifts toward the ceiling, the sound of her certainty in God's existence being wheezed out along with the flame.

Looks like someone's having a baby.

* * *

I'm not sure how long I kneel, reading wishes, eavesdropping on prayers, ensuring that people's greatest desires will never reach anyone's ear, omnipotent or otherwise.

Misery loves company.

I lose time, sometimes, listening to the fingerprints. Sometimes I wipe out the dreams of an entire congregation's worth of worshippers; sometimes I pick just a few, just a few to really piss off God, the most desperate prayers of the meek who need a miracle the most.

Once I blew out a candle lit by a single father in his twenties, swearing he'd realize his dream of the seminary and priesthood if God would only cure his only daughter of leukemia. Blowing that one out felt good. It felt like vengeance, from one man who had everything taken away against another one, against the God that has abandoned us both.

I sense movement behind me and remove my hand, lest anyone see me plucking wishes from the well. An older man—someone pious, someone devout, someone damned anyway—approaches the altar, steadies himself against the balustrade, and drops to his knees on the cheap green velour cushion.

I nonchalantly rest my fingertips upon the wood of the rail, feeling the vibrations pulsing through every fiber of the grain. I hear the inner monologue of every person who has ever touched this banister and left a print; I hear the voice of the tree itself. I hear the man's thoughts. I have his headache.

I swear to God, when she wakes up...

I startle at the venom in the prayer, my teeth closing involuntarily on my tongue. This man is *enraged*; anger is radiating from his very psyche through his hands, tightly clutching the balustrade, his knuckles white, even his fingerprints infuriated, which I read through the white noise of the wooden rail's past lives, when it housed baby birds and cried red leaves in the fall and was felled, finally, by a chainsaw and man's short-sightedness.

I will burn that house to the ground, I swear I will...

This caricature of Christianity, this refined gentleman, looking every inch the successful professional and

God-fearing lamb, means exactly what he says; I understand that intrinsically. There is indeed a woman, and there is indeed a house, and if she wakes up, he will burn them both to the ground, and I have no more reason to doubt this than I do reason to suspect God answers prayers at all.

The man, his jaw clenched, reaches out a hand and plucks a votive from the pile. He grabs a match, pinches it between his finger, flicks it alight with his thumbnail in a near-unimaginable show of manliness and manual dexterity belied by his polo shirt and shiny shoes.

He lights the candle, the alcove infinitesimally brighter with the added illumination, and shakes out the match. The pungent stench of sulfur fills the air, like hellfire—like Revelation.

As quickly as he has come, the man rises to his feet and exits the periphery of my vision, the receding echo of his footprints sounding like a dying heartbeat. I hear the towering oak doors with the giant bronze knockers open, then shut, and he is gone.

Quiet again, and I edge over to the newest candle in the chorus of light, resting a single finger against the gummy wax.

A shriek as loud as a siren fills my head, and I see her, his wife, probably, unconscious, bleeding, supine on a bed that is soon to go up in flames. Images flood my nervous system and bounce around, relentlessly, like a million tennis balls hit, again and again, against the walls of my skull: a fight, yelling, pervasive terror, the moment she was choked unconscious and a small child peeking around the bedroom door at the dreadfulness of it all.

Well, *shit*.

I feel a stirring, foreign, alien. It takes my breath away.

It's been so long since I've felt anything but rage that I almost don't recognize any other sentiment. And as I clutch the candle and see the eyes of the child, my mind flashes back, unbidden, to the children, my children, my family, the only thing that mattered, taken from me by a supposedly omnibenevolent God, and I feel paternal, and I feel grief, and I feel sorrow, and I feel, suddenly, like a dam has broken, thousands of other things I can't even identify.

Now what?

Is now, I ask myself, *the moment it all turns around? Is now my chance to set things right, to balance the cosmic scales, to forgive God and ask for his forgiveness in turn? What if now is my last chance?*

Emotion is filling me up like water in a bathtub, punctuated by flashes of the hatred at God I've never been able to let go. I feel uncertain; I feel lost. I feel alone.

I've been alone for what seems like forever, of course, since he took my wife and kids and house and job, but the ache of this loneliness is different. This is the loneliness of solitary, and this is the loneliness of being on your own in a foreign land, and this is the loneliness Cassandra felt after Apollo cursed her.

Is this the moment?

I stare, transfixed, at the flame. I try to dredge up a memory, of my children, of when I was last happy. I see the light, dancing, and understand in my lizard brain that, if given the chance, this tiny fire would burn out of control and eat everything in its path. I stare, and the flame merges with the fire in my mind's eye, the fire that is probably about to be set and which might take the life of a child in addition to its mother.

Is this the moment?

Nope.

This candle I leave. This prayer keeps shining right up to heaven, a prayer to make things right and not get caught, but right is wrong; and I have no problem letting wrongs play out as they may. After all, if I'm in perdition, I don't give much of a shit about the *rest* of the world getting there eventually, too.

Why, I've asked time and time again, *have you forsaken me?*

It took a while, but the answer struck me one day, out of nowhere. It is not that God has forsaken me; it's that he doesn't care enough *not* to. Back then, before, when he called me Job, I put everything on the line for him; and like any gambler down on his luck or with a crooked dealer, I lost it all.

And now?

Now I leave that candle burning. It's the least I can do, for revenge, for my family, for the love we shared that became a mockery, to pay back this debt I feel I am owed.

It's not like I'm going anywhere at the end of the day. I've lurked in churches for millennia, chuckling inwardly as sermons praise my faith, plotting, blowing out candles, destroying fantasies and hope. And I'll stay, too, until the debt is paid.

This is my penance.

Perdition. Because God isn't dead . . . He's just a sadist.

Shannon Frost Greenstein is the author of Pray for Us Sinners, *a fiction collection from Alien Buddha Press, and* More., *a poetry collection by Wild Pressed Books. She is a multitime Pushcart Prize nominee and a former PhD candidate in Continental philosophy. Follow her at shannonfrostgreenstein.com or on Twitter @ShannonFrostGre.*

The Weight of It

Thalia Geiger

When I walked in, Ella was waiting for me. I had only put my keys in the dish by the door. Dinner had already been made; I could smell the chicken, surely cold now on the stove. Daniel was sitting with her at the table, drawing, crayons and colored pencils sprawled around him. I greeted Dan, who chirped a happy, "Hi, Dad," back to me, but Ella said nothing. I would have hugged and kissed him, but Ella's position told me to keep my distance. Her legs were crossed at her ankles as she gripped a glass of water, condensation trickling over her hand. I imagined she must have been pressing the dripping hand to her chest before I arrived, holding onto the cross around her neck and bracing herself for what came out of her mouth, slow and controlled.

"Is there something you need to tell me?"

I didn't answer her at first, just waited for the moment, like a dream, to sink into reality. But it was reality; I just made her wait.

"I guess I'll just ask," she said. Her face was still. She held her arms stiff. "Have you—been . . ." She stopped, looked at Dan as he colored.

I let my head drop to the side. "Really?"

"I have to be sure." We stared at each other. "Wally. *Have you?*" Dan finished his drawing, placed the green crayon down, and looked at Ella, about to ask to be excused. I could see the concern on his face, a cry soon to come if his request was denied.

"Wally. Answer me."

"Because I'm late, you jump there?"

"Why not?"

I pivoted, my shoes scuffing the hardwood. This was exactly what I didn't need: to be ambushed. What made her so sure? I kept my hands on my hips, radiating disbelief.

"Mom," Dan whined.

"Wally. Answer me."

I pinched the bridge of my nose, a headache suddenly flashing there. "You're ridiculous."

"Then just answer the question."

"I don't want to answer the *fucking* question!"

Ella didn't blink, but Dan broke into a blubber. Tears gushed. A throat-catching cry stuttered out of his body, so breathless I thought he was going to choke on his own spit. My head was pulsing.

He whined through his tears, "Stop yelling!" He raised a weak hand to reach for her. She sighed and let him crawl onto her chair with her, cries muffled in her neck.

"Shh, D. We're not mad at you. We're not mad at you." He stifled the tears, settled to whimpers as he slumped back against her and, with her, stared at me.

When she let him go, he stumbled upstairs, forgoing the need for permission. Ella's dark eyes didn't move from me as she folded her arms. "Whatever's going on with you right now, I see it. He sees it. Soon other people will see it, and then next thing you know, you're out of a job."

"Jesus, Ella—"

"Don't." She put up a finger and started to count on her hand. "You've been coming home late. You're always mad at something. You say you're swamped with work. Passing out early, sleeping in. I know what this leads up to, if you haven't done it already."

Itchy, I scratched at my neck. I wanted to roll my eyes. She was so prepared for this. She must have just read one of those pamphlets: *How to Confront an Alcoholic: 1) Be firm and clear. Remain calm and list the facts.* She thought she had me all figured out. As if I hadn't already started and finished the 12 steps two years before. As if the whole reason we got married that year was because I proved to her that I could do it.

"I'm just stressed, Ella," I explained, rubbing my eyes again. "I try to blow off some steam with other teachers at that grill, Ray's." I told her that the new principal was cracking down on us. There were new teacher evaluations, and I had just started a new unit on US government and the kids weren't getting it. All of it was true, though I still stuttered. "And then I come home and you do this."

She assessed me a moment, her stern brow shifting. She became passive enough to let me get to the couch where I took off my shoes. As I unlaced, she sank into the cushion beside me, eyes no longer narrowed and cold as she looked me over, but tepid and watchful, her hair falling into her face.

"You never tell me these things." Her nose pressed against my neck as she toyed with her cross again. "We'd be a lot stronger if I didn't have to guess what's going on with you all the time." She pulled away from my neck and looked at me.

"You're right. I'm sorry." I rubbed her thigh, her back. "Good interrogation, though. I'm gonna change."

"Okay," she said and nodded. "I'll make your plate."

* * *

The spill was invisible by the time I checked myself in the bathroom mirror. It smelled faintly, though I had run warm water on it earlier and it had dried long before I came home. It could have been rubbing alcohol, if I said so. *I cut myself shaving. Spilled some.* It happened sometimes. Or I could have told the truth, that David spilled it on me at Ray's Grille. The genius lightweight had hooked his arm around my shoulder and spilled his shot of vodka down my shirt. I just said it was no problem, dabbed it with a napkin, excused myself to the bathroom. They didn't know. Under the fluorescent light, my hands trembled. I stared at the stain for a while. Ella wouldn't know about the pep talk I gave myself, laying my forehead against the wall's cool tile. How I had cried. How I had lifted the alcohol-suffused cotton to my nose and held it there before I realized the wetness trickling down my arm was from David, too, and, convincing myself it was harmless, licked the lone stream off my skin. At the sink, I splashed my face. At the table, I told David he owed me a shot.

I took the shirt off, shoved it in my hamper and packed dirty clothes on top, then put on a fresh T-shirt. My head still rattled. I could hear Dan running around through the halls upstairs making race car noises, probably dragging his Hot Wheels along the walls. Eight-year-old things.

On the bed, I held my head and focused on the TV console—Ella's perfume on the ledge, my slumped figure reflected in the black screen—and waited for it to still the room that always seemed to be spinning. Getting through life staying sober was like trying to break down a wall by endlessly scratching at it when all I wanted to do was use a sledgehammer. Ella didn't know how hard I tried.

* * *

"I miss Ol' Garehart." David stuffed onions into his face as he spoke. "Though he probably used to shit himself in that desk. He was an okay principal. Landon is *such* a dick."

"I know," Parth said. "How do you walk into a new school, a new district, and decide to size up everyone there? He's the new one here, and one of us might get booted out?"

"If it's gonna be anyone, it might be June." David laughed as I swirled my beer in its bottle, watching the suds swim to a thin layer of froth on top. She was the new art teacher, still in her first year, and making so many mistakes.

"You're still fresh, Wally," David said. "Landon could be eyeing you, too."

"I heard June was encouraging erotic images in oil pastels," I said.

"That little five-foot woman?"

Parth nearly shot his drink out his nose. I watched it splash across his napkin. "Amazing," he said, wiping away dribble.

We talked, argued, and joked across the varnished wood table. The grill was becoming busier as we ate, getting louder with each new table filled. I watched the servers dole out dinner menus and happy hour specials. A group of young girls struggled with the table, the folders too tall and bulky for the small chairs their elbows stuck out of, the tables not big enough for all the drinks they looked ready to order.

I kept track of the time: it had been two and a half hours now, but since it was Friday, I had one extra hour before Ella got as suspicious as the night before. I kept track of my drinks: two beers, two shots, and I needed the bathroom. On the way, I calculated the time and beverages consumed, allowed myself one more before I had to cut myself off, then water, so much water, six Altoids, a cigarette, and an extra spray of cologne before heading home. If Ella still smelled something on me, I'd blame David.

In the bathroom mirror though, it was undeniable. Wally, slightly swaying. Wally, eighteen and drunk again, smiling at his reflection, hoping he'd stay that shade of happy forever. But I was thirty-one. Early grays came, one stray hair at a time. My eyes squinted to slits I could hardly see through, crow's feet crinkling. My smile came easily, and I laughed at myself, laughed at him.

Water splashed everywhere as I washed my hands. I missed the trash can with my wet paper towel and watched it bounce off the side, hitting the floor. On my way out, I was too busy rubbing still-damp hands on my slacks and bumped into a girl. I had knocked something out of her hand and said sorry, and her long blur of hair dipped and resurfaced to grab it quick: a white baggie.

"Whoa," I said. "Be careful with that."

She glanced up at me, worried, and I realized I had seen her earlier, that group of girls with the too-small table. She looked about seventeen with her freckles and blushed face, but her familiar sway and vacant look told me she was drunk, too. She saw me staring, jiggled the bag back and forth.

"I can tell you want some." A smile spread across her face. "Keep it quiet?"

I didn't say anything, couldn't say anything, then she laughed.

"Is that a yes?"

"Uh, sure," I said.

She nodded and fished the bag open, grabbed my hand from my side and poured out a small mound on my pinkie. "First snort's free," she said, closing it up and pushing past me. "You want any more, you have to buy."

She slammed the door behind her, locked it. I turned around, not wanting anyone else to see the powder I held precariously on my finger. I was numb, frozen. On the wall above my head was a picture of a cowboy riding in sepia, his face hallowed out to a skeleton. Around the corner, the chatter of the grill rose. My hand started to cramp. Heat prickled as I stared at the picture. It taunted me. Like the girl, it didn't seem to fit. And yet it folded into reality, as if all this was a dream. And if all this was a dream, it meant nothing. It was harmless. I would wake up.

I went back to the table, feeling fine. David and Parth didn't notice a thing. Soon, it kicked in, and I didn't need to think. I tilted my head up to the ceiling tiles and noticed how they glittered from all the tacky string lights, then closed my eyes and gazed at the blackness there. I could feel it happening all over again. I missed it.

* * *

In the corner of my eye, she shook her head. "Are you kidding?" She laughed then. It was a short one, so loud and wild she put one hand over her mouth then stifled a cry. Tears welled in her eyes. "God, Wally."

* * *

I had plans to meet up with an old friend, Mica, the night before to celebrate our friend Joan's birthday. She would have been twenty-six like us, and Mica planned to go to a concert at a new place, since our usual spot, Hell Hole, had closed earlier that year. It didn't take much for me to take a shot myself after we poured one out for her, and with Mica struggling to hold himself together, I needed something stronger than a soda to get me through the night. We managed to meet the band backstage and join a ten-minute smoke session in their tour bus before they kicked us out, where we paraded through the streets, looking for more bars, drugs, anything else we could find.

I had fallen asleep at Mica's in Jersey and, in the morning, drove across the Ben Franklin Bridge too fast. The sun glinted white-hot off everyone's hoods. I was still fucked up and didn't want to die, didn't want my stupidity to kill someone else, but I was late. In front of me on their morning commute, cars blurred.

When I got home, she was upstairs, grabbing her coat. I wanted to shower to get the stink off me, get rid of the fog still hovering about my brain, my eyes. Her interview was in a half hour. I slapped on cologne, rubbed my nub of deodorant into my armpits, and vigorously chewed several wads of gum at once. Downstairs, only a look—standing in my presence was all it took for her to know. She glanced downward but held her head steady, clutching little Dan in her arms, almost tight enough to make him cry. I could see the discomfort in his face. I could tell he wanted to suck his thumb by the way he held his hand close to his open mouth, though he had just stopped that a year ago. He was going to howl and wail, wrinkle her purple blouse, muss her neat bun. A glance at the living room clock showed she was going to be late, but she had to wait with Daniel, for me.

"It was Joan's birthday," I said.

"Wally." I could see her trying not to shake. "You know I need this job, and for the job I need this interview."

"I know."

"So. Then we just fix it," she said, and put Dan down, smoothing her shirt. He shuffled over to me and clutched my leg, tears subsiding.

All that time, that weight in my chest. I couldn't breathe with that weight, until she could look at me again, proud. And she didn't, but when she looked at me, I swore an inch almost lifted.

* * *

In the morning, I felt like shit. My head was pounding, throat closed and so dry a gallon of water wouldn't fix it. Sunlight streamed through the windows, warming and blinding me. I rolled over in bed. Ella was gone. She must've been downstairs, avoiding me. She had found me at the grill, drunk, high as a kite, and drove us home.

In the bathroom mirror, my eyes were bloodshot; red lines threatened to strangle the white. I tried to tame my unruly hair, brushed back the frizz with my hands, wiped my mouth clean. It was early. From our window, I could see Vanessa, a neighbor from down the street, leading her dog back into her house from a walk.

I had an idea as I showered and put on my clothes: new day, fresh start. Moretti's Bakery was around the corner. I'd get a dozen donuts, all different flavors. The baker would throw in an extra raspberry crème for my troubles. We'd all sit at the table and watch Dan gorge on them, and Ella wouldn't be able to stop herself from smiling at the whipped frosting gathering at the corners of his mouth just like I would, and our eyes would meet, and though she wouldn't forget, she'd remember. Everything.

In the hall with his toy in hand, Dan looked at me. I grabbed him up in my arms.

"Ahh!" he squealed, then said, "You stink!"

I frowned. "It's cologne."

He scrunched up his nose. "Cologne smells weird."

"You smell weird. Hey, you wanna smell like donuts? I'm gonna get some."

He flashed a big sunny smile at me. "Yes!"

"Okay." I put him down. "I'll get them right after I talk to Mom."

* * *

There was hardly a talk. More like a call that had been made.

I couldn't stop sobbing enough to get the words out. I hadn't touched her. The drugs weren't mine. But that didn't matter. My body rocked with guttural cries against the cold metal of the handcuffs. Ella's voice from last night in the car came back to me, *God, Wally. What were you doing with that girl? That kid?* She had looked at me so simply, flatly, as if she were reading a script and didn't mean the words: *I'm gonna fix this.* I hadn't done anything.

My fingertips went for Dan's head but only brushed the soft hair before Ella pulled him away. Red and blue lights flashed, coloring me as an officer's hand palmed my head and ducked me into the squad car. I listened to the silence of the neighborhood watching, the leather flexing as I sat in the seat. And all the while, they're thinking this will make me better. They think they can help me.

Thalia Geiger is a poet and fiction writer born and raised in Philadelphia. She has a BFA in creative writing from the University of the Arts and serves as an editorial assistant at the American Poetry Review. Her work has been published in Pamplemousse, Coffin Bell Journal, Santa Ana River Review, Black Horse Review, and is forthcoming in Aurora—the Allegory Ridge Poetry Anthology in 2021.

Manayunk

Peter Cunniffe

"Toady, there's some boxes from Pittsburgh outside!" Jeannie shouted up the stairs.

Toady lay unresponsive in the bed she had climbed out of over two hours ago, the same bed he had slipped into only an hour before that. This was the life the two had come to accept, if not love. Jeannie was a dental hygienist. Toady played bass in a jam band. Nights kept him out till the wee hours. Mornings got her up. "The secret to a happy marriage," Jeannie sometimes joked.

They had met in Manayunk at the Grape Street Pub. He was not playing that night, just drinking with his softball buddies. She arrived with some friends from Textile. Toady was wearing his team jersey, which was why Jeannie called him Toady. Sometimes she called him "Toady #7" and playfully perished the thought that there could be six other like souls. His shoulder-length hair was tied in a loose ponytail, with a carefree stream of orange running past his left cheek. He approached Jeannie—a very un-Toady-like move by his own admission—and introduced himself as Todd Newtson. Something about her eyes compelled him. They were brown and persistently sorrowful. They contrasted her smile perfectly. At night's end, she offered her phone number, and he promised to call. That was seven years ago.

At the beginning of their courtship, Toady was working for Corpmark by day. When a gig could be gotten, he performed in a band dubbed Thump Momma. He had studied philosophy at the University of Pittsburgh eleven years earlier. He learned to play bass because his college roommates wanted to start a band. He enjoyed it so much that he gave up his pursuit of philosophy and dedicated himself to the hell that was musicianship.

The jam band Toady now played was called Gorge. They had a local following and a steady enough go at it that Toady no longer worked by day. Whispers, rumors, and dreams circulated about Gorge landing a record deal. Toady was more amused than optimistic.

Just about three years ago, Toady and Jeannie had married. Jeannie's sister came down from East Orange to witness the nuptials. Toady sent his mother and sister a postcard from Atlantic City, where the newlyweds spent a long weekend: *Hope all is well. Jeannie and I are honeymooning. Yes, honeymooning! Will call soon. —Todd*

Jeannie had only recently met Toady's family—actually, his sister. That was Toady's family now. In the seven years Jeannie had known him, he had driven across the state only once—when his mother died, two months before the boxes arrived. Seven hours in the Saab, and Toady barely spoke a word. Jeannie stroked his neck, offered to drive occasionally, and changed CDs. It was exactly what he needed. That was love. He was certain. Jeannie was less certain, but banking on the same.

Toady and his sister hugged stiffly before he introduced Jeannie. Toady immediately walked to the backyard and plopped himself in a deck chair. Angela treated Jeannie with genuine kindness and spoke highly of "Todd", as she called him.

Toady forced himself out of bed when a Philadelphia Suburban Water crew set up shop below his window. Clanging and shouting made grown-up sleep impossible. His clock said it was 11:43. Toady lumbered downstairs in tartan boxers. Summer sunlight entered his house as uninvited as had the shouts of sewer workers. Opening the front door, he saw the boxes shipped from Angela. With considerable effort, Toady hoisted the two boxes closest to the door. He lugged them to the seldom-used sofa in the seldom-used living room and dropped them unceremoniously and then did the same with the third and fourth, only after watching two amateur cyclists heading toward the famed Manayunk wall.

Toady loped past the boxes to the kitchen. After breakfast, he washed his dishes, ignored the boxes by the sofa, and headed to the shower.

As he pulled on a pair of cut-offs and a John Lennon T-shirt, Toady noticed the blink-blink of messages on his answering machine. He hit the play button.

Beep. "Toady. Romero. Listen. Steiner thinks that BMG might send someone to tonight's gig. I'm telling you so you're ready. Steiner says BMG thinks the bassist is weak. I want you along for the ride, man. Bring it tonight. Okay? Maybe show up early for once, huh?"

Beep. "Hey, Toady. Not sure if you heard me this morning about the boxes outside. Grab them before they walk away. Love you."

He smiled at hearing Jeannie's voice, her considerateness. He scoffed belatedly at Romero's message. Romero was always poking.

***

Kara was Toady's first love. It had started in high school, junior year. Unbeknownst to Jeannie, it lasted until death did them part. That was when he left Pittsburgh, why he never talked about Pittsburgh. Jeannie should maybe know this.

There was so much maybe Jeannie should know. It would all be exposed by the contents of these boxes. Why would Angela ship his past to his front door knowing that Jeannie would say, "Toady, what's in all those boxes?"

Kara was by far the most beautiful girl in his school. That she dated him was baffling, not just to him. But everything was right between them. He didn't have to pretend to be anyone except himself. Kara felt the same way.

The summer before senior year, he worked as a lifeguard at the Collins Avenue Swim Club. Kara wore a blue bikini that turned every head in the place. Kara was the kind of girl who jumped in the water without testing it first, an observation that only a former lifeguard could make. Everything Kara did, she jumped in with both feet. The pool. Their relationship. Marriage. Death.

Toady picked up a yearbook from one of the boxes but tossed it back in without opening it. He carried the boxes out to the garbage.

He had gone to college mostly because Kara expected him to. Kara would be attending Pitt to study biology and continue to medical school. She talked about how great it would be if they could go to the same college. He took the hint.

Three years later, Kara was wearing his engagement ring. They married a year later, after graduation, so they'd be ready to move as a couple to Boston for her medical school. They were back in their Pittsburgh suburb home, dropping off the things they wouldn't take to Boston, when their friend Sully suggested they get together for a going-away party: Sully and his girl, Christy; Ed McD and his wife, Donna; Kevin Dowd and Blair Thompson; Toady and Kara, the new bride and groom. For old times' sake, Kara suggested the quarry. All the nights they had spent drinking beer and sneaking off in couples made the location seem ideal.

The girls packed a picnic lunch. Kevin and Toady toted a cooler of Rolling Rock. The day was slightly overcast with the expectation of rain, so they had the place to themselves. They spread blankets and relived scenes from what seemed a lifetime ago. They laughed away the afternoon, drinking beer and swinging with ease from the past to the future tense, giving scant attention to the present.

Three beers into the day, Sully took the first leap. The trick was the same: fifteen feet the minimum distance to clear the bottom ridge. He shouted into the sky as he descended. Ed McD followed on his heels despite Donna's urges that he not. As Sully and Kevin scaled the west wall, Kevin egged Toady on. He had his head in Kara's lap with no intention of moving. When he said as much, Kara squirted from under him. "Well, I'm going," she exclaimed. No surprise. Kara was one of the few girls that would jump. She had done it the first time they came to the quarry together. She liked the thrill—not just the jump but also the climb that followed. Kara feared neither. Kevin joked about Toady's wife having bigger balls than him.

Kara locked her eyes straight ahead and set off in a sprint. What happened next, he could still see in slow motion: After her last full stride, her ankle rolls. She shifts hard left. Her body keeps moving. No sound as her body scrapes over the ledge. Then Donna and Blair screaming.

Toady sat frozen until he heard Sully's shouts echoing around the quarry. "No! Kara, no! Shit, oh shit! Todd! Todd!"

Before his voice stopped, Toady was flying. He could still see the images that registered as he plummeted through the air. Her twisted body on the rocky lip. Sully and Ed McD staring from the wall. Water moving closer. Kara moving farther away. The cold water stung, pulling harder than ever before. He wanted to keep going into its darkness. Surfacing, though, and reaching for the ledge, he was greeted by pink water. He struggled to pull himself through it, already knowing she was gone. Her blue eyes beamed from a lifeless and misplaced head. He pulled her onto his lap. Rocked her. His wails echoed around them. He patted her sticky hair.

He could remember no other details of the day. Who came? When? How she was taken from the quarry? How he was? What happened to the others?

The next morning, Toady left. He didn't want to be seen. Not by her father or mother. Not by her brothers. Not by Sully. Not by anyone. Angela kissed him when he snuck down the stairs at four a.m. She cried and cried but never said a word. Never tried to stop him.

He didn't even stay for her funeral.

This, too, Jeannie should know.

* * *

The Clash were rocking "Death or Glory" on the radio. Toady was curled up in a ball. He noticed a new blink-blink on the answering machine. More messages. Toady killed the radio, pressed the button on the answering machine.

Beep. "Toady. Prelish. Did Romero call you with some bullshit about BMG not liking the drummer? I swear—"

Toady deleted the message.

"Hey baby. I miss you today. I thought I'd say hello between patients. Maybe tomorrow we do something fun, huh? Love you."

Toady rewound the message, listened again.

Toady went back into the shower. He stood motionless, letting the water wash over his body. When Jeannie came home, he would tell her everything. She would understand. Maybe she already did. She'd hold him tightly.

Toady didn't hear Jeannie enter. She had navigated the stairs while shedding her work scrubs. She playfully intoned, "Toa-dy, I want you!" She entered the shower, and Toady was shocked by her touch. She responded to his vacant stare: "My last patient canceled. When I heard the shower, I thought there's nothing I'd rather do than . . . you." She giggled in that throaty way he liked and kissed him deeply.

Toady responded in kind. Her warm hands worked at him until the water turned cold, at which point they spilled naked into the bed and made love hungrily. Toady's wet hair whipped Jeannie's face. She laughed at these tiny flagellations. Toady laughed, too, until such point their laughter turned into hurried moans, and Toady fell into an exposed heap next to Jeannie. The two were drifting into a soft sleep when Jeannie whispered, "Oh, what was in the boxes?"

"Some shit from Pittsburgh," Toady heard himself say as he drifted away from Manayunk and into Jeannie.

When they woke, the clock read 6:04. They dressed and walked to Azteca for dinner, holding hands. Over a plate of tamales and looking directly into Jeannie's eyes, Toady told all, without trepidation: the boxes in the trash, Kara and her blue bikini, their marriage (all three weeks of it), and the quarry. He was both passionate and unharmed in the telling. He spoke about Kara's eyes, both when he first met her and when he last saw her. Everything flowed naturally. As he knew she would, Jeannie understood. She cried. She cried, but he knew her tears were not inspired by feelings of betrayal or insecurity. They were an expression of sorrow for Toady—no, not for Toady but for who Toady had been. She cried for Todd Newtson. She interlocked her fingers with his. At some point, Jeannie slid into the booth next to Toady. She whispered her love. She stroked his neck as she had in the Saab on the way to Pittsburgh.

* * *

Toady strutted into Drunken Ben's Olde House like he owned the place. Romero was onstage, holding court with Prelish and Steve. "Nice of you to show, Toady. Didn't you get my message?"

Toady looked at his bandmates. "Sometimes . . . life just kind of . . ." Toady smiled without finishing.

"You all right, Toady? You're not gonna fuck this up, are you?"

"I've never been more ready in my life, Romero. Try your best to keep up with me, huh?"

"Fuck off, Toady. What's with you anyhow?"

Toady looked past Romero. "Prelish, you are the best drummer in Philly. And Stevie, your guitar rocks just as hard as his." He pointed his bass neck at Romero. He turned from them all and began tuning.

The show was hands down the best they'd ever played. Right from the start, Toady wrested control from Romero. He embraced the improvisation. Somewhere during their second jam, Toady stepped into Romero's face as if challenging him to a duel. Toady hammered away. For a moment, he sensed fear in Romero, but Romero found the flow. Everything clicked. The band pushed a new groove. Romero, Steve, Prelish—they were all swept away, at Toady's insistence, into a single vision, expressed musically. Toady struggling through air, all Pittsburgh gray and bruised. Falling in slow motion. Moving away from Kara, toward cold water. He saw her twisted form, saw Ed McD and Sully on the wall. Falling. Without warning, Jeannie's eyes flashed from above. His head jerked. To his surprise, he began to elevate as slowly as he had been descending. Toady was being pulled toward Jeannie, who floated above like an angel, like a savior—two long-repressed possibilities. He chanced a downward glance, saw the wall morphing. Sully and Ed McD were cyclists; the wall was Manayunk's "wall". Toady watched them ascend with determination. Threatening gray sky and grayer rock became the hills and houses of Manayunk reaching up, spires to the heavens. The quarry crumbled to nothing. Jeannie above it all, Toady stupid for her.

Toady worked an end to the jam. The room was ecstatic. Toady, all sweaty and lanky, unplugged and floated off the stage. His Gorge mates were baffled. Toady heard Romero's shouts as he pushed out the back door. He sprinted to his Saab and raced for Jeannie. So much did Jeannie mean to him. He'd pull back the boxes from the garbage. They'd sit on the floor and explore them together. So much to tell.

The Schuykill welcomed him more readily than usual. His windows were down. Summer air swirled. Everything was right. Sure, Romero would be livid, Steiner apoplectic. But what could they do? The suit from BMG—if there was a suit from BMG—would ask, "Who the hell is the bass player?" Toady had been that good.

Toady would look deeper into Jeannie's eyes than he ever had. He'd tell her about the show. He would call Angela. He needed to call Angela. The wind roared in his ears as he eased past boathouse row. He could see the GP tower as he weaved through the sparse traffic. He was almost home.

Peter Cunniffe is a husband, father, business professional, and writer living in Malvern, Pennsylvania. His short fiction has been published by Philadelphia Stories, The First Line, Wheelhouse Literary, *and in the anthologies* Chester County Fiction *and* Works Write: Tales from the Couch.

Amalgam

Selene Lacayo

4:15 a.m.

The solitude was something that Andrés liked most about his job at the parking garage. It was not that he wasn't grateful to have a place to live, but sharing a two-bedroom apartment with nine other men never allowed time for his thoughts to grow. He liked the quiet Friday and Saturday nights watching over the security screens from his post at the parking garage. Best of all, he didn't have to say much to anyone. His English, though it had improved since his arrival almost two years prior, he felt was nothing to be proud of yet. He spent some of the lonesome evening hours trying to learn the language from a set of books and CDs that the other guys he lived with had used to learn it. One of them was now working at a call center. That's what Andrés wanted to do, so he was studying during his evening job, on the bus on his way to work in construction during the week, and every time he found himself with some time on his hands—like at the Laundromat.

It was Sunday, and Andrés still had one hour and forty-five minutes before his shift was done and he could head to his favorite place in all of Philly: Albert Street Tacos y Desayunos. Sunday breakfast was the only meal a week that Andrés allowed himself to splurge on, eating menudo or barbacoa de borrego instead of the ramen noodles in a Styrofoam cup that kept him fed during most of the week. He loved the feeling of belonging that surrounded him and his roommates that would meet him there. He didn't feel unwanted at Anita's restaurant. The best part was that he got to see Brenda, Anita's daughter, who was always quick to smile and never minded when Andrés used any of the English phrases he had just learned when talking to her.

5:00 *a.m.*

The alarm clock resonated through the Southside row home. It really meant nothing more than the announcement that Sunday had officially started, for everyone in the family had been up for a while. Anita had already headed to the restaurant, with her camioneta full of pots of the barbacoa de borrego that she'd finished preparing the night before. It was a labor of love: the selection of the best lambs, their placement in the cooking pits, then the careful shredding of the meat, making sure that the fat and the meat cuts would be evenly distributed among the large pots. Early Sunday morning, Anita's family would help her place them into the truck that would take them to her restaurant. Anita would start the fogones to warm everything up while her comadres made tortillas and finished the menudo and the assortment of salsas before the customers started lining up.

Anita had been living in Philly for a few decades now but had only managed to open her humble restaurant five years ago, when she and her husband looked at their savings and decided to take a leap of faith and follow at least one of the many dreams they had brought with them across the border. What started as a breakfast place offering chilaquiles, quesadillas, and egg-and-chorizo tacos evolved into a proper taqueria during the week and a breakfast place on the weekends, with an extended menu and the added art of authentic lamb barbecue.

Anita wanted a place for all Mexican workers to have a warm and properly cooked Mexican meal. Every time she passed a lawn service crew or a construction site or saw a paisana boarding a bus to head to a job cleaning offices or houses, she thought about her first years in the US. The isolation and homesickness she experienced at every moment of the day was only made better by the warmth and love she enjoyed while preparing and eating a meal with her family. She wanted her restaurant to be that place for all Mexicans in Philly looking for a taste of home.

She had been lucky to open her restaurant in a neighborhood where young people with college degrees and a sense of culinary adventure lived. Soon after expanding to a bigger venue, with a menu that included breakfast foods on the weekends, the locals started to frequent it—even the mayor had come and dined with them. She was so proud to have a picture of her displayed on the wall.

Her children, who were now eighteen and twenty-one, had been born in Philly. They pushed her to start a Facebook page and accounts on other social media platforms. Their online presence seemed to be the biggest reason for the latest boom they were enjoying. Now, all weekend long, there were big lines of people trying to eat her food—imagine that! Anita felt proud of the success of the family restaurant but was troubled by the idea of turning customers away. Most of the time, the people who couldn't get a taco de barbacoa or the expected menudo bowl were her regular customers, the Mexicans for whom she had opened the place and for whom she cooked with such love. This made her feel as though she was taking away their safe place while depriving them of a taste of home.

The conflict inside her had been spreading to the rest of the family. They were all happy about the tremendous success but felt that something needed to be done to cater to their community while inviting the rest of Philly to share in their culture through food. Anita had not come up with a solution yet. She realized she might have to turn customers away again this Sunday.

6:30 *a.m.*

The sound of the rubber track under new jogging sneakers was one of Alfonso's pleasures. He didn't have much time for running when he was driving to and from the office and to and from his children's activities, so he dedicated time to his hobby on the weekends. He was especially happy this Sunday because his family had gifted him a new pair of running shoes.

He liked running at the college track by his house because it brought back memories of his student-athlete days in Monterrey, Mexico. They seemed so distant now that he had been living in Philly for seven years, after his American company relocated him and his family to the States. It was an opportunity of a lifetime as far as new adventures go, but it had been hard on his wife, Alicia, who had not been able to make many friends since the move. He felt guilty for leaving their extended family back in Mexico and watching his wife lose her cheerfulness. Therefore, he was sure to get them plane tickets every spring break so that they could spend a couple of weeks visiting Mexico. This year, though, he'd been set to travel to close a big deal for his company, so he couldn't accompany Alicia and the boys. He was a bit homesick for Mexico, but more than anything, he was missing his family, which was how he found himself at the track so early on a Sunday morning.

Tired and more relaxed after running ten miles, Alfonso thought it would be good for his soul to have a proper Mexican breakfast. After a shower, he headed to Albert Street Tacos y Desayunos. He liked going there, where he could be the Poncho of his Mexican childhood instead of the Al that people in the company that brought him to Philly started calling him when they deemed Alfonso "too hard to remember".

7:05 *a.m.*

When the Uber driver pulled up, the line at the Albert Street Mexican breakfast place was already at least twenty-five people long. Angélica was a bit mad at Robert, who had overslept and now made them late for breakfast.

"Who would have thought that a little spot far away from the Center City scene would be so popular?" Robert ventured to say, closing the car door after him. But he knew full well that good Mexican food, especially the authentic kind, always had a loyal clientele mixed with an enthusiastic following of foodies in search of the best brunch in town. Besides, Angélica had been talking it up, saying that it was the closest thing to her grandma's barbacoa tacos that she had tried since she came to college in Philly—and she had warned him of the giant lines if they didn't arrive early enough. He knew he had messed up.

Meanwhile, inside, Beto and Brenda were struggling to convince Anita to take a little risk and give their idea a try. It had come to them when they had gone to a beer hall the night before. They had met a group of their friends there for some grub after work. The place was a big warehouse with long wooden tables, where every single spot was used. People sat with strangers at these tables; the whole idea was to enjoy the company of strangers while still hanging out with your friends. They thought this concept could be implemented at Albert Street Tacos y Desayunos, but their mom was not so sure that people who didn't speak the same language would agree to such an arrangement.

"Ma, you just have to listen to us. Por favor, let's try it today, and if it is a mess, I will take full responsibility for it. Lo prometo," insisted Brenda, the youngest. Since she was still in high school, she was the child who spent the most time at the family restaurant.

"M'ija pero ya está la gente ahí afuera esperando. It's too late for us to be rearranging tables right now—just look at the line!"

"Precisely because I'm looking at the line, I can tell you that we can do this. Look: ahí está Andrés y sus cuates. I'm sure they'll be glad to help us out, and I will explain what's going on to the people in line. We'll put a quick sign on the window too and add a message on social media. No hay problema!" Beto was very affirming as his dad, Arturo, came to inquire why they had not opened the doors yet.

"Okay, pues, está bien. But if we have angry customers, you two will be dealing with them!" Anita lifted her hands and headed to the kitchen to inform the staff.

7:10 a.m.

"I have an announcement to make. Atención por favor." Brenda was addressing the crowd outside, alternating between English and Spanish so everyone could understand. "First of all, thank you for your patience. Please help yourselves to some coffee on the house. We are overwhelmed by the numbers of great folks showing up every weekend to try our family's recipes and be a part of our community. We don't like turning anyone away, so we came up with a solution. I hope you are open to it." Brenda continued explaining their plan of putting tables together to make long dining areas where even the lonely could eat in the company of others.

People in line didn't seem to mind, and as expected, the regulars, including Andrés, volunteered to help configure the restaurant while the rest of the customers waited patiently nursing their coffees outside.

Angélica was very excited to be in the line at that moment and started tweeting the action: *Mexicans and non-Mexicans are coming together to eat in a family-style setting by joining their tables and creating three very long ones. Extra chairs materialized and now the public is helping with the set up #LOVEPhilly.*

7:20 a.m.

The line started moving in large groups. The newcomers heard from people in line that today everyone was invited to break bread, or in this case, tortillas, with whomever happened to sit at their table. Alfonso was happy to hear that, being that he was there without his family. Organically, people in line and at the tables who were bilingual took the role of interpreters.

Robert dove into getting to know the people around him. "Hi, I'm Robert, and this is my girlfriend, Angélica." Angélica nodded but continued explaining what menudo was to the people on her right. "I noticed you spoke English. I wonder if you could tell me if I should go with the chilaquiles verdes or rojos?"

"I'm Alfonso, or Poncho here. Sure, I'd be happy to help you." He leaned in closer to Robert. "So, your girlfriend is Mexican, huh? I say you go for the chilaquiles divorciados. They are called divorced because half will have green tomatillo sauce and the other half, red tomato. You'll get to try both, and your lady will be so impressed that you knew to order them that way. Y qué, te está enseñando español?"

"Sólo hablo un poquito," said Robert shyly. "But I'm going to be completely immersed in the culture for at least six months. When the semester ends in a few weeks, Angélica has to return to Mexico, and she invited me to meet the family and all that. We've been dating for a few years, but I haven't made it down there to meet the extended family. We're here today because she wants me to get a sense of what her grandma's cooking is like. I'm so looking forward to being with Angélica in her own element. She's been in mine for a while now, you know?"

"I get it. And good for you, hermano! I'm sure you are going to have a terrific experience. Just make sure to always say yes to the food from la abuela, eh!" Alfonso advised, concluding the exchange with a wink.

7:45 a.m.

The plates arrived steaming and fragrant, filling strangers-turned-friends' eyes with colors and their watering mouths with great expectations. Andrés was so excited to have been able to help Brenda—and Anita—with the new setup that he lost his inhibition and readied himself to help those new to the restaurant choose what to eat. "Hey, mira, I really like the barbacoa. You can't go wrong with that. If you like tacos, then you have to taste los tacos de borrego de Anita. Really, that is what I'm eating. They make me feel close to my family. They taste like Mexico!" Andrés said it with such conviction that many around him placed the same order.

Anita couldn't believe it. The social experiment that her children had imposed on her was turning out to be a success. "I don't know how you're getting people to agree to sit elbow to elbow with complete strangers. Y oyes eso? I hear a lot of Spanglish and laughter going on!" She was talking to Beto at the host station as he managed the influx of people with ease.

"Ma, people are usually open to new ideas. Besides, esto es lo que hacemos los jóvenes. The newer generations are open to this family style. I told you about the brewery, but I had seen it in other places before. Now, if you would only let me install some software and apps that would help us do some crowd control . . ." Beto started again with the idea of modernizing the restaurant a little bit. After all, he was learning just that in his hospitality courses on campus.

Anita sighed and said, "Una cosa a la vez, Beto. This is not a race. Let's try new things little by little." Then she rushed back into the kitchen to tell her comadres the great compliments the food and the restaurant's new atmosphere were getting from many different customers. "I'm glad I listened to you, m'ijos!" She called back before the kitchen door closed behind her.

2:10 p.m.

It was time for Anita's family to sit together at the table and enjoy a meal after the first successful family-style dining at Albert Street Tacos y Desayunos. They all were very satisfied with the large numbers they were able to serve. They'd still had to turn some people away, but it was not as many as the previous weeks. If there was ever a place to bring together an amalgam of different people to share a table and form a community, Philly was the right one.

Selene Lacayo (she/her) is a graduate student of English and creative writing at West Chester University. She was the 2018 judge's choice runner-up for the Write Michigan Short Story Contest. She is currently working on a memoir centered on the themes of belonging, identity, and motherhood. When she moved to the greater Philadelphia area close to three years ago, she was charmed by its diverse community and rich history.

Obligation

Herman Beavers

Jurush is sitting at his desk, talking to a Mrs. Townes. Even though the sun is shining and there is not a cloud in the sky, she is in a man's raincoat. Mrs. Townes is a short white lady who wears horn-rimmed glasses. They're the kind of eyeglasses a man would wear. In fact, the glasses don't fit her face and she is constantly pushing the temple over her ears so they will stay on. Jurush is telling her that he's gone over her loan application four times and he's concluded that it's just not possible for her to refinance her home loan. She's five months behind in her mortgage payments, and so what he knows is that, at the end of this conversation, he is going to tell the raincoated Mrs. Townes that her loan is in default and the bank is going to foreclose on it. When Mrs. Townes hears the bank is foreclosing on the home where she's been living with her four children, she gets so angry she pulls a straight razor out of her purse and swipes it across Jurush's neck.

* * *

He always wakes up when he puts his hand to his neck and it comes away covered with money.

For a moment, Jurush doesn't know where he is or what day it is. There is the sound of pigeons cooing, a jet plane drilling across the sky, and the breeze wending its way through the leaves of the tree he fell asleep under last night. He tries to piece the sounds into a mosaic of what might constitute reality, but sitting up, he feels an overwhelming sense that waking up means another shard of normalcy has fallen away and he'll spend the remainder of the day trying to find it. But the hunger pangs ringing in his stomach make him know finding something to eat is more pressing. He looks across the street and the dumpster calls out to him. He visualizes the feast meant just for him. Today will be the day that he finds a bag containing a meal that hasn't been discarded after a few bites. No, Jurush thinks, today is the day someone who's seen me sleeping under the tree has decided to buy a meal and leave it in the dumpster for me to find, meant for me and me alone.

As he walks across the street, Jurush begins performing his favorite mental task. He looks over, sees a burned-out husk that had once been a luxury car. The Acura badge on the front grill of the car sparks a flow of numbers through his head. Nearing the dumpster, he runs through the formula for calculating interest: interest rate divided by the term of the loan multiplied by the principal would be the interest owed over the life of the loan. The car still has three of the four tires, and only one of the windows is missing. So he begins to work the numbers: 45 percent interest divided by 72 payments equals 0.625. Multiplied by $56,000, equals $35,000 interest, bringing the cost of the car to $91,000. Jurush ponders what the car would cost if it had four tires, but he quickly pushes the thought aside because he knows that there is someone someplace willing to buy the car "as is".

Crossing South Street, he reaches the dumpster and lifts the lid. At one point in time, his nostrils would have been assaulted by the smells issuing from all the trash: rotting fruit, moldy bread, general decay. But what keeps dumpster diving bearable is that when he got ill, he lost his sense of smell. Two years later, long recovered from the virus, it has still not returned. Standing on tiptoe and peering inside the dumpster, he is startled to see a woman's body wrapped in a man's beat-up raincoat. The corpse looks fresh, but the woman's face is gone. With his body growing slack at the sight of a dead woman, Jurush is about to shut the lid and head toward the dumpster behind the diner on Front Street. But he glances at the corpse's left hand and notices an expensive wedding ring. If she was the victim of a vicious attack, as he had assumed, why didn't her attacker take the ring? He peers down to examine the diamond. It's substantial; a ray of sunlight strikes the gem in just the right way so that a defiant glint shoots off the stone. Jurush feels challenged to act.

In his first life, when he worked at the bank, news of a dead woman's body found in a dumpster would have triggered a scintilla of sadness, that would then fall away, replaced by thoughts of all his obligations. But today he has nothing else to do. His only obligation is to find out who this dead woman was. Why would someone take her life, but leave the expensive diamond ring on her finger? Who was this woman? What excited her when she was alive? With so many questions to answer, Jurush wonders if there will be time enough . . .

No, time is not the issue. He recalls something his boss told him the day he was let go. "The best way for us to ride this thing out is to get leaner. That's why we have to shed middle management salaries." The boss was wrong, of course. He'd failed to anticipate how the pandemic would drag on till the banking system collapsed.

The task before him feels immense, like standing in a dark place at night, a railroad crossing perhaps, awash in awe and fright, with large fuel tanks looming in the darkness, the loud rocking of railroad cars hauling freight. Jurush steps toward the dumpster, his hunger slaked. Finding a plastic milk crate, he sets it down in front. Stepping up on the crate, his left hand hesitates over the dumpster lid like someone holding pen over paper, wondering what to say. Lifting the lid, he reaches down to get a better look at the ring. Holding the dead woman's left hand in his right, Jurush feels a wave of sadness pass clear through him and rise into the bright Philadelphia sky. He searches for words, anything to commemorate this woman's suffering, to give her death attention.

He feels he's gotten back to something he can't remember feeling since before the virus took so many lives and communities came unraveled. Stepping down off the milk crate, moving toward a street teeming with clues, Jurush suddenly feels purposeful, necessary . . . caring.

Herman Beavers has taught at the University of Pennsylvania since 1989. He continues to be active in the Philadelphia poetry and writing communities.

Charlie Parker Has a Voicemail

Sophia DuRose

Sent to voicemail. The tail end of a Charlie Parker solo plays. Is it "Body and Soul"? "All the Things You Are"? "Autumn in New York"?

"Is that 'Melancholy Baby'?" I ask myself.

"That's just *music*, baby," I answer myself.

* * *

People of all colors and classes ebb into Rittenhouse Square, sometimes flooding the greenery like hungry wasps and sometimes leaking in, in gentle trickles. There are bifurcated benches lining the wide paths like urban knights. The brunch-specializing restaurants frame the park with color all up and down 19th and Walnut Street. Steam seems to waft off their garnet and yellow awnings. Men with close-cropped hair and crisp suits crush the signs of the homeless in mad dashes to and from scattered coffee shops. Within the dirtied grout of the brick-lined heart of the main square are the particles of people's lives—a dropped bobby pin, an "I Voted" sticker, a highlighted pamphlet advertising hair removal. Tossed like pennies into the central fountain sporting Neptune's head are zinc and copper testimonies to the human condition of always wanting more.

In the sun-bleached months of winter, the bare air welcomes the warmth of all different kinds of people. Barneys boots and Reebok sneakers trample fallen pennies that ping in the tinny wind, rattling through the cold sighs of Philadelphia's fall. Variegated leaves dot the path like freckles.

And, of course, there is music.

Not always. But sometimes, the wind's limbs stretch like wavering ledger lines, soaking up Jafar Barron's music. A YouTube video posted two Octobers ago shows Barron playing in Rittenhouse Square. As chilly bursts of wind slither into the empty spaces between held hands and warm embraces, Barron's playing is a welcome version of the wind's wavelengths invading conversation.

* * *

Barron plays a lot of free-bop jazz. Free-bop music bridges the distance between jazz and hip-hop. Miles Davis's Second Great Quintet is widely known as a pioneer for this sort of music, the genre of free-bop as a playing style being characterized by "time, no changes". Rooted in this principle, Davis allowed the five men in his quintet to play as equals, instead of maintaining himself as leader while other players peeled off the melody in unrelated solos. As Davis became more interested in funk, his Second Great Quintet unraveled. By the time Barron was born in 1972, the Second Great Quintet had all but evaporated, as Davis and his new collaborators began exploring other elements of jazz fusion, on such albums as *Bitches Brew*.

"The only time stamp in life is chance," Barron says.

David Rittenhouse, a Philadelphian astronomer, is the namesake of Rittenhouse Square, one of the five original open-space parks planned by William Penn. Barron, age forty-seven, grew up in Philadelphia, attended Central High School, studied briefly at Temple University, played for hours at a time in Rittenhouse Square, yet insists that the city of Philadelphia isn't any more special than any other city. "The art culture makes it a great city," not the city itself, he says. Despite his insistence that it is people who make a place, and not the other way around, watching him practice in the park still makes you feel like this park could truly have been built as a repository for native talent. Something about the gentle laughter of the scuttling leaves, like a violin's bow stroking the exact right string, makes the park feel very alive.

Small wire-frame glasses encase his view of the world. He holds his trumpet like he's holding a time machine.

* * *

Barron sends a text. It is nothing but a picture of a cartoon character from the show *South Park*. The character is Butters, and he is sporting a light pink coat, black slacks, and a ridiculous half smile. The laugh of a twelve-year-old girl enchanted by Christmas lights bursts from Barron's lips. The deep resonance of his voice as he chirps, "Peace!" should clash with his laugh. But as a professional musician, Barron knows more than most about the importance of harmony and rhythm, and he manages to string his sentences and laughter together as if compiling notes for a melody far more important than any typical conversation.

I reached out to him on social media, hoping that he would be willing to divulge his life story to a complete stranger. He was beautifully eager to speak with me.

I found myself increasingly eager to hear from him. I am not an expert, will never be an expert in the collage of language he chooses to exist in. I feel no pressure to respond with witty jokes or impress him with my knowledge of Coltrane fun facts, because to do so would be useless. All I can do is sit back, listen, and truly take what he is willing to give.

"Great understanding of music and all its techniques can bridge any gap between any genre. If it's music, then it's related. You know what I'm saying?" This is why he can bridge jazz and hip-hop, navigate the barbed trails leading between the two that are invisible to many. He forges ahead on uncertain ground, certain only in the music.

* * *

Barron, the son of George Barron (a widely recognized saxophonist) and Janet Simmons (a fine pianist and jazz singer), started playing music when he was about eight years old, along with his older brother, Farid. Farid Barron is older than Jafar by only one year and three days.

Winding through an explanation of his childhood, Barron offers no information that doesn't relate either to jazz or his nuclear family. He attended a music program at a local elementary school from the second to the fourth grade. His childhood self floundered from one instrument to the next, piano and then drums until landing safely on the shores of the trumpet. By the time Barron was fifteen, a freshman at Central High School in Philadelphia, he was proficient enough at the trumpet to perform for Miles Davis on an episode of Bill Boggs's talk show in 1987. At the time of its filming, Boggs was married to his second of four eventual wives. Boggs, a graduate of the University of Pennsylvania and native Philadelphian, mistakenly called him "Jasper" Barron when introducing him to Davis and the live studio crowd.

"It's Jafar," Barron said.

Clad in a black suit and dress shoes to match, Barron stood as tall as his fifteen-year-old frame could manage. When he started to play, it looked as if he were channeling energy from the very ground he was standing on, allowing it to shoot through his body like a bolt of electricity. His eyes rolled upward. His silver trumpet glinted under the stage lights like an eighth gilded wonder. The thirty-two years since this TV appearance, Barron has swapped his silver trumpet for one that glitters in gold.

When Barron finished playing his sampling of music,

he joined Boggs in front of Davis. Barron's head remained high and proud, though only reaching Boggs's shoulder and despite the pressure of having just performed for one of his musical idols. He opened his mouth to ask a question rather than waiting for Davis to address his playing. "What are you going to be doing in the future?" Barron asked.

There was no hesitation. "Playing trumpet," Davis said.

The audience laughed, but Barron persisted. "What kind of music?"

Barron tucked his bottom lip under his top while listening intently to Davis's answer, which was pregnant with pauses. You can almost see the reflection of young Barron in Davis's black sunglasses, which remain on his face for the entire forty-five-minute show. Davis's answer, convoluted and a little standoffish, is unimportant. The important part is that Barron was already thinking ahead, wondering about what Davis wanted to do with the future of jazz, which he basically held in the palms of his hands.

Fifteen-year-old Barron turned into sixteen-year-old Barron, a trumpet player at Central High School and a member of their orchestra, and then into eighteen-year-old Barron, a first-year student at Howard University in the jazz studies program, and then into nineteen-year-old Barron, in Temple University's jazz studies program.

"I didn't stay there, because I was doing other things in music." Those other things included a stint in the army, playing and performing drills with their marching band on the weekends.

* * *

"Music is music. The only thing that isn't music is if it doesn't have any music in it, no melody and no harmony," Barron explains. It seems as if he truly believes his body is nothing but loosely held together limbs, the fishing wire connecting his tissues composed of pure chance. He's quick to pause while he talks, unwilling to say something he hasn't truly thought about, something he doesn't absolutely mean.

Barron is also a self-proclaimed Raja yogi. Raja yoga shares a great deal of philosophical beliefs with Buddhism, though Barron makes no mention of any other formal religious faith. He emphasizes his extensive knowledge in the "studies of spiritual science".

"There is only the self," he says, his voice sliding down into a more serious octave. All of the subtleties of his words can be excavated from his voice, which is steady no matter what he's saying.

The term *science* comes from the Latin word *scientia*, meaning "knowledge". But spirit, according to Barron, "is a concept that refers to an invisible essence of all creation. The knowledge of essence is the knowledge of self. You better know thyself if you want to do life to the fullest. Everything that is transient is not real. That which is real is that which is constant, which is the self. The body dies, personalities die, but not that which supports the body."

Barron continues, "That's when you're able to still the thinking mechanism. Like when you're asleep and there's nothing going on. Or when you're not in the body. When you're not affected by anything. That is the self. The transcendent Self. That's reality. When you have a dream in a dream . . . Actually I'll just put it to you like this." Then he starts to sing. "Row, row, row your boat gently down the stream. Merrily, merrily, merrily, life is *but* a dream."

"Life is but a dream?" I dare to ask.

"Yes."

When Barron is not playing a professional gig or practicing, he offers lessons to students who seek him out. In this moment, as he is determined to impart this knowledge of spirit, this so-called science, it is easy to see that he is the kind of teacher who doesn't dole compliments easily, making him the kind of teacher everyone always wants to impress.

"You're not in the same body you were in eleven months

ago, because every cell in your body, from your biggest cell, that's your skin, renews itself. They go through some change. You know how dogs shed?"

Cats shed too. And if you're going to be a cat who sheds by Barron's standard, you've got to know what rhythm is.

"People say they're a musician if they rhyme. No, they're a poet. That's bullshit."

*　*　*

When asked if his spiritual studies and beliefs influence his musicianship, a heavy pause fills the air.

"Just think about it... Of course, it would be the importance of all matters. Or the root of all matters. Or the essence of all matters. Right?" He guillotines the word *mat-ters* into two distinct syllables. He nods as he does so. "Mm-hmm."

Barron isn't the only jazz musician to believe in a divine link between music and science.

Stephon Alexander, a Dartmouth professor and astrophysicist, radically claims that the same geometric principles that motivated Einstein's theory of relativity were the foundation for John Coltrane's highly regarded jazz "diagram", which looks like a color wheel but with musical notes. The mysterious way that quantum particles move in our world, that is, traversing all possible paths, parallels the way jazz musicians improvise, according to Alexander. Watching a video of Barron's fingers flying between the three keys of his trumpet, as if governed by a different gravity, it isn't difficult to equate his hands to quantum particles, tangoing eerily in the parts of our world that we can only feel, and not truly see.

Barron continues to slither out of his shell. He jumps from an explanation of his father's influence on his musicianship (never mentioning his mother, save her choice of career), then to the time he played for King Britt on Baby Loves Disco, then to his 2000 recording of *Who Is Jill Scott?*, in collaboration with the Philly artist Jill Scott. They met when they were both attending local Philadelphia high schools.

The impressive list of people Barron has played with doesn't end there. "Google me," he advises. Most of his work credits him as the main trumpeter, but on the album *Jafar Barron: The Free-Bop Movement*, Barron is listed as the primary artist, producer, arranger, trumpet, and composer; the album was distributed by Atlantic Records, which was founded in 1944. Atlantic Records is credited with producing such hits as John Coltrane's *Giant Steps* and Aretha Franklin's *Lady Soul*.

* * *

The world of professional jazz musicians is a small one, pockmarked with unexpected yet celebrated cross-pollinations. "There's a relationship between the Marsalis family and the Barron family," Barron tells me with pride.

He explains that he "was influenced—still am—by Wynton Marsalis. His brother, Branford Marsalis, is in fact my frat brother. It was a professional musicians' fraternity." A few years later, Farid would play in the Lincoln Center band, still led by Wynton Marsalis.

"There's a lineage of trumpeters from Louis Armstrong to Miles Davis to Dizzy Gillespie to Wynton Marsalis to young musicians like Nicholas Payton, because we're all centers of influence. John Coltrane is a great influence of mine. Thelonious Monk is a great influence of mine. All the musicians of note."

Barron feels strongly that any mind "has the ability to create because of the creator within them". The generosity of this perspective is refreshing, a warm and golden ray in a silvering world.

"If it has to do with life, I can answer that question," Barron assures, the shadow of a giggle lurking beneath his words. The bowing sun is alive against the metal of his trumpet, spearing passers-by with lances of light. A dog barks somewhere. A car horn sounds. The shade from waving trees shimmies from right to left and back again, leaves untangling themselves from their tethers like dry clothes unpinning from a line. An older gentleman's cough folds itself into the breeze. A little boy asks for a dollar to give the "trumpet man".

It almost feels like it could be "Summertime".

Sophia DuRose is a twenty-two-year-old former circus performer and current writer from Florida (unfortunately). Her work has appeared in such literary magazines as Rainy Day Magazine, Revelry, National Poetry Magazine, *and* Apricity. *Her first book of poetry,* Losing Teeth, *was published by Shantih Press in May 2019. She is an English major at the University of Pennsylvania, happy to call the city of Philadelphia her new home.*

Graves & Glory

Jeannine Cook

It's just a fever. I am not sick. I am not afraid of the shaking. I will not die.

My hands are not trembling. I am not tucking my hands under the covers. I am not sleeping on the floor. I am not dying on the floor. My children love me. I love them more. My oldest is giving me Tylenol every four hours when the fevers return. I don't have a mattress.

I gave The Man my paycheck. The Man is my man, kinda. Some say The Man is for everybody. He is teaching me a lesson on saving by taking my paychecks. He is flipping my money. We are eating sweet potatoes every night for dinner. We have a sweet potato song. The song is high-pitched. Out of tune. Sweeeet potatoes. Sweeeet potatoes. We jump up and down when we sing it. My children hate sweet potatoes.

Our electric is cut off. I am working full-time for a Philly homeless shelter and giving The Man my rent to "save". I should live and work in the homeless shelter. There is no money. I am not sick. This is just a fever. It will pass. Give me the Tylenol. I am not a broken dishwasher. I am not a leaky roof. I am not a lint-filled dryer caught on fire. I am not a dirty carpet. I am not fingers on walls. I am not on the floor in a fetal position. I am not calling my sister in South Philly. Give me a Tylenol. I pop four. Fevers stop.

Marie, my childhood friend from Tidemill in Virginia, stops by to visit. How does she know where I live? She brings other friends. High school friends. All scared to catch it. I don't like people knowing where I live. I don't like people knowing *how* I live.

Why don't you have furniture?
Where are your tables and chairs?
Why are you in a robe?
Why are you so thin?
Why do your children have no toys?
What's with all these sweet potatoes?
Marie feels my forehead. "You have a fever."
Let us take you to the hospital.
Who is going to watch my children?
Who is going to take them to school?
Why he got y'all living like this?
Why you got you living like this?

I need a blanket. One more blanket. More Tylenol. Tuck me in. Tuck me in. When y'all getting on the road back to Virginia? Please, Marie, feed my kids before you go. Tylenol me, please.

My oldest wakes me up. I am not moaning in my sleep. I am not seeing dark figures. There is no white tunnel. The dark figures aren't holding my eyelids shut with staple guns. I will not eat. No sweet potato soup for me.

The Man's friend is an electrician. The Man pays his electrician friend to come jimmy-rig my electric back on. Why doesn't The Man just pay the electric? Where is The Man? He is not gone. He is coming back soon. He is not coming back soon. With his other family maybe? Buying trees with my rent. Raising other women's babies with my electric.

My two babies, they sleep on the floor in my blankets with me. Try to hold my shivering body still. Try to keep my warm self warm. My skin is a California wildfire burning. My insides are Colorado ski slopes chilling.

The baby feeds me sips of water.
Drown a fever.
Feed a cold.
Drown a flu.

Feed a fever.

Drown a family.

Feed a family.

I am not drowning.

The electric company finds out about the jimmy-rigged electric and jimmy-rigs it back off. Adds a red tag. We will be fined.

Where is Marie?

Good-bye. Good-bye.

Thanks for the Tylenol.

I am fine.

We are okay.

Thanks for stopping by.

Thanks for sweet potato soup and tucking me into the floor.

Thanks for feeding my babies.

No, I am not hungry. I'll bake a sweet potato when the fevers pass. More Tylenol, please. My youngest puts a wet towel to my head. So wet it soaks the blanket. I am steam.

I'm too hot to lie with.

I'm too hot to speak to.

Too hot for my oldest to check my heart rate.

Do you feel it? He feels it.

He is like my mother. There with more Tylenol.

Maybe you should go to the hospital, he says.

No, it will pass, I say.

I don't call my sister. We aren't friends like we were. Who are my friends?

I don't call Nia. Lion.

I don't call Phil. Ostrich.

I don't call Aaron. Muskrat.

I don't call B. Turtle.

I don't call Tasha. Ape.

What's the point?

Who cares?

Mom, you were crying in your sleep. Here's more Tylenol.

The Tylenol stops working. The blankets are not working. The wet rags are dry. My dry pillow wet.

Dear God, don't take me from my children. Who will they have without me? My oldest wants to call his auntie, my sister.

I am the Peshtigo fire. I am the Move 9.

Isn't it funny that we say it's our body, but we control so little of its functioning.

I am not peeing myself in my sleep. I am not peeing myself when I wake up. I don't need help getting to the bathroom. The carpet isn't stained. The blankets are not soiled. My eyes are not floods flowing forward. My ears are not Alexander Graham bells.

My oldest calls my mother.

Grandma, here she is.

Speak to her.

My mom is not stuck on an island.

She is not six hundred miles away.

I'm okay, mommy.

I am not four years old. I am not Noah in this flood.

Jeannine.

My mother is a humble lullaby.

She is a sweet supplication.

She prays for me in the name of Jesus. Why in his name? I don't know why. Is Jesus God? Is God God? God, will you watch my children for me? Mom, will you watch my children for me? She binds the devil. She tells God to put his hand of protection around me. The Quran speaks of angels. One is writing down my actions. The other is writing down my deeds.

She refuses to take medicine. Check.

She allows medicine to run out. Check.

Takes pills before board meetings. Check.

Takes pills before events. Check.

Takes them before job interviews. Check.

Will not take them every day.

I am not a crackhead.

Mommy says I need to call my sister. My sister I don't

talk to. My sister who kicked me out on Christmas. My sister who is like my twin. My sister who used to ride me on the back of her bicycle to and from school. Who I traversed a six-foot snowstorm with to Shalonda's house in Tidemill. Only for Shalonda's mean-ass momma to tell us, smaller than the mounds of snow, that we couldn't unfreeze our decaying toes in her foyer. Shalonda's mom, do you know everyone in the neighborhood hated your angry bitter ass? How you gon let two frostbitten black girls from up the block die from cold shock while you wave them off through your bitter ass blinds? Why were you so damn mad all the time? No type love for the community. What the hell was going on in your spirit?

When mommy's prayer is over, I roll over in my pee pee pants to call my sister. I don't know what's said. I don't remember the car ride. I don't remember checking in. I don't remember my vitals. I am not the Black Friday bushfires. I am not the Ice Data Center.

I wake up on a cot in the hallway of the hospital with the lights blinking. Nurse says I have the flu. My heart, the sly motherfucker that it is, takes off running in sprints when no one is looking and returns to normal when they come back. My fever is an ocelot climbing Mt. Aripo the second the nurses walk away.

Sleep is the cousin of death. Dreams and death are similar. Who gave death such a bad name? And dreams such a good one?

I am not on a cot.

This is not a hallway.

This is not the flu.

Do you have any other conditions? No.

I am not lying.

Growing up in Tidemill, we ate at each other's houses. We'd walk right into each other's kitchens. We lived around the corner from Langley Air Force Base. A cultural hodgepodge of sorts. We somehow work. We drink NASA water. We bike air force air. We speak Tidemillian. Tidemill, where are you now?

I am in a hallway on a cot. I am the Great Chicago Fire. I am the Russian Oymyakon. My blood pressure is a sunrise over Mt. Kabru.

The nurse on duty insists I have the flu. He gives me a Tylenol. I don't trust him enough to tell him about the impending storm. It's gonna rain. The eye of the storm is in my neck.

I don't pee my cot.

The nurses switch shifts.

She checks vitals between dreams. It must be the flu. I seem fine, she says. I don't have a fever. Sneaky bastard.

Miss, can you check my fever now? I assure you I am not making this up. It climbs Mt. Davis when you walk away. Maybe check my record.

I am not lying. I am still not telling the truth. I have not been taking Tylenol every four hours for days. I do not have diarrhea. I can see from her eyes that she smells me. I am not a bum.

Do you have a history of disease?

No.

Let me check your vitals.

No.

Ms. Cook, hold still or we will have to . . . He does not lunge for my neck. He does not choke me with his claws. They are not holding my arms down while he feels me up and down. This is a simple medical assessment.

I fade to the alley between the big streets in Tidemill. We pop petals of honeysuckle in our mouths. There's a fence here in the alley that we have to jump to run from stray dogs. Rumor is someone died in that house. Out of breath we'd have cursing competitions. Who can go the longest. Fuck those fucking motherfucking fucked up shitty ass ghosts. You said that wrong. No I didn't. Yes you did. You supposed to say, I don't give a fuck about those stank ass shitty ass fucked up dead ass bitch ass motherfucking ghosts, they can't catch us for shit.

The doctor checks my heart.

My heart checks him.

I don't pump Kool-Aid, my heart straight talks.

Nurses hold my arms and legs to the cot.

My teeth clack together like cartoons.

Ms. Cook, do you have a history of disease? He shines a light into the back of my oversized left eye.

I do not have a history of shit.

Take that fucking light out my eye.

I don't need your shots or your pills.

Ms. Cook, the doctor/captain says, you are experiencing a storm. We are flying through air clear turbulence. Unsteady winds are tossing us in between the in-betweens. *Get her a change of clothes*, the captain orders. Nurses scramble. *Get her a bed.* Nurses scramble some more.

In Tidemill our house came with cute furry bunnies. Our neighbor said she needed to take one of our bunnies for a few days because she thought it got loose and bit her cat. Bitch, bunnies don't bite cats. When she gave us the bunny back, its head got fatter and fatter and its feet got skinnier and skinnier until one day our bunny's head exploded in the cage. I am not a cute cat-biting bunny.

When I come back, Nurse Ann is at my ankles tugging my soiled pants toward my feet. I am not wearing underwear. My children are with my sister. They can't go to school after this. What will they say? Yes, ask me stupid ass questions about trapezoids as I stress out about my Tylenol-filled mother. She is not in a hallway hospital on a cot fighting nurses. She is not in the eye of a self-induced storm. Our electric is not jimmy-rigged and red tagged.

What keeps us alive?

My grandfather died like this. In a hospital hallway alone. Uncared for, ill and overlooked. My father was three. Rumors in the family say that my grandmother took a high-heeled shoe to my grandfather and punctured one of his vital organs. Others say he sauntered into the hospital inebriated and they laid his drunk ass down in the hallway and he never woke up. Did he die in that hallway a battered murdered husband? Or did he drink himself into the eye of a storm? Could he sing like my father? Play guitar? Had he really slaughtered a family of white sharecroppers down south? Am I his generational curse?

They just don't ever stop taking vitals, do they? Blood test. Pills. Heart rate. Fever. Pills. Vitals. Blood pressure.

How many pregnancies have you had?

More than I care to admit.

When was the first day of your last menstrual period?

None of your goddamn business.

Can you tell me what medications you're on?

Does weed count?

Hi, Ms. Cook. I am the hospital social worker.

No, I am not crazy. No, I am not sick in the head. No, I don't feel safe at home. No, I don't have the virus. No, they aren't going to take my kids.

The concern here, Ms. Cook . . .

Yes, I do believe that sweet potatoes can heal me. Vitamin A, sweet social worker lady. Vitamin A. Ever hear of it?

Short letter I write on my heart to my children: I brought you here. I will not leave you here. I am not Marvin Gaye's dad.

We *want to support you.*

I try to say, I hear you, sweet social worker lady. But I cannot because *my body* starts to convulse.

When in a battle with *your body*, the slightest mishap can kill you. I stop convulsions with poems. Recite them from the base of my spine two at time for urgent results.

Did you hear about the rose that grew

You see these hands?

from a crack in the concrete?

These is my hands.

Proving nature's law is wrong it

These are not your hands.

learned to walk without having feet.

These are my hands.
Funny it seems, but by keeping its dreams,
All mine.
it learned to breathe fresh air.
You see these feet?
Long live the rose that grew from concrete
These is my feet.
when no one else ever cared.
You see this mind.

   I am surrounded like a stickup. A team of blue uniforms poking and pulling and prodding me. I am fine, I say. They disregard and continue stealing *my beat, my blood, and my breath.*

Jeannine Cook's work has been recognized by Vogue, MSNBC, *and the* Washington Post, *among others. Her writing has appeared in* Philadelphia Inquirer, Root Quarterly, Printworks, *and* midnight & indigo. *She recently returned from Nairobi, Kenya, facilitating social justice creative writing with youth from fifteen countries. She is the proud new owner of Harriett's Bookshop in the Fishtown section of Philadelphia. She's lived, birthed, worked, cried, and sighed in Philly for the last nineteen years.*

Road Show

Liz Kerr

On the day Diamond McSorley was hired as the assistant testing manager for the university, the woman in Human Resources told her she was a good fit for the position.

"You'll be responsible for overseeing the MCATs and the LSATs."

Diamond nodded her familiarity with these tests. She had spent the last three years working for the Philadelphia branch of a company that guaranteed, to those who could afford the tutoring, a higher score on these exams.

"I think you'll find the benefits package generous." She handed Diamond a binder. "It covers full tuition up to a master's degree level. Nice, right?"

Diamond did a Keyser Söze of the woman's desk—Phillies bobblehead, two blond grandchildren on the beach, a birthday card "From the Gang".

"Yes," she answered, "very nice."

"What is it you're pursuing, Diamond, history?"

"Anthropology."

"Interesting," the woman said in a flat tone that indicated she didn't find it particularly so. "If you turn to the last tab in your binder, you'll see another wonderful benefit."

Diamond flipped to the last tab, a photo of a redbrick row home with the caption "The Community Initiative Program".

"If an employee purchases a home within this zip code, the university will pay up to five thousand dollars toward the settlement costs." Diamond must have appeared confused, as the woman went on to explain, "It's called gentrification."

Diamond wondered, since she had lived her entire life within this zip code, if it was demographically possible to gentrify oneself. She smiled at the thought of how this might muddle the statistics of the Community Initiative Program, and the woman smiled back and said, "Welcome aboard!"

Now, six months into the new position, she questioned the woman's assessment of her as a good fit. She questioned whether she should come back tomorrow or ever again. Today, she had wrecked someone's life.

The day hadn't started well. It was an LSAT day, and it never went smoothly with the future lawyers of America. They were a group who had chosen, basically, to spend the rest of their lives arguing. Despite the fact they had been notified well in advance of the list of prohibited items—no purses, cell phones, digital or electronic devices—there were always a few who tried to bring them in. The women were worse than the men.

"Do you have any idea how much this cost?" they'd ask, as if she'd give them special dispensation because they paid seven hundred dollars for their iPhone or their purse was a Gucci.

When she made it clear they could not enter the testing center and would have to wait four months to retest, it set in motion a sort of reverse Easter egg hunt, with students scrambling to find good spots to stash their devices—behind vending machines, under trash cans, or stashed deep inside the artificial plants in the lobby. Some demanded that Diamond or her staff hold onto their prohibited items during the testing, but the rules forbade it.

She had to be strict; she was responsible for two hundred fifty test takers spread out in six classrooms, with a staff of six room monitors, six proctors, and two university security guards. Once the test began, any student found with a prohibited item was immediately ejected and a security cancelation notice would display on their exam report. It was a permanent black mark for an aspiring law student and could ruin their chance of acceptance at the most competitive top-tier law schools.

During the October LSATs, an irate ejected student had threatened to have her fired. "Do you know who my father is?" he yelled. Diamond remained unfazed. "Sir, your iPhone is a prohibited item." Her demeanor pissed him off more. She heard him mutter "black bitch" under his breath as the security guards approached, and she wanted to correct him, wanted to tell him that, technically, she was a biracial bitch, but he wasn't worth the argument.

A woman whose ringing cell phone gave her away in the December LSAT jabbed a finger in Diamond's face and hissed, "My dad is mobbed up," and Diamond wondered whether that was supposed to elicit fear or pity. It never made sense to her, this invoking of the powerful father. It was nothing she could relate to. If they really wanted to appeal to her sympathies, they'd tell her their father was broken and disillusioned and so lost he couldn't find his way to the road back.

Diamond and the security guards kept hallway vigil over the six classrooms in her charge. At any point a proctor could signal, by opening the classroom door, they needed Diamond to step in. The room could not be left unmonitored. An hour into the test, the door to room 2 opened. As she walked down the hallway toward the open door, she wished it was an MCATs day. The future doctors of America never gave her any problem. They knew how to follow rules. This crowd made her feel like a bouncer at a Jersey Shore bar.

She stood in the room 2 doorway, and as per protocol, the room monitor revealed the location of the offender and the charge.

"Aisle three, seat five. He's wearing a digital watch. I saw it when he pushed his sleeve back," the room monitor said in a whisper.

Diamond counted three over and five back and took a deep breath. The "he" in question was oblivious to her approach.

He was hunched over the test with an almost childlike concentration, his elbow propped on the desk, forehead resting on his left hand as he penciled in a circle with his right. As she approached, other students realized her mission and slinked down in their desks as if from the grim reaper.

From a distance of a few feet she could see that the article in question was, indeed, a digital watch, a seemingly innocuous item that could be used to photograph and sell test questions. She had no choice; this one was written in black-and-white. She tapped him on the shoulder.

"Follow me, please."

He looked up at her with an open-mouthed expression of abject horror, comprehension of the shoulder tap swiftly making its way to the panic-room center of the brain. She was familiar with that look. One day your little brother is just a boy, and the next day he's looking at you across a courtroom, trying to comprehend the words *adult time*.

She lifted his test from the desk, and he followed her out to the hallway where the security guards waited to escort him from the building. She was about to explain the violation, but he was already removing the watch from his wrist.

"I completely . . . I meant to . . . oh shit . . . I'll throw it away, okay? I'll drop it in this trash can right here—"

The older guard, Maurice, took hold of his elbow. "Son, you have to leave now."

The young man looked at her but made no threats. He didn't invoke the name of his father. Worse, he had started to cry.

"Miss, please," he whispered, and she noticed his wet eyelashes had formed into pointy triangles, the way her brother's had when he was an infant and her mother had bathed him in the kitchen sink.

"You can retest in June," she said but knew that was little consolation. The four-month delay in testing would put him a year behind in the law school admission process.

Maurice led him away to the exit, and Diamond paced

the hallway. Tomorrow, she thought, she would check the university's job postings for another position, maybe something in research, where she wouldn't be responsible for ruining a kid's chances.

When Maurice returned to the hallway, he patted her on the shoulder. "Don't feel bad, Miss Diamond. He wouldn't a made a good lawyer. He would of got a brother sent to the chair, crybaby like that."

It was dark by the time she made it home to the apartment she shared with her boyfriend, Tyler. They had met in college, the semester he dropped out to concentrate "24/7" on his art. He had worked a variety of day jobs—bike messenger, sandwich maker in a campus food truck—so that at night he could express himself artistically, or, as his mounting police citations described it, doing graffiti.

The apartment was a decent size but felt cramped due to the stacks of unfinished paintings propped against walls and stacked behind furniture. She thought his work was beautiful, that he was able to portray the city from a perspective unfiltered by the experience of having grown up in it. She'd argued with him about wasting his talent and encouraged him to show his paintings, to try to place them in galleries and make some money, but he said art and materialism were "divergent pathways".

"Hey, babe," he greeted her from the sofa, where he was watching TV. The room smelled like stale pot and Febreze. "Check this out, *Antiques Roadshow*. This guy just found out his *chair* is worth a hundred grand." The way he dragged out *chair* confirmed he was stoned.

"You can't smoke your shit in here," she said, feeling suddenly and completely exhausted. "We talked about that before."

"My dad has a mint Fender Stratocaster," he said, ignoring what she'd just said. "I bet they'd appraise that at a few thousand."

She thought about what she owned that could be brought

for appraisal to *Antiques Roadshow*. Going back generations, hundreds of years, to the veldt of Africa and the bogs of Ireland, back through millennia, nothing had been passed down, nothing of value, nothing that would appreciate.

Tyler got up from the sofa, stretched, and began to load spray paint cans into his backpack while Diamond microwaved leftover pasta. He tucked his blond dreads into a wool hat. "I'm working on a new project," he said with an enthusiasm she knew would be short-lived. "I want to create something, street art with a message that goes viral."

"What's your message?"

"I haven't figured it out yet but something that tells the truth, like what Banksy is doing in England or Shepard Fairey is doing here. A message that makes you stop and ponder, you know? I think I need a new tag name, something with a *y* on the end."

The name that came to mind was Lazy, but she kept it to herself. She was too tired to start a fight.

"You seem depressed," he said. "Any LSAT dudes in your face today?"

"I had to eject a guy."

"So, you've done that before and it didn't bother you."

"He cried."

"Like, sobbing cried or silent tears?"

"Silent tears."

"White guy or black?"

"Black," she answered.

"Not that it makes a difference," he said, but she knew, to her, it did.

* * *

When the June LSATs came around, she scanned the crowd for him. She would make sure he checked his pockets, that he rolled up his sleeves, that he carried nothing on the prohibited list. She would tell him that, if he was interested, there was a part-time opening in the testing department and it paid pretty well, but he never came back.

She thought she saw him one day on Broad Street, when the traffic had come to a stop due to road work and a young man in an orange safety vest holding the sign with *Stop* on one side and *Go* on the other waved her on. She couldn't slow down enough to get a good look; she had to keep moving because the car behind her was leaning on the horn.

She hit the red light at Broad and Erie. The bookstore on the corner had a huge sign fixed to the front window—"We Ship To Prisons". She thought of telling Tyler that if he was looking for a tag message that told the truth, that was it, but she didn't feel like calling him.

The day she signed up for the Community Initiative Program, she didn't tell him. She put a bid in on a house, a clean little corner row two blocks off campus with windows that faced the center city skyline. She could handle the mortgage on her own, the realtor told her, and she had already decided she'd put window boxes on the front of the house, and they would overflow with flowers and cascading vines, and she would have, for the first time, something that would appreciate.

Liz Kerr has had short stories, poetry, and commentary published in Philly Fiction, Galway Review, The Lancet, Philadelphia Inquirer, Philadelphia City Paper, Sixteen (*Dublin*), Jewish Currents, Irish Central, Ice Colony, Rust Belt Rising, New York Times, Mayday Magazine, *and* Beyond Words. *She is a registered nurse in heart transplant and oncology at a Philadelphia hospital, earned an MFA in creative writing from Arcadia University, and holds dual Irish and American citizenship.*

Mysteries of the Street

Ann de Forest

The woman jogs around the park swathed like a beekeeper. All in white. Hat and gloves, a veil over her mouth and nose, her legs and arms covered no matter the temperature or the season. She runs at a steady pace. She circles the park, around and around, oblivious to the stares she draws, the questions she raises. Why does she cover herself? Is she religious? Ill? Allergic to sun or air? Is she scarred? Paranoid? Is she protecting herself or us?

There is another jogger. I've watched her for years. Everyone laughs at her, the way she runs, dragging her feet, her body bent to the side, head drooped, shoulder lifted. She looks exhausted always. She appears everywhere. In the center of town. On the path by the river. Crossing the bridge. I even saw her indoors once, jogging out of an elevator. She smirks as she runs. Or is it a grimace?

Once on a bright fall day I saw a man sitting in an alley contemplating a tray of pomegranates on his lap. A few were cracked open to reveal the tiny seeds of fruit inside, glistening like rubies. Did he know how to eat them? Would he eat every one? Did he know that I spied him sitting there in his rapture? Did he know what impression he made, so sharp in the morning light, about to taste the fruit of the dead?

One guy I call Retro Man. His sunglasses have silver frames. His hair is cut short at the sides, longer on top. A little slick. A little shiny. Everything he wears or owns seems to want to make a statement. He rides a Schwinn Classic Cruiser, black with cream trim and white wall tires that match his black high-top Keds. He drives a two-tone Citroën, burgundy and black. The headlights bulge like eyes. I spot it all over town, crossing the bridges, parked at the gas station, in back of the shut-down supermarket, down by the basketball courts.

Another man walks through the park mumbling to himself. His eyes dart about and he casts evil glances at anyone who dares look his way. Sometimes he bursts into laughter at his secret jokes.

There is a woman who wanders into the park to sing to the trees. Hymns and Aretha Franklin songs pour out in her loud, clear voice.

Retro Man never says a word. At the park or at the pool, he speaks to no one. Except his own children. Wherever he is, he turns so he can face the sun. He tilts his chin up to catch the rays. Behind those dark glasses does he keep his eyes closed?

Who smashes the car windows in the night? Who slashes the tires? Who walks over the cars leaving the tread marks of sneaker soles on the windshields? Who digs up the tulips? Who eviscerates them? Who scatters the mangled petals and leaves, the twisted stems, across the sidewalk? Who writes in code on the lampposts? Who reads these nocturnal messages? Who walks down the street at three in the morning, spewing insults up at the streetlamps? Why does the broken glass look so beautiful in the morning, glittering green in the sun?

I did meet Retro Man once. At a neighborhood Halloween party. I forget his name now. I forget if we were ever introduced. He sat on a couch and told horror stories about houses where blood dripped from faucets. No visitor came out alive. He spoke in flat, expressionless tones. Nevertheless the children shuddered. They squealed and shrieked on cue. He told these stories as if they were true, as if he and his wife, Melissa (he always called her that: "my wife, Melissa"), had seen the blood, had watched the victims die, had been threatened themselves. They alone had lived to tell the tale.

His wife, Melissa, sat beside him on the window seat. The children's upturned faces horrified, delighted, reflected in the glass walls of the porch. She—his wife, Melissa—was dressed as a belly dancer, or maybe she was supposed to be Jeannie, from I *Dream of Jeannie*. Her long blond hair coiled above her head like a turban. The perfect magician's assistant, she never raised an eyebrow. She never said a word.

Why does his car look like a cartoon character? Why does it stare with those round insect eyes? Why do I see it on blocks at the gas station, the passenger window covered with cardboard and tape?

The woman is stuck on the same song. *You better think think think think think* . . . All day. All night. My window overlooks the park. I hear her even when she's not there.

Who leaves behind the residue of the night? Chicken bones, burnt embers, banana peels, potato chip bags, syringes, malt liquor bottles, plastic bags the size of postage stamps printed with the silhouettes of naked women, wilted condoms still sticky with the evidence of passion and release.

Why do men leer when they see me on my bicycle? Why do they ask their questions: *Are you wearing underwear under that?*

Once late at night I was riding through a deserted intersection. The street was covered with women's shoes. Pairs and pairs of pumps, all different colors, scattered over the asphalt. Where did they come from? Who did they belong to? Did they fall? Or were they dumped there on purpose? Did anybody miss them? Did anybody wonder why they had vanished without a trace?

The wife Melissa disappears. I never see her anymore. Retro Man is everywhere. Always with his kids. He picks them up in the Citroën at the school. He splashes with them in the pool. In the park, he bounces them on his lap, tosses them baseballs and footballs and Frisbees. Is that him pushing his daughter on the swing? I can't see so far away. His daughter must be too old to be pushed. He is always so animated when he talks to them. I strain to catch the stray words: *Batman . . . ilex bush . . . tomorrow we will . . .*

Public exercise has become the fashion. Some men come to the park in the morning with swords. They gather on the old stone shuffleboard court. They lunge and thrust and draw slow loopy arcs in the air over their heads. They slice the sky with their silver blades *swish swish* then slash at the air in front of them.

Where has their mother gone?

How do fashions begin? One year, for example, everyone wore varying shades of pale green. Apple. Mint. Lime. Chartreuse. Shoes. Handbags. Dresses. Hair ribbons. Scarves. This winter it was puffy coats, plump as marshmallows, in black or taxi yellow. There was the summer of unbuckled overall straps. The spring of bright plastic barrettes. Lately I've noticed faces scarified in elaborate tribal patterns. And brands—geometric shapes, initials—seared into human flesh.

I choose a pumpkin at the farmers' market. I want to carve a face. I consider the shapes, the sizes, assess the symmetry. I hear a voice behind me. Mock whisper. *Watch out for that woman, she's dangerous.* I look back to catch Retro Man nodding. At me. How does he know me? His little daughter stands beside him. She blinks behind her glasses. I try to decipher her code. "Hey," he says. Is he smirking? "Hey," I answer. Why do I feel a shiver? Why do I call that feeling connection? Why do I sense that this is the beginning of something between us?

You better think think think

What you're trying to do to me . . .

Brown ribbons of tape flutter and sparkle in the tree branches. Sometimes you see a strand coiled and knotted in the gutters. Unwound, the wind catches it so easily it looks like something alive. I flinch when I see it fly up, startled by that sudden movement. There's sound on that tape. Music perhaps. Or maybe voices. A lecture. A conversation. All that sound, tangled in the gutters, woven through the trees, never to be heard again. I don't know how to hear it. Does anybody?

Halloween night I spy his wife, Melissa, out on the street. She wears blue jeans, a pea coat, her blond hair unbound. I don't really recognize her without her harem costume. But she is walking with Retro Man's kids. They both have pushed their masks up on top of their heads to see in the dark. The son lags behind. His mother turns her head to yell out his name, and I see her face clear in the streetlight. *Jasper*, she calls. Her tone is harsh. Another kid, a teenage boy, joins her, coils his arm around her waist, pulls her toward him. Was I wrong? It must not be her after all. It must be just the babysitter. She turns again, calling. *Jasper.* Her hair flips like a whip around her shoulders. She looks exactly like her. Who else could she be?

Hey! Think about it. You! Think about it.

Once I was riding by the river and had to slow down to steer around the police cars parked on the grass, blocking the path. As I pedaled by I glimpsed the policemen puzzling over some object on the bank. A pair of yellow work boots stood neatly placed at water's edge, socks folded and tucked inside each one. A dead man's shoes, I figured, shuddering as I rode past. By the time I reached the bridge I was mourning for a man I never knew. I had built an entire story on those boots. I could see the dead man carefully removing his shoes and socks and lining them up on the bank before he stepped into the water. It was a beautiful morning. I crossed the bridge and peered out over the falls, hoping to see more, to know something. The bend at the boathouses blocked my view. The water washed over the falls as always. White birds bobbed on the surface. Or were they debris? I searched in the next day's paper for some kind of notice. I never learned anything. There was never any news.

"Hey," he says when we meet at the park. "Hey," I answer and wait for him to say more. The woman sings to the trees. Children shriek from the playground. Would he answer my questions if I asked him? For example: Who is the kid I see with your wife, Melissa? He smokes cigarettes and wears his baseball cap backward on his head. I heard him introduce her as his girlfriend, Melissa. She curled her lips at the stranger, a half smile of acknowledgment. I watched the exchange, wondering. I've seen the boyfriend at the park with the children, Melissa's kids, Retro Man's. He tosses them baseballs and Frisbees. Why do they look so happy? I say nothing. Retro Man removes his glasses. To reveal his eyes? To look at me? The sun is behind us. The afternoon rays are long and low. Our shadows show two giants, side by side on the green grass. He squints, rubs the corner of his nose. He puts his glasses back on and turns away, tilting his chin to the unsparing light.

In the playground at night, I pass by the swings. Girls sway on the seat, boys standing before them, catching the girls as they swing forward. Or do the girls catch them? They wrap their legs around the boys' hips, hold on, pull back again, boys' bodies attached to theirs. They rock together, swings amplifying that natural rhythm, widening that natural arc of back and forth, up and down, give and take. I see other couples lounging on the slides and someone else on the monkey bars. They're kissing I think. Maybe they're doing it? How should I act? Pretend I don't see? They don't care if I watch them. Is this a commercial transaction? Or are they in love?

Retro Man slowly unties the laces of his high-tops. He slips off his shoes and his socks. His bare feet surprise me, so white and vulnerable. He unbuttons his shirt. His chest is golden brown. He lies down in the grass beside his bicycle. It makes an inadequate screen. His kids find him easily. They jump on his back, pummel his shoulders with their fists, tug at his arms. He doesn't budge. I keep out of sight, behind the sycamore. Is he hurt? Does he need help? Should I say something? Tell someone? Ask him what's wrong? With a roar, he jumps up, swinging his arms, scattering his children. They run off shrieking. He chases them down.

Is that Melissa I see down in the bowl of the park wearing camouflage? Her face is sharp, focused as a weapon. She is practicing some form of martial art. I notice for the first time the tattoo on the back of her calf, a black rectangle, dense with writing, a language I cannot read. Why did I never notice how strong she is? Her face shows no pain as she walks barefoot over the broken glass. Slowly, slowly, she raises one leg, her knee bent, then kicks straight up at empty air.

Freedom. Oh oh. Freedom.

Why won't that woman stop singing?

Why do the streetlights conspire against me? They give me two shadows instead of one. I worry that someone is following behind me, watching me. I spook easily. I jump to conclusions. I forget that it is an illusion of light. That both shadows, stretching ahead and behind on the sidewalk, belong to me alone.

Ann de Forest lives and writes in West Philly. Her work has appeared in Coal Hill Review, Noctua Review, *and* Cleaver Magazine, *among others. She contributes to* Hidden City Philadelphia *and is currently editing* Slow Going *(New Door Books, forthcoming in 2021), an anthology of essays about walking, inspired by her perimeter walks around Philadelphia. "Mysteries of the Street" was originally published as "Mystery and Melancholy: After De Chirico" in* Hotel Amerika *(Spring 2010).*

Pests

Sofia Rabaté

The first one I see alive is trekking across my carpet. It is a surprise to see it moving after finding so many poisoned husks. I watch as it tries to clamber into my recycling bin before I kill it. I can't figure out what is appetizing about cardboard boxes. I must look very tall, holding a tall can of Raid, as it lies on its back, trembling. You can tell exactly when they die: it is very sudden. I am running out of paper towels to scoop up their corpses.

    I have been thinking recently about all the ways in and out of this apartment, the places where a roach might breach my defenses. I have heard of them coming in through the pipes in bathtubs. There is a new theory that the virus can circulate through the vents of apartment buildings. HVAC filter sales are going through the roof. I find a crack underneath my kitchen sink where they must have been filtering through. All jittery, I spray Raid in there, expecting one to come at me in a rage. I am afraid of insects. Specifically, I am afraid that a roach will fly at my face and into my mouth. Nothing happens. I plug up the hole with industrial sealant. It all smells awful and I am suddenly aware of my raggedy lungs.

    I still haven't bought paper towels, when the next one tries to dart behind the microwave. I smash it with my frying pan, then regret having put bug juices and perhaps chemicals and diseases on my frying pan, even though it's only the bottom part that never touches my food. I scrape the remains into the trash. They stick, brown goo and bits. I need paper towels, but I am tired of suiting up like an astronaut and being afraid of that lady that gets too close to me with her mask slipping under her nose.

One appears while I am already vacuuming, so I suck it up, still alive. It makes the worst crunching sound I have ever heard, so horrible that I throw the machine on the ground, even though I need to continue vacuuming. I am trying to keep a clean space. The pest control forums warn that an unclean apartment invites vermin. I try: I sanitize my hands whenever I handle anything from outside, I spray Lysol on high-touch surfaces, I even do laundry twice a week in case any of my clothes were contaminated.

The next few are in the bathroom. I shriek when I see one nudging at my toe. Spit and toothpaste go flying everywhere. I smother it to death with a towel that happens to be close. I peel the corpse off and the towel goes into the laundry. I start to wonder whether I ever forgot to sanitize after spraying the Raid and maybe I touched my face and maybe it got into my system somehow.

I am Googling symptoms of poisoning—stomach pain, fatigue, appetite loss, and irritability, but I have been feeling this way awhile—when an ad informs me of a miracle cure that involves ground ginger and something else that costs $29.99 to find out. For a while, a large portion of my family was circulating an email that claimed that it could not survive above 80 degrees and that the summer was sure to bring salvation. I find out that roaches' supposed ability to survive nuclear fallout is a myth. They are actually quite mortal. I see one across the room and lunge at it.

There is a very effective system called bait. It is better than poison because the cockroaches do not merely eat it and expire on the spot, they also bring it home to their families. My mother is calling but I don't answer, I'm busy sneaking up on one with a rolled-up magazine. She doesn't understand why I won't visit—she thinks it's fine as long as I wash my hands and take vitamin C.

Boric acid exploits their cleanliness. It clings to their bodies as they walk through it, and they later eat it when they clean themselves. But further research reveals that they don't have tongues, instead they have taste receptors all over their bodies. I don't understand the details, but the end result is that their nervous system breaks down. I imagine that this death is much like the others: twitching upside down, a mad short dance.

There is a story of a woman who had a cockroach crawl into her ear, where it died, of course. It had to be surgically removed.

There is also a story of the virus coming to Washington State floating in the ocean. Another chain email claims that the virus lives in fluids for weeks and that it could even be inside your bottled water. I think this story is made up.

I start tasting the boric acid through my feet. The Lysol tastes awful when I run my hands on the counter. I have to wash my hands so I don't accidentally touch my food and consume Lysol. My whole apartment smells like a hospital, a slaughterhouse, an illicit drug lab, but one still has the audacity to appear, vibrating with life, inside my old biscuit tin. I shut it and shake it around violently, hoping it will kill the thing, but he looks unharmed. He scurries out with the glee of a child getting off a carousel.

There is one giving birth placidly behind my sneakers, squeezing out an egg sac that looks like a roach-textured jellybean. She needs no epidural, simply depositing it and running to hide behind the laundry basket. A single sac can contain up to forty children. Some females remain pregnant for life with the offspring of one mate.

The exterminator says they live in the wall. He will not come to my apartment, though, because of the current situation. He offers a virtual consultation: yes, those are roaches all right.

His advice is to put all my food into plastic containers. I knock on all the walls, trying to find a hollow spot where they are building their home.

The ground is sticky from all the stuff I have tried. I feel the soles of my feet sticking to the fabric of my bedsheets. They are so sticky that maybe I could walk upside down on the ceiling, as I imagine they are currently doing. The progression is obvious: the chemicals touch my feet, my feet touch the sheets, the sheets touch my hands, my hands touch my face, maybe in my sleep, and I have gotten the chemicals into my mouth.

I cannot be safe. They have probably touched every surface in this apartment, their low bellies leaving crisscrossing trails of bacteria. Traces of their fecal matter must line the little crevices where no one looks.

I see them everywhere, in the shadow underneath the radiator, in the dark spot on that old junky pillow, in the smear on the wall that I should paint over, in the cracked baseboard that needs replacing.

It's really my fault. I remember all my sins: the disappointing sandwich I left out all night, the bacon grease that slipped in the crack between the stove and the counter, the orange I forgot to eat that grew a moldy beard.

They are nocturnal creatures. I stay up late one night, pretending to sleep so that they will feel they have the upper hand. They can live for a week without their heads. My blanket rustles from the weight of a thousand tiny lives. Of course, cloth barriers are not the most effective, with shoddy pores that let in their little bristly feet, but what other options are available?

The blanket slides off under the tugging of so many mandibles. Already a few are walking on my thigh, feeling like the rough side of a sponge being dragged across my skin. As soon as the first few do this, the hordes advance. They move together. They are all related, all cousins brothers sisters, all descended from the original two cockroaches that mated underneath my refrigerator.

They are walking over me like I am furniture, like I am the floor. I stare at them, daring them, imploring them. I will let them crawl anywhere they want as long as they don't go into my mouth.

Sofia Rabaté is a Philadelphia native who currently attends the University of Pennsylvania. She is pursuing a bachelor's degree in English with a concentration in creative writing. A multilingual musician, her life is constantly in translation.

Mr. Friend

Jeffrey S. Markovitz

The home was called The Villages, though it was a singular structure and on the seam of the city and its nearest suburb, and was in a neighborhood called Chestnut Hill, though there was no hill and the chestnut trees had either been lumbered for the buildings there or had been nothing but a romance in the first place. A green-railed bridge by the college wed the ridges of the Wissahickon ravine by the trailhead to the park. Trailhead, he thought, or trail end, depending on the orientation of the walker. He drove over.

The trees on either side betrayed the fact that the road upon which he drove was paved only after felling a number of their fellows; the entire city, he thought, was once this woodland, where all that remains of its native people was a stone statue deep off the trail—white and commissioned by a wealthy, nearby denizen—that covered, with saluting hand, the brow of his forehead against the sun or against the divinity from above that brought to his woods saviors with saws. He looked up and out of the windshield, the bare winter branches set against the sky like the bronchial tubes of anatomy textbooks: trees and lungs on opposite sides of breath.

They'd cut down the trees because no one had reverence for trees even though they gave life, as all things progeny underestimate the vitality breathed from paternity. Never more climbed, sheltered under, never more rested against nor slept among, never again scratching the backs of bears nor sharpening the tusks of elephants, never more shadowing the sun nor describing the wind, never living nobly: satisfied of their roots and place—this shaved Earth a razor burn of stumps, and yet it is the *people* who now tramp the open ground like amputees.

The hopeless, antiseptic smell reminded him of the sacristy. A sign reading *The Villages* was illuminated from behind by buried lights behind the letters, the one behind the second *l* out, emphasizing the last two syllables by its shade. There was a man in a wheelchair by the fireplace in the lobby, where flames ate the empty space above themselves, and his eyes refocused from the eating to the man who'd just walked in and was signing the register. When the eyes of the chair-bound man met the eyes of the visitor, there was at the same moment a plea and a fear: the yearning came from the wish (not the only wish but the deepest) that he'd be the visited for this visitor, and the fear came from the vestments. The black. The sterility and stoicism. Priests only showed their faces around there when someone was close to death, though the joke on them—and on all—was the proximity in which death always waited.

But it was true: the priest was there for last rites. It was a trail end.

* * *

"Hello," the priest said. This would be his last sacrament. He was old enough, too old, for it anymore and so would retire after performing the anointing of the sick on the man in the bed before him; it was his last sacrament, the end of a long life of administering such sacraments, and he would withdraw to a quiet home—not unlike this one—and wait for his own priest to come. The room told of faux home: carpeted in colors not easily stained and wood paneling at the edges that looked less like wood when approached and hotel-style lamps and prints in frames and the lavatory with stainless steel rails around the toilet and bath and the one beeping machine the thing out of place. There was no hum to the room, no life, no vibration. It was a holding pattern, a cell, into which were placed people for whom medical advancement stalled the natural progress of the body, for a time. So much had been spent on the extension of life, only to find little for it to extend into. These rooms, all rooms like it, multiplied across the country, to hold medicine's greatest accomplishment—life everlasting, ticking hearts in limp bodies—and to be a priest in all of that science felt just a little validating, as if the net gain of corporeality still came laughably short of the old thing, of faith.

He said hello again to the man lying in bed before him, but the man did not answer. The priest pulled the single chair of the room to the edge of the bed and sat. "Hello," he said once more. "Do you know me? Do you remember me?"

"Mr. Friend," the man said, looking at him with a clarity that the priest knew wasn't there. It hadn't been there for a time. The man was in the later stages, the last stages, of the disease that took his memory—the most unjust disease—where the body can live on while the mind whips in panic at an entire life seen through ever descending screens of increasing opaqueness.

"No," the priest said. "It's me."

But it was no use. The man puckered his lips against the toothless ridges inside and shook his head slowly, turning away. "Mr. Friend," the old man said again.

The priest sighed. He began.

In the name of the Father and of the Son

The old man turned back at this start, at these words, as if startled, and mouthed again—this time with no sound—what seemed to be his only phrase.

and the Holy Spirit. Amen.

The priest took the man's hand, the skin phyllo thin and transparent, and held it gently. He rubbed his thumb against the knuckles, displaced the hair between them, sighed the resignation that comes when what was expected still strikes suddenly. He knew he had to continue the ritual but felt less adept than usual, as if the power of God, through which he worked, was somehow truncated at the bedside of this father, this power.

The peace of the Lord be with you always. The Lord is our shepherd and leads us to streams of living water. Coming together as God's family, with confidence, let us ask the Lord's forgiveness, for he is full of gentleness and compassion.

He was not a parent, but the moniker *father* taught him of that vantage. He leaned into the old man and kissed his cheek. "Do you know me?" The cheek was soft; the kiss, wet, lingering.

The faint almost breath, among the last of a long sequence: "Mr. Friend."

He knew then that a child would never love their parents the way or to the extent to which their parents loved them. But those parents did not love *their* parents the way or to the extent to which they were loved by them. Children would love their own children this way without this way or this extent being requited. It was this generational one-way comprehensive love that united parents and progeny; it was the love for one's child that completed the love felt for them by their own parents, which they never before truly understood.

"No," the priest said. He looked out of the window. There were no trees. "It's me, Dad. It's your son."

"Mr. Friend."

Praise to you, God the only begotten Son. You humbled yourself to share in our humanity and you heal our infirmities. Through this holy anointing may the Lord in his love and mercy help you with the grace of the Holy Spirit.

* * *

Before the old, bed-ridden man was old, he bore a son and

loved him. On Sundays, his wife, a Christian, went to church; he went into the woods. There was a spirituality there, as if the Gnostic Gospels' insistence of God in things—the Eastern recognition of divinity even in gnats—called him away from all edifice and into the trees, where he could saunter for the hour she was in a different prayer, she always bringing the child, always a church wall away from her husband but loving him no less. He brought his son often to the woods, but it was the wooden rafters of the stonewalled church with dusted stained glass and martyred statues captured in their various agonies and the repetitive chants, songs cycling through celebrations, and stoicism of the priest before his congregation, that won the child. From a young age, his son wanted to follow into the cloth.

The man was raised in the church and married his wife in the church but when he became a father, he stopped being a Christian because the Christian God could not be thus. The need for supplication. The conditional love. God: the essential third-person omniscient absentee father. To father was no such thing. It was a verb. To father was to submit control to the will of the universe, not need omnipotence against it. To do it gladly. To understand that the act of creation made the creator *less* relevant, *less* sentient, *less* powerful. To accept the novelty of that reduced agency.

When his son took the holy orders, he gave him an inscribed Bible of sturdy leather and gold-embossed lettering—the epigraph, his heart.

* * *

Kilbourne Hole was where they did it, where the earth sunk into itself, the basalt cliffs block-fragmented and arranged by the awesome power of angry things below the surface, a mile-wide ditch in the desert offering no panacea from sun or thirst or refuge from travel but where the travelers rested anyway, the cliff edges' sinking feeling like enough of an aberration of land to sink with it, be born to be killed, and breathe what was supposed to be freedom but felt no different than home, where they did it: took the child from his mother's nipple. The attorney general went to church every Sunday, supplicated himself in front of the Lord and had the Ten Commandments framed and hung in his office in DC, exactly two thousand miles from Kilbourne Hole, where he'd never have to meet the woman or her son; he slept under a crucifix and prayed on knees in pajamas by a bed near the Capitol for goodness to enter his heart—he said it was about "deterrence".

The man's son had been a priest for a year, had delivered weekly homily in quaking voice but quickly commanded himself in the faith that diluted doubt to nothing. He had traveled to New Mexico to make his body a vessel for the transport of water and prayer but was a fence between coyotes and snipers—the former gold-toothed and rank, the latter begging him to move out of the quadrants of their crosshairs. (They, too, Christians.) His father was proud of his going there, of his human kindness—the one thing he wished of his son the day he was born: kindness in the face and wake of humanity. His father did not go to church, did not believe, but hugged his son at the airport, grabbed his neck behind the clerical collar, and looked into his eyes, saying, "I am proud of who you are," to which the son replied, "I hope only to bring some peace to those poor people," and the father nodded, pulled the son close, touched foreheads, and waved through the sliding doors where went his boy, grown, a father of sorts himself, to the West, where he could hold people without country against the vilification privileged to patriotism.

He was in Kilbourne Hole when it happened.

And when he returned, more human, because he was more hurt by the world, he embraced his father and moaned into him, "They took the boy, right there, and put him in a van. Drove away."

The father squinted against the dark of his son's soutane.

"Her breast dribbled, as if it was looking for the mouth that had been wrenched from it."

He was weeping openly at the same airport where they had departed a month before.

"And I could do nothing. I pleaded, ran after the van, came to the woman and spoke to her, prayed for her, and it was nothing. Then another van came and took her, in handcuffs, without her son, a different way."

The two negotiated the transient personality of the airport, the space where nothing lived but where life flashed match-head temporary.

"They call themselves Christians, Dad. Christians. They say they follow Christ, then do this. This to people who don't even speak their language, can't understand what they're saying, why they're doing it. This basic human truth. To never take a child from a parent. But they say they are Christian. What am I doing? Me, a leader to them. A parent to them."

His father thought about what he said, the basic human truth. Wondered what he would have done had someone stolen his son from him. Wondered how he would survive.

"This hurts worse than anything I've felt." Christians hanging the cross itself on a cross of their own hatred in the name of a god-man who, if there, would have held the mother and child together against the most violent force.

It was Kilbourne Hole that first tested his son's faith, and it would take a father's selflessness to restore it. A conversion.

He told his son, "The worst kind of fear is an abstract fear." It was something a father should never have to explain to a son: that there was ugliness in the world and it would surround him and try to get in and it would likely get in but what he wanted most was to help his son develop a skin against it. Like the skin he gave of himself. But it permeated and we must watch the crude innocence be eaten by it, a cancer that catalyzed the final transformation to full person: to lose faith in people. He said, "Our country's coasts, I'm

sorry, are parentheses that sometimes hold an aside of hate."
Fathers were men, too.

* * *

Soon after, in an awkward moment in the very woods to which his father retreated and where he had raised him, when they reached the part of the trail that felt closed in enough by trees (it was faux, but if they breathed deeply at that exact spot, they could just believe that the air those trees provided made the inhale somehow fresher), the son asked his father to call him *father*. He didn't ask for the validation commiserate with naming; it was a deeper petition. The Wissahickon woods were sacred in that they smelled of their ownness: wet brittle rock and leaves cycling through the dying and fertilizing of new growth, the trails soggy with the held dregs of past weather and scented similarly: of rain that was in a mud that stuck and a river somewhere—the namesake—that called to the first from the ships to cut there, build there, make a city of that scent. Those first colonists knew the sacredness of those woods and knew the city that would occupy that space would somehow hold the same potency in rising from such a place. So the trees of that place became the lumber for the beams of the houses that would rise there, transmitting from tree to beam a sanctity inexorably attached to what quiet, woodly people could recognize as holy. In the moment he asked his father to call him *father*, then asked him to join his flock, there was no force in his shepherd staff's ground strike, no urgency in his asking, because he knew paternity could not flow upriver. His father might call him the new name, but it was only language, sound and code, and he could not hope to think of his father as his child or lamb. Nor could he believe his God capable of sending his father to damnation, sinner and nonbeliever though he might have been; it was, as if, in this man, God would make an exception for sacrilege.

Still, he wanted him saved.

His father knew that this was Kilbourne Hole sinking his son deeper and that he had to do what was called of him, his own sacrament (brother to sacrifice), to father, a verb, his son.

He converted.

* * *

The deeper into the systems of man, the further away from peace, the man knew. He came to his son's church every Sunday—no different than if he'd come to the ballpark where his son pitched—was baptized and confessed, knelt at the appropriate times and blinked when the holy water fled the aspergillum and coughed at the sage ghosts leaving the censor; he memorized the creeds and hummed through the homily, took the Eucharist, offered offerings, clasped his wife's hand, and pretended.

His son knew the conversion and attendance was for him, not for faith, but he was a priest who felt an insatiable responsibility for the members of his congregation and so hoped for osmosis, that the spirituality of the building would seep into his father and bring him in. What he felt most deeply was the need to be with his father, that there could be no peace in heaven without him; he feared an eternity without his father, where he, having failed to save the man he most needed to, would wander through paradise in the dread of this most precious lost soul burning. He was a good priest, respected and loved, and believed truly in his devotion to the church; he felt joy in seeing his father in the pew but realized it was only for support—bleacher cheering—and not a true belief. He thought of what he'd do as father to *his* congregation, if his children were wrenched from him. He wondered how far off love was from salvation, if any distance at all. Religion and biology, parenthood, the father preached and his father listened—what greater hope could mankind wish for but to be a shield against the rot of itself?

***

Father in heaven, through this holy anointing grant my father comfort in his suffering. When he is afraid, give him courage, when afflicted, give him patience, when dejected, afford him hope, and when alone, assure him of the support of your holy people. We ask this through Christ our Lord.

All forgot that the miraculous city that rose and spread before them, with its bisections of time in the various architectures of colonial homes to corporate towers, was culled from a forest in a valley, with three rivers and their eternal flowing ignorant to the chopping of their bank trees and damming of their own bodies. In that city, the homes were built with shared walls between, brick being better than trees at shielding one's life from their neighbors.

Roots and schist, shadowed by dusklight, turned his ankle toward sprain and yet he proceeded directly to the place, the sky through winter branch striations a royal blue shade deepening to universe. The Wissahickon, last bastion of woodland against the imposition of city, showed little sign of the population density surrounding; no cars could be heard, no voices, none of the weep and lamentation of the priest as he walked to the place, having come from The Villages, having come from his last sacrament, having sat thumbing a thin-skinned hand as someone unplugged the out-of-place machine. It would be dark soon. The branches, finger skeletal. He was going to the place. On the inside of his coat he portaged the small book, gold-embossed, heavy in the odd off-balance weight on one side of the body: the text bearing everything to which he'd dedicated his life and something more than life, something metaphysical and unknowable and endless—it was faith in script and it was not to be challenged, but it banged against his ribs, stopped no bullets, took from him no violence of loss, but reminded him of itself in its banging. His father had given it to him on the day he received his holy orders, became a father himself, and he took it and kept it and read from it all those years. Now the darkening woods and precarious roots and schist threatened—they were not the pleasant reprieve of day but something worse, sinister. No, he knew, trail bound, momentous, agile for his age, done—it is only me that is this darkness. What I am of and by this virtue was of me is gone; these primordial woods care nothing. Yet he went on to the place.

* * *

"Dad, do you remember? Can you tell me who I am?" The home's staff hovered around the room, unsure of themselves in the face of a priest that was a child. All fathers were at first sons. The old man was in and out of consciousness, the machine removed from the room, all bodies still save for the hearts.

"Mr. Friend," he said again.

The priest breathed, defeated. The surface of the world was mottled with disease, desperate with despotism, a visage that would slow a growing man's faith for goodness. It was a sun that could never be known because it could not be seen but was ubiquitous in its warmth. Too long looking away from such a sun while still feeling it could turn a man from life, frustrate him against his fellows. It was a decaying and corrupting surface. But there was purity below. It must be held out for, dove for.

"Okay."

God our Father, we have anointed your child with the oil of healing and peace. Caress him, shelter him, and keep him in your tender care.

* * *

He was in the place.

It was a special place in the way that it was completely inconsequential to anyone but him and his father, the way the most banal place took special precedent over other geographies in the minds of those who found love there, who harvested indescribable energy from the feel of it and returned to feel the same energy because it was there that there was connection. Such places held the purity below, they must have, because how else could they bring so much peace in the otherwise tumult? (Passing a sidewalk bench in ignorance, it is heaven for someone.) His father, at the last, did not remember him. But in the place, the place in the woods where they would go, that didn't matter; they were both there, perpetually, in paradise. Home is, after all, just a place people agree to meet their family.

It had been years since he'd opened the book; he didn't need to; after so long, so much knowledge of it, the book was more a representation than words. But then he remembered his holy orders, his father's giving of the book, the epigraph within. He opened the cover and with a penlight read:

My son, on this day of your devotion, I hope you feel some of what a father feels for his child, that you know just some of the love.

When you were small, just born, for no reason whatsoever and with no rationality, I would call you Mr. Friend. It was a pet name that fell from my mouth one day and stuck for some months but didn't mean anything. Now, in the strange way of things, I know how the accident of my calling you that came to fit you. You are a friend to the world.

I am proud of you.

With love,
Dad

* * *

The Wissahickon woods held the last trees, which were the first trees. The place was sacred. The priest wept. The sick were anointed. The sacraments administered. Nothing was ever gone; the woods cared. It was full dark then, but he felt no fear.

May God the Father bless you.
May God the Son heal you.
Amen.

Jeffrey S. Markovitz is a writer and educator living in Philadelphia. His books include The Sharpest End *(Sharp End, forthcoming in 2021),* US VS *(The Head and the Hand, 2020),* Permanent for Now *(Unsolicited Press, 2018),* —for Olivia *(The Head and the Hand, 2013), and* Into the Everything *(Punkin Books, 2011).*

Chuck Taylors

Robin Jarrett

Vivid colors appeared suddenly—the red kind, blue, deep purple, pale yellow, and pea-soup green, as if radiating throughout every cell of his lithe body. Thinking he was anchored on all four corners of his feet, he felt grounded. Yet moments before, a cinder block had crashed over his head. It had felt like a cinder block at least.

Maybe it had really been the barrel of a semiautomatic. He wasn't clear whether blood was actually running or he was imagining it.

Overwhelmed with confusion, he sat up and scanned one-eyed in every direction. He realized he was all alone. Night had fallen and clouds had formed. He hoped it would rain. It was warm enough, and he needed a cleansing.

* * *

"What a wake-up call," Pedro exclaimed. Holding his head, completely startled, he heard himself saying aloud that he should never take anything for granted and then noticed his distended belly. Pumpkin-filled ravioli, toasted pine nuts, sage, ricotta, and a splash of beurre blanc . . . He recalled the combinations of delicate, savory herbs in the shaved-parmesan and arugula salad. He could almost see the chunks of roasted butternut squash. The high-end catered dinner the evening before had left him with a larger than usual girth. A once-a-month gathering of his now former roommates had been a moving-away celebration this time.

Pedro felt the gash above his right eye that was bleeding profusely. His blood tasted unfamiliar. It was salty and thick. He savored his blood as if he'd never taste it again. Taking his left hand, he began smearing blood over his eye and his cheek, covering his nose, onto his mouth and down his neck. Stopping before he reached his chest, he felt the blood still flowing downward at a rapid pace.

He felt like a warrior and recalled a book that had carved a significant path through his early high school years, inspiring him to conquer jump splits, leaps, and many other physical feats. Spirits still flowed in his head, and the abundance of wine still permeated his body. He felt awake, alive, and bloodthirsty as images of painting came flooding, as did the sensations—the tastes and smells and textures—from the feast the evening before.

* * *

It was three thirty in the afternoon, and Pedro had taken an alternate route through Germantown, a northwest section of Philadelphia, to have keys made at a local hardware store. He knew this shortcut, littered with debris, used needles, and industrial castaways—it was off the beaten path, but it shortened the trip from his new digs considerably.

The day was warm, and he was enjoying the walk, excited about creating his new home. He imagined how he'd apply the newfound feng shui skills he'd picked up from his most recent ex-girlfriend, Amanda. She had had impeccable taste and a home with a flow like none he had ever seen. A fountain, wind chimes, and ceramic frogs filled her living space. He'd felt more at home in her place than he felt with her. That realization had left him wanting someone else, or perhaps no one. She was so pretty, though, and smart, with long auburn hair and light brown eyes, and lithe like him.

Initially, their conversations stimulated him. After ten months, though, he couldn't bear her bullshit existential crises. Pedro was a spiritualist, but her endless new-age banter left him lusting for any kind of interruption. If Pedro looked away or seemed slightly distracted, Amanda expressed profound hurt and repeatedly said, "If you really care, you'd attend to me and listen. Please care enough to listen to me." The thought of sex wasn't even enough to keep him interested. Her repetitions became exhausting. He began to only appreciate her in passing, like a landscape best viewed from a distance. They both cried when he left. He suspected that she was more angry than sad.

Pedro heard whistling from far down the alley. It was quickly getting closer, and the pitch had become disturbingly piercing. He picked up his pace and tried to hurriedly detach from his mounting fear. The whistle breathing down his neck disrupted the flow of his thoughts and the rhythm of his flight. Pedro felt assaulted by the shrill sounds.

An imposing figure, he introduced himself as "Big John" and then quickly bulldozed Pedro's body.

"I have a gun, and I will shoot you without hesitation," he slurred.

Big John invaded Pedro's space at an alarming rate and began speaking in a quieter tone than one might have anticipated based on his sheer size. "What's your name?" the large man asked.

Pedro thought about the limited cash in his pocket (just enough to pay for his new keys) and glanced at his outlandishly expensive watch, given to him by Amanda on his birthday three months prior. "I'm Pedro," he said casually, trying to appear relaxed and confident.

He assessed his other valuables, of which he had none,

except for his cherished red Chuck Taylors. Pedro sighed on the inside. Big John was bone bald with a skull tattoo on the right side of his thick neck. He had a big, bulbous nose and thin lips that seemed to be swallowed up by his throaty gruff voice. *Scary fugly*, Pedro thought. Amanda had hated when he used that expression.

Pedro was focused on his beloved sneakers as he remembered that he'd left his phone in his new living room on the makeshift coffee table, a cardboard box. He thought about what he might make for his first dinner party and felt relieved that he had left his phone behind. If he survived, at least he'd still have all his contacts.

"Look me in the eye," Big John grumbled. "Why are you fixated on your goofball red sneakers? Take them the fuck off and empty your pockets."

"You want my sneakers?" Pedro quivered.

Big John stared in his menacing way, and Pedro reluctantly began removing his favorite Chucks, shoes that he wore for important events, life-altering events, like moving. He unlaced them in his usual meticulous fashion. Kicking them off would be disrespectful and wouldn't show the love and admiration he had for them.

He sat with his shoes neatly in front of him, now staring up the barrel of Big John's gun. Pedro, suspecting Big John was a seasoned criminal, and possibly drunk or on drugs, smiled a crooked smile in disbelief.

"What the fuck are you smiling at?" said Big John, raising his voice ever so slightly.

* * *

Pedro wondered how long he'd been out. He checked his wrist; his watch was gone. His socks had been removed, and his Chuck Taylors were nowhere to be seen. No keys, no money, no watch, no Chuck Taylors. He replayed the events; they switched on and off like passing headlights. Pedro mourned as it began to drizzle. He sat up against the wall littered with graffiti. He leaned into the wall and stood, continuing to paint as he watched the drizzle wash away the multitude of colors.

Robin Jarrett has an insatiable appetite for the creative and performing arts as an actress, voice-over artist, writer, and jewelry/crafts designer and dance teacher. She was born and bred in Philadelphia. She's relocated a few times and inevitably comes back to her hometown.

Turnabout

Will Clattenburg

If it wasn't depression in the clinical sense, it was close. All her days, all her hours. Here she was, just graduated from college, living at home. A prestigious college that her grandparents paid for, and no real job afterward. Every morning, she drove the forty-five minutes to Emmaus, New Jersey. Radio personalities talked in between songs for somebody else, a soundtrack for a life she'd outgrown. The grass along the highway was green, the color of magic markers. She parked at an office building with blue-tinted windows, took the elevator to the seventh floor, and found her supervisor each morning at five minutes to nine. The tests were already stacked in a small metal bin labeled TEMP on her supervisor's desk, about four or five standardized tests sealed with red, orange, and yellow stickers on which bold text read, "Do Not Break the Seal," and which when opened released a mild floral odor from the soybean-based ink that came off on her hands like pollen. She carried the tests back to her desk in a generic cubicle that she shared with no one and then sat and read them; read the directions that never varied, the questions with five answer choices; matched what she read with the diagrams and visual accompaniments, the rather crude stick figures whose purpose was to demonstrate relative velocity or forensic science. It didn't matter if she understood the content—what mattered was grammatical correctness, that everything made logical sense. After the temp agency processed their fee, she received eleven dollars per hour. So she read tests. Her eyes sometimes hurt, but the higher-ups weren't cruel taskmasters. She could take breaks, have a coffee, gaze out the window at the field that horseshoed the parking lot. At 5:00 p.m., she handed her supervisor both her opened and unopened tests and drove in true rush hour back to her parents' house in Flourtown, Pennsylvania. Day after day, week after week. And then one day, she decided she didn't want to sit and read tests anymore. She called the temp agency and spoke with a nice woman named Angela who urged her to reconsider her decision—if she quit midweek, without giving two weeks' notice, the agency would have no choice but to terminate her contract; she would no longer be able to apply for future assignments! But she said, *That's okay, thank you for everything*, and hung up before Angela could give her more valid reasons for staying on the job. It was Wednesday; the month was July. She drove on I-95 south. Starting out, the sky was the color of sediment in a river. She approached Wilmington, Delaware, on a stretch of blanched roadway, passing the brick buildings and factories. In a short while, she was in Maryland, where deciduous trees, Virginia creeper, honeysuckle, redbuds, sumac, and forsythia curtained off and almost touched the road. Two hours later, she crossed the Potomac. The rain had held off until then, and now it looked like a faraway stippling against the surface of the Potomac, where the river turned. Then, without warning, sheets of water began to hit her windshield. Still she drove, slower, following the other cars' brake lights, her car cutting through the crystal-like opacity of rain. The rain stopped, then resumed, then became very bad, her windshield wipers only capable of glazing her view, leaves and twigs striking the sides of the vehicle, getting wattled on the hubcaps and undercarriage. The car crunched and absorbed slaps and gentle swipes as it crushed along, spraying water and sliding in water and breaking water into a thousand droplets. There was never any danger of flooding; the car was heavy, stately, a safe car for a safe girl who had always made safe decisions, a car her parents had bought her with safety in mind. So she observed the culverts and runoff and the new grass from the safety of her car, still pelted with rain. She hadn't checked her phone. It was going on noon. The storm had slowed her down. When it let up, she was driving through hills and copses of trees, dark foliage in the axillae of the landscape, everything washed and blurred, except at a distance, where she saw a heap of garbage bags. She slowed, then slowed even more. What looked like garbage bags was in fact a dead cow on the side of the road, legs spread as far as the rumble strips. In the light of recent rain, the cow was copper colored, darker the closer she got. She didn't stop. Even then it didn't look real. But the incident was filled with a gravitas that seeded itself in her mind. She didn't feel like she was in a hurry to understand its meaning. And for the next part of the drive, she was lighter; she could have laughed. She was not someone to make spur-of-the-moment decisions. She had been expecting something different, some uneasiness to work on her and reshape her mind, an uneasiness that would give her a new perspective on herself, a culminating answer to questions about her future. But the future comes slower than she'd anticipated. It would be future when the world was dry and all the leaves fell off her car and the grass in the gullies could breathe. She was not stopping. Be brave, she thought, be brave. She was entering a new phase of her life. The bloated cow had vanished from her rearview mirror. Ahead the road shone like obsidian.

Will Clattenburg is the author of The Art of Fugue: Short Stories (Uncollected Press). *His writing has appeared in* Crack the Spine's 2019 anthology *The Year, as well as in journals like* Toho, Cagibi, Litro Online, *and* Wraparound South. *Born and raised in Philadelphia, he is now living and teaching in Albuquerque, New Mexico.*

Balayage

Debra Leigh Scott

The city itself had come to life hours before. It was an early spring morning chilled by frost, but tourist season had already begun. Horse-drawn open-air carriages lent an air of charm to the streets, the drivers regaling their passengers, who huddled under scratchy blankets listening to the stories of events and people of the colonial past. They coaxed their horses around cars and busses, as the steaming breath of both driver and horse met and mingled in the sharp air. Trolleys offered less exposure to the elements and provided tourists with guides who spoke through microphones, pointing out the sites, reciting the scripted histories of the rogues and pirates and revolutionary heroes who once walked these cobblestone streets.

Some of the buildings and pubs in this part of the city dated back to those colonial times, each one with a street sign announcing its history and the famous people who had slept, met, ate, or died there. These venerable sites now shared the streets with museums, tourist shops, tattoo parlors, a few movie complexes, a variety of restaurants offering everything from American bistro to Middle Eastern fare, pizza joints, banks and ATMs, open-air parking lots, a few grocery shoppes (always spelled in that dated way on their signage to add to their ambience and prices), and, of course, a liquor store.

It was to this liquor store that Rona was headed. She left her home on Delancey Street, which had a brass plaque near the front door announcing that, in the eighteenth century, this house had belonged to Thomas Cosgrove, sea captain and suspected privateer who had served in Ben Franklin's rag-tag fleet, fighting the British at sea. She averted her gaze and walked quickly past the three high-rise towers she hated, so incongruous and ridiculous in a neighborhood of charming two-story colonial brick dwellings; then she passed the Sheraton Hotel, Lamberto's Italian restaurant, the City Tavern, the Baskin-Robbins Ice Cream Shoppe, the crusty and shifty-looking storefront announcing "passport photos and palm reading". She wore a silver and gray fur shrug, which she pulled tighter around her shoulders as the sun moved behind a cloud and a biting wind began. Rona was dressed well, as usual. Today she wore lean slate-gray slacks tucked into darker gray leather boots, a black silk blouse with pearl buttons, black leather gloves, and black sunglasses. Her jewelry was set in antique silver. The shrug around her shoulders had a bateau neck and hook-and-eye closure, made with the kind of quality craftsmanship that today's late twentieth-century clothing manufacturers, with their overseas sweatshops and mass production, could no longer accomplish. It was one of the many beautiful pieces she'd inherited from her late mother's closet. Her hair, which would have matched her fur had it been allowed to go natural, had just been balayaged with copper, caramel, and honey tones and freshly cut into the long bob that had become her signature look through the years. Rona was the kind of woman who thought seriously of things like having a "signature look".

There was a slight commotion across the street, in front of The Plough and the Stars Irish pub, but Rona only gave a quick glance as she entered the liquor store. Inside, she chose three bottles of Moët & Chandon for a birthday luncheon she was giving the next day, exchanged some friendly conversation with Patty, the longtime store clerk, then headed back out onto 2nd Street.

The ruckus at the pub was continuing, with the restaurant manager now out on the sidewalk, attempting to calm the situation. A ragged female voice from the center of the growing crowd was howling, "I'm havin' a *baby*! I'm havin' a *baby*!"

Rona, who always thought of herself as a take-charge person, was certain she could offer some assistance and strode across the street to lend a hand to the manager, a red-haired, harried young man in his twenties, who seemed entirely out of his depth.

Rona approached with the polished hauteur of a museum docent, determined to get to the root of the disturbance.

"Let me through, please," she said, elbowing her way to the front of the crowd.

He was little more than a boy, really, this manager; he stood akimbo in his starched white manager's shirt with a stunned and frightened look on his pale and slightly freckled face. A shocked and nervous young Asian couple sat at the high-hat table nearest the door, holding their drinks with both hands and leaning toward each other, afraid, since this woman was nearest to them, crouched and howling, almost beneath their table. Patrons at other tables leaned to take in the scene but didn't rise or approach, didn't offer help. Inside, the pub was filled with highly polished wood and brass and had a roaring fire in an enormous fireplace. The two-story vaulted ceiling held and dispersed the light that entered through its many windows. Within, most patrons seemed unaware of the drama taking place on the sidewalk and were happily eating and drinking and enjoying their afternoon.

On the sidewalk was an old black woman, rail thin, uncombed steel-gray hair like swirling, stringy clouds of smoke from a trash can fire. She wore brown canvas sneakers with no laces and had bare legs with raised white and purple scars down both shins. Wrapped in a filthy, oversized military-issue coat that hung to her knees, she had a backpack that may have once been green, slung on her back. A moth-eaten black knit hat was pulled unevenly over her head so that on one side, the wiry gray hair exploded and flew about her face. She was nearly lying on the cement, clutching at her knees, her stomach, her chest, and rocking, rocking, rocking, all the while moaning and crying out. Suddenly, she turned and fixed her attention on Rona.

"Who are *you*?" the woman said.

"My name is Rona," Rona said.

Rona saw that the old woman's face was nearly as dark as her hat, smeared with grease and dirt. One eye was milky white and turned in toward the nose; the other was dark and oozing and darted violently, like a caged bird.

"I'm having a *baby*," she shrieked.

"I'd just gotten her to stop screaming," the manager said.

The woman crawled toward Rona, and her voice came out like a ragged whisper. "I'm havin' a baby," she repeated. "Right *now*. Right *now*. Mama cut my head off, left me bleedin' to die. That's why the baby's comin'."

Even twisted in pain, there was something of a child about the old woman's face, despite the wildness of gray hair and the filth that covered her. A look of being lost and helpless and small. A look of being hungry for love, not just in this current moment but through all of life. A truth existed on her face that, should anyone be brave enough to travel into it as it beckoned, would reveal decades of that helplessness, subjected to harsh and brutal living, unmet longing, violence and abuse, a life that began in shreds and tatters and only advanced into deeper misery. The moaning that came from deep inside her was an ancient growl, heavy with winds full of dust, raw with nightmares of vicious and ravenous creatures, battered by hurricanes and floods and human ruin.

Rona's impulse was to reach out and touch her, but she recoiled and stopped herself. She looked at the manager. "You've called for help?" she said.

"Cops don't come for crazy vagrants," he said. "I just need to get her away from here. She's upsetting my customers. I'm gonna get *fired.*"

"I'll help her," Rona said to the manager.

"She's *not* having a baby!" he said. "*Look* at her!"

"I *said* I will help her," Rona repeated, this time in staccato, beckoning and leading the woman away from the pub toward the corner, where she could speak to her directly.

She was clearly too old to be having a baby. Rona estimated that the woman was in her seventies or so.

"Are you having pain?" Rona asked.

"Yes!" the woman hollered. "The baby's coming *now!*"

So Rona asked her, "Do you want me to get help?"

"Yes!"

"Shall I call an ambulance?"

"Yes!"

Rona began to search in her purse and realized that her phone still sat on its charger on her bedroom night table. She looked quickly around and saw a meter reader writing a ticket on the other side of Chestnut Street.

"Stay here," she said to the old woman, and ran across the street to the meter reader to ask for help.

The woman wore a uniform with the Parking Authority logo on the pocket. She was young and blonde and disinterested.

"She'll only get arrested for panhandling if I call this in," she said.

"We don't want the *police,*" Rona said. "She hasn't asked anybody for money. She's asked for help. We need an ambulance."

"Oh, that's different," the young woman said. "I can call directly for an ambulance."

Which she did.

But as the two women were moving back toward the old woman squatting there at the corner, they saw her rise unsteadily to her feet, clutching at the wall, and begin to move away with halting steps, heading in the direction of the river, still hunched over in abdominal pain.

Rona called to her to stop, and she did. Once they reached her, Rona explained that this young woman was not a policewoman, which is what she assumed drove the old woman into trying to run away. She told her that she had called an ambulance and it was coming.

"She's a civil servant," Rona explained. "She's offered to help."

The old woman began her litany again, first about the baby, then about her mother cutting her head off.

The young woman stayed as long as she could but had to leave before the ambulance got there, because she was late ending her shift. She seemed very uneasy about this old woman and a little bit scared. Rona imagined she was a suburban girl with her first city job and that she was unused to what confronted her here. Others hurried around the three of them there on the sidewalk, casting side glances at the trio or staring outright at the old woman, sometimes with curled lips and judgmental looks on their faces.

The young woman ultimately hurried away, too, with much apology. Rona stayed.

"Thank you, civil bitch!" the old woman hollered to the blonde girl. "Thank you!"

They waited together for a while. Time seemed to have slowed down. The old woman was moaning more quietly now, sitting on a bench in front of a building that used to be the old Corn Exchange. She rocked slowly. Rona didn't know what more to say to her, so she repeated at intervals that the ambulance was coming, even though she wasn't entirely sure that it would ever arrive.

The old woman looked up at her after a time, squinting and turning her face sideways so that she could see Rona with her darting eye.

"I like that little coat you got on," she said. "Is it bear?"

"No," Rona said slowly. "It's chinchilla. It's a chinchilla capelet."

The old women squinted her eye tighter and shook her head. "They ain't real words," she said slowly, pointing at Rona with a bony finger. "You ain't talkin' real words to me."

The scream of a siren suddenly pierced the air, and Rona was relieved to see the flashing lights of an emergency wagon heading through the traffic light two blocks farther west, heading toward 3rd Street as other cars pulled aside to make way.

The ambulance finally pulled through the 2nd Street intersection. Rona motioned to them. The driver cut the siren and kept the flashing lights on, then double-parked, there in the middle of Chestnut Street, tying up traffic rather than pulling over to the open spot at the curb. Two medics jumped out. The younger man went directly to the old woman, and the driver, a dark, squat, balding man, scowled at Rona, then opened the back of the cab and climbed inside.

The young man was trying to talk to the old woman, who was still holding her stomach and rocking.

"Do you know her name?" he asked Rona.

Rona walked closer to the old woman. "You need to tell him your name," she said.

The old woman mumbled what sounded like a string of names, the last one being something that sounded a little like "Liza".

"Is Liza your name?" Rona asked.

The old woman nodded, then recited a different string of names. "Never got any real names 'cause of my mama killing me," she finished up by saying.

Rona looked at the young man again as she spoke. His ID said, "Sean MacNeil."

"Well, this nice young man is named Sean, and he's going to help you and get you to the hospital, so they can find out what's going on, okay?"

"It's a *baby*," the old woman insisted.

"Oh, fuck me." The older medic had jumped down from the cab and approached. "It's the nitwit again."

Rona looked at him, shocked. "Don't call her that!"

"That ain't my name," the old woman said. "My name is Rona."

"No, it is *not*," the older medic said. "It's Junie, same as it's always been. Junie the nitwit."

"Wait," Rona said. "You *know* her?"

"Know her? Don't I drag her ass to Pennsylvania Emergency every damn month?" He looked over at the younger medic. "Sean, get her in the back."

"I don't want to go in there," the old woman said.

"Well, that's just too damned bad," the bald man said, and tried to take the woman's arm.

She pulled away from him and let loose a string of words that didn't sound like English. But instead of actually resisting, she seemed only to want to be allowed to move toward the door of the ambulance on her own. The younger man took her elbow to help her climb in and jumped in behind her.

"I'll do the exam," he called to the older man.

Rona had moved into the street so that she could see inside the cab and watch to be sure that the old woman was settled. A small group of onlookers had gathered on both sidewalks, and a few cars were lined up behind the ambulance, one of the drivers honking in frustration. A couple shopkeepers had come to their doors to watch. A few tourists huddled near the Corn Exchange Museum entrance, looking nervous.

Rona looked at the older man. His ID said, "Nick D'Annunzio." He scowled at her again and then raised his square palms at her, shrugging his shoulders.

"What?" he said. "You got something to ask?"

"I don't understand," Rona said. "You've taken her to the hospital before? Why don't they take care of her?"

"You think maybe they should give her a private room? Round-the-clock care?"

"Mr. D'Annunzio, you could have a little compassion."

"You want this job, lady?" he asked. "I'll see how long you keep your compassion."

Sean had managed to quiet Junie and was taking her temperature.

Rona motioned toward the old woman. "She's in pain."

D'Annunzio scoffed. "Yeah, yeah, she's always in pain. We're *all* in pain." He looked Rona over and smirked. "Well, maybe *you* aren't. Maybe *you're* doing just fine."

Rona had dealt with his type many times before. *Resentful*, she thought. Workmen, plumbers, landscapers, exterminators, electricians, repairmen. All so resentful. She drew herself up and lifted her chin, glaring right back at him. Balding, unkempt hair. Wire-rimmed glasses taped together on the right side. A rumpled and stained uniform that looked like it was pulled, unwashed, out of a hamper and reworn.

"It is your job to take *care* of this woman," she said, putting her hands on her hips. "Are you going to help her or not?"

"I'm gonna do what I always do. Take her to emergency and dump her. She'll end up back on the streets, and we'll do it all over again. We're street sweepers, lady. That's all."

"I don't think that's very nice."

"Well, who do you think we do it for? We're here to sweep up what *you* people in Society Hill Towers don't want to see."

"I do *not* live in the Towers," Rona said, insulted.

Horns were honking as traffic continued to back up on Chestnut. Cars on 2nd Street couldn't turn. The intersection was clogging up, and drivers were yelling out their windows. D'Annunzio motioned to the noise.

"You happy now? See this mess? You shoulda walked past her like everybody else. She's gonna wind up back here anyway."

Rona turned a bit away from the cab and lowered her voice. "And if she dies?"

"You think you prevented that? You haven't done shit but prolong everybody's misery, lady. A month from now, she's a huddled corpse, turning blue in one of these alleys."

Sean had come to the back of the cab. "We have to bring her in, Nick. She has a temperature. Her pulse is really rapid."

"My name's gonna be Rona now," Junie hollered from inside the cab. "Like the lady with that tiny bear coat. I'm gonna name my baby Rona, too."

"Ah, Jesus Christ," D'Annunzio said.

Rona moved to peer into the cab. "You get well, now," Rona said, as the young medic turned back to attend to Junie.

"You *too*," Junie said, wrapping the sanitized blanket that the young medic gave her around her shoulders. "We *both* gotta get well now."

The older medic looked at Rona again, looked at her packages, her hair. Rona felt the wash of his hatred flow over her.

"You can go on home now and enjoy your wine, enjoy your nice, safe, well-swept neighborhood. You'll have a Good Samaritan story to tell." He leaned toward her. "But newsflash for you"—he motioned around, his hand sweeping in the air—"*this isn't your story.*"

He turned his back on her and climbed back into the driver's seat of the ambulance, gunning the engine a little.

The younger medic had secured Junie into the cot, and before he closed the doors, she lifted her head and looked at Rona.

"Thank you, lady bitch," she called. "Thank you. Get well."

The young medic looked at Rona, embarrassed. "I'm really sorry," he said. "I'll take care of her."

He hesitated for a minute, shot a quick look over his shoulder, then leaned out and motioned Rona closer. "Please don't report Nick," he whispered. "He's having a hard time. His wife is sick. He's got insurance troubles."

Rona held up her hand to stop him talking. Suddenly she imagined this nasty, horrible man standing in the door of a darkened bedroom, a wife huddled under piles of blankets. She saw him eating cold, stale pizza alone in an empty kitchen, still wearing his rumpled, unwashed clothes.

"It's okay, Sean," she said.

"He's not wrong, though. What he said. It just goes round and round. They won't help her."

Rona shook her head. "I just don't understand."

Sean shrugged. "Look, I'll take care of her best I can," he said. "Try not to worry."

Rona nodded but realized with discomfort, as she watched him close the back of the wagon and climb into the passenger's seat, that she hadn't planned on worrying. She hadn't expected to.

D'Annunzio gunned the motor again and turned on the siren. As the ambulance pulled the rest of the way down Chestnut Street toward Front, the crowd started to disperse. The tourist family still huddled, whispering to each other, staring over at Rona. She waved, and they all looked away quickly. She made them uncomfortable. From now on, when they think of Philadelphia, they'll think of her and the ambulance and Junie howling and clutching herself in pain. She felt somehow responsible, a little sorry, about that.

You happy now? Nick had said.

She felt bad about herself, about her antique jewelry and leather boots and expensive, styled hair, about her champagne and her life of luncheons and how meaningless her existence appeared. She hated the woman reflected back to her from the eyes of Nick D'Annunzio.

Rona was frozen, even though the sun had begun to warm the air. She knew she couldn't stand on the sidewalk forever. The tourist family had left. Traffic had resumed, moving easily again. The shopkeepers had returned to their stores and restaurants. But her legs remained disinclined to carry her in any direction, and her mind, newly torn open by what she still failed to understand, offered little by way of rational thought.

Still, it was spring. The buds on the trees were beginning to open. Cherry blossoms. Magnolias. Flowers would bloom in the gardens again, as they did every year. Snowdrops, daffodils, tulips, buttercups. Rona closed her eyes, imagining the city fragrant and in bloom, seeing the dogwoods on her street gently unfurl their pink and white flowers.

She knew that she would eventually begin to move, that her legs would begin to feel like her own, her feet would follow their often-traveled path, that she would return to the ship captain's home to put the champagne in the refrigerator, brew herself a pot of Darjeeling tea, curl into that favorite overstuffed armchair in her well-appointed study, and look out onto Delancey Street. From there, she would imagine that she was miles and miles and many centuries away from the worlds inhabited by angry ambulance drivers, frightened restaurant managers, and insane homeless women. She began to hope that, if she were very careful from now on, she'd never again have to feel the ancient winds that howled around and through them all, and with even the smallest bit of the kind of luck that defined her entire life, she'd begin to feel, soon enough, like her old familiar self.

Debra Leigh Scott is a writer, playwright, singer, and filmmaker; founding director of Hidden River Arts; and editor in chief of Hidden River Publishing. She lives in Headhouse Square. Her Quaker ancestry arrived in the region in the 1600s, and they've been here ever since.

Take a Joke, Leave a Joke

Neil R. Wells

"Before you were afraid of terrorists and Republicans, you thought about how quicksand might get you, right? Quicksand is a great starter fear for a child because it doesn't chase you. You have to go to it. And even though it's called *quick*sand, you sink in it very slowly. And if you really want to escape it, all you really have to do is fall backward and pull yourself out."

The crowd was eating the bit up from the start. Relief.

I continued into the mic, "When my daughter was in her quicksand phase, at age five, we'd look at videos on YouTube. One time we clicked on one that had an attractive woman in tight spandex, and you couldn't tell from her squirming whether she was trying to get herself *out* of the quicksand or stuck even deeper. I started to worry and read the comments. Yup, it was a fetish video for men who get turned on watching women struggle in quicksand. Who knew such a thing existed!"

The crowd was into it. As long as these millennials with their short attention spans pay attention from the beginning, they get hooked. Their own sets are typically good-natured one-liners about the befuddling disarray of their lives and clever complaints about jobs, society, relationships, and, of course, parents, so being somewhat traditional and having actual content at open mics made me something of a freak. That and the graying hair.

"Now I understand what people mean when they say having children shows you things about the world and about yourself that you wouldn't otherwise know. Because without my daughter, I never would have known such a genre of porn existed, and well, I'm not saying I'm a fan, but, in its way, it was entertaining."

Big laugh right on cue. The Wednesday night crowd at Fergie's was always kind to me. Except, well . . . Anyway, it had been *six months.*

"So my daughter's sitting on my lap, and we're both enjoying this video, but on *completely* different levels. I wanted to change it, but she was riv-e-ted. She had to see if the woman would get out, whereas *for me*, it was all about the journey. Then my daughter starts doing commentary, which was terrible, because she was saying the exact same things I imagine a perverted man would say: 'Oh no, now the mud is up to her thighs. She's really messy now. And the bottom of her butt's all wet too. She must hate that. She must really hate that. Do you see, Dad? Do you see?' And reluctantly I say, 'Yes, yes, I see it.'"

The applause and thumbs-ups were enthusiastic and sincere. Most of the people there didn't know me. I looked at David, who ran the mic. He nodded. Apparently, all was forgiven.

*   *   *

When I got home, my daughter looked up from her phone. "How did it go?"

"Great."

"You did the quicksand bit again, didn't you?" she said.

"Hardly anyone there had heard it before. And you know I had to do something safe."

"You need to let me grow up," said the now eleven-year-old. "I want you to do my dog park joke again. 'Dad, look, that dog is licking that other dog's butt.'" Imitating me perfectly: "'That's how dogs greet each other.' 'Hmm. You know what? I think I'm gonna stick to shaking hands.'"

I couldn't help it. I laughed every time she told it.

"Shh. You're going to wake up Mom."

"Time for bed. You have school tomorrow."

She got up and gave me a hug. "Time for bed," she said so pleased with herself. "You have school tomorrow, too."

* * *

Lunch the next day at Sabrina's Café on Callowhill with Jackson.

"How did it go being back?"

"Fine. Great actually. Remember Billiam? You met him once."

"Billiam?"

"It's his stage name. He sort of invited me to do some shows with him in the summer. He's the guy who does the circuit through clubs in central Pennsylvania."

"Actual paying shows. That would be great. What do you mean 'sort of'?"

"He wants to see me one more time. He'll be at the Grape Room next week. We'll finalize it there."

"Look at you. Already reaping the benefits of being on good behavior."

"I did not misbehave that night."

"See, you get triggered like everyone else," Jackson said. "So you're going to go to Pennsylvania. I wonder what it's like there."

"We're in Pennsylvania right now."

"No, we're in Philadelphia. Big difference." Then he added, "I'll bet your anti-LGBTQ jokes will be a big hit in Pennsylvania."

"Don't say that. You know I'm not anti-LGBTQ."

"I know that," he said. "But that's because I've known you since I was Jacqueline."

"And because you think for yourself and have a sense of humor."

He shrugged, conceding some doubt. "I'd like to think so."

"And my jokes did not make fun of your community that night."

"But they were not appropriate jokes to do at an open mic directly after an LGBTQ showcase."

"I thought I was doing material that the particular audience would especially appreciate," I said.

"Not coming from a middle-aged, white cis male."

"Why do you always have to remind me of that." Then, as if we hadn't had this conversation a bunch of times in the last six months, I said, "What is so offensive about saying, 'I'm all for people choosing their gender, but as an English professor, I got to tell you, I have some issues with *they* as a singular pronoun. I've been correcting *they is* my whole adult life. Now what do I do?'"

"You *know* that's not what upset everyone."

I kept going. "Using plurals to describe individual people also has a history of being an insult. Like referring to fat people as 'they'. 'Hey Russell, have a seat. Guys, move over so *they* can sit down.' Or for equating a woman with her breasts: 'Open the door. Stacy's here. Let *them* in. Wait until you see *them*. *They* are awesome.'"

"Keep going. Get it out of your system."

I did. "Schizophrenics are now saying, 'I've been asking to be a "they" for years, and now these singular nonbinaries come along and *they* get to be called "they". No wonder I'm so paranoid. It's not fair.'"

"That was funny. Lots of people laughed."

"And when people put their preferred pronouns in emails, why do they always put 'he/him', 'she/her', 'they/them'? Can't we deduce the preferred object from the preferred subject? Who would ever say, 'When I'm *doing* the action, refer to me as "she", but when I'm *receiving* the action, I want to be regarded as "them"?' And why are the pronouns that will help to liberate us from our implicit binary thinking presented as unnecessary binaries?"

Jackson said, "You know I don't like to speak on behalf of my community, but this one time, let me say, no one knows."

We both laughed.

"Okay, now I'm done."

"We all took that part in stride."

"Remember when we were kids? You'd call someone something crude, and they'd say, 'Sticks and stones can break my bones, but names could never hurt me.'"

"I hated those kids," Jackson said. "They were the only kids I wanted to throw rocks at. And you know how much I was teased growing up."

"I didn't like them either," I said. "But they had a point. Now words trigger everyone. We respond to words like we've been punched in the face."

Jackson said, "That's the trade-off educated, upscale, delicate people make for living in a culture where they don't actually punch each other in the face. They have to *feel* the brute force of the words."

"Good point."

"And you understand that, by 'delicate people', I was referring to your ilk: oversensitive, ultrawoke, white-cis virtue signalers. Not my crew—who can be punched in the face or burned alive without a moment's notice."

"I understood," I said. "I was just trying to say that I should not have so much power that I can traumatize people with a joke."

"Don't flatter yourself. You didn't traumatize anyone. And you *know* what got you banned from Fergie's for six months. 'You know how back in the day enlightened liberals taught us that one's sexuality is an orientation, not a choice, and that conservatives don't have to worry that gays would turn their straight kids gay by exposing them to homosexuality? Remember that?'"

Jackson was going to make me listen to the whole thing, doing an impression of me every bit as good as my daughter's.

"'Now the same liberals are telling everyone that sexuality is on a continuum and that we all have different degrees of fluidity. For some people this is a revelation, but you know who knew this all along? The conservatives. Yes, it's ridiculous that your totally or near totally straight son's gay friend is going to make him gay. But if your son has dormant gayness in him, has some murky alluring parts of his sexual continuum he's never explored before, what about then? Well, then that gay friend just might help him take a little personal journey he'd otherwise never make. Conservatives knew about fluidity all along. They were ahead of their time on this one. Their only problem was, and still is, they want to keep the flow of their impressionably fluid ones going in what they feel is the right direction—very, very straight and very, very narrow.'"

"I made it clear at the beginning that I believe everyone should be who they are meant to be, that people should explore and flow and not be afraid or ashamed of what gives them pleasure. I even talked about the importance of consent. I was very sex positive."

"It doesn't matter."

"But you see my point about conservatives and fluidity."

"*Everyone* sees that point. It's not *yours.* But saying something to that crowd that comes off as pro-conservative, after everything they've put us through and *are* putting us through . . . it's . . ."

"Offensive?"

"It's not generous."

"Comedy is about pointing out inherent contradictions."

"Exactly. And some contradictions hurt when they are flung in your face. Someday that bit will be funny to that audience. When it can't be weaponized against them. Us. Me. You weren't being generous, my friend. You were showing off how clever you are."

We took a moment to tend to our neglected coffees and plates.

"What is the point of going onstage just to entertain people?" I said finally.

Jackson was dumbfounded. "I think you answered your own question. Why can't people just laugh? Why do they have to laugh *and* think? You know that's painful."

"I can't help it. I'm a professor. A professional sadist."

"No, you're self-destructive. Self-sabotaging. You are the only person I know who is trying to get canceled before you've even been activated."

"Do you want to hear the latest bit I want to do?"

"I always do."

I cleared my throat. "Isn't it amazing after everything that's happened that there are still people who support Trump? Well, I think I have a way to help them. The solution comes from a movie from the nineteen seventies. Has anyone seen A Clockwork Orange?"

"Oh jeez."

"What you need to do is invite your favorite Trump supporter to your windowless basement. You are going to have to restrain him. But let's face it, from all the bondage porn none of us is watching, we're all experts at tying people up." I pause with question-mark eyes.

"Funny," he conceded.

"First, we deal with the gun obsession. There are two types of men when it comes to guns: those who see a gun and their balls curl up and look for a place to hide and those who get a little hard. Testicle retreat when you see a gun is normal. That fear is what makes a person cautious. So, while holding electrodes to the nuts of your favorite gun nut, show him videos of guns until he is conditioned to have a healthy fearful response. Well?"

"Not bad. Keep going."

"To make them understand climate change is real, show the supporter videos of all the things we are doing to destroy this beautiful planet, while burning his thigh with sunlight concentrated through a giant magnifying glass."

"How are you getting sunlight in a windowless basement?"

"Good point," I said. "'Never mind that this is all happening in a windowless basement, people.' You've given me an additional joke."

Jackson waved for me to continue.

"To help them get over their homophobia, have your supporter watch videos of gay men having sex. And that's all you have to do. Those supporters who are homophobic because they are secretly attracted to men will have to confront their true nature. You will be doing them a favor. And those supporters who are hateful because they aren't used to seeing men making love, well, like anything else, they will get over their squeamishness just by being exposed to it."

"So it goes on like this."

"Pretty much."

"How's it end?"

"Remember, Republicans think of torture as enhanced interrogation. So I guess you can call this enhanced education. And if you take away the restraints and things that cause pain, all you are left with is basic civics education, which—if these voters had gotten that in the first place, the country would not be in the mess it's in today."

"Bravo to that. You are an equal opportunity offender. I'll give you that."

"Not offender, provocateur maybe."

"But you're not going to do this on Tuesday."

"No way. Not for Billiam. I'll play it safe."

"Good, this would not play well in Pennsylvania."

* * *

Tuesday night when I entered the Grape Room in Manayunk, the mic was already underway. I had gotten an ideal time slot online earlier in the day. Billiam and I said hello and agreed we'd talk outside after our sets. Jackson arrived ten minutes later. We talked in the back.

"Energetic crowd tonight," he said.

"I go on in about forty minutes."

"What are you going to do?"

"'Playground Moms.'"

Jackson said, "That's the one that goes, 'All the moms I

meet in the playground are there because they either made all the right choices in life or all the wrong ones. Either way, they always like talking to me. The moms that made the wrong choices have no man in their lives, and the ones that made all the right ones are so fed up with their perfect husbands who don't listen to them anymore they are thrilled to have any man's attention.' Good choice."

"If I were famous, you and my daughter could impersonate me on talk shows."

"Oh my, look."

Four men I had never seen before at a comedy show, or anywhere, were taking their beers to an empty table close to the stage. Two of them were wearing MAGA hats.

"I've never seen anyone wearing those hats in the city," I said.

"I've never seen those hats in real life," Jackson said.

Others were giving them sideways looks as well.

"Do you think they're deliberately trying to be antagonistic?" Jackson asked.

"How could they not be being antagonistic . . . here . . . with those hats."

I kept watching how they responded to the different comedians. They were as into the various bits (or not) as everyone else. They were completely respectful to the two women who went up.

Thirty-five minutes later, Jackson said, "They just seem to be regular guys who made a bad fashion choice for the night. Like regular guys so often do, I might add."

"Yeah, but none of the material anyone is doing is really challenging them. It's been easy for them to laugh along. I'm surprised no one has taken them on from the stage." I looked at Jackson and said, "I mean, what's the point of just making people laugh."

It was right at that moment that the host called out my name. I hopped up on stage, shook his hand, and unhooked the mic from the stand. "Hey, everyone, it's great to be here."

Billiam moved closer to the stage and was watching me eagerly with such goodwill.

The four men, friends, with those hats and jovial smiles, just sitting there staring up at me, *doing* nothing offensive whatsoever—it was maddening. Were they profoundly ignorant or just profoundly clueless? Did it matter? Did they have a sense of humor? Did that even matter?

I looked at Jackson. He shrugged. Whether it was resignation or *go for it*, I couldn't tell. It didn't matter. My mind was made up. I cleared my throat. "Isn't it amazing after everything that's happened that there are still people who support Trump? Well, I think I have a way to help them. The solution comes from a movie from the seventies. How many of you have seen A *Clockwork Orange?*"

Neil R. Wells has a master's degree from NYU in creative writing and teaches writing and public speaking in Philadelphia. He performs stand-up at various locations in the city. His most recently completed project is a novel, still looking for a publisher, called Three Love, *a heartwarming hard-core romance told from the perspectives of three travelers who find love with one another. Follow him on Twitter @NeilRWells and on medium.com/@neilrwells.*

Penny Ante

Roland Williams

It was the 1976 inventory day at the Thimbles department store. The staff had to count the entire stock by hand. Mostly, they dreaded it. Sterling Hart was an exception. He anticipated the event with excitement. For him, it was key to a promotion.

The young black salesman arrived an hour early. He headed for breakfast in the cafeteria. Hart wanted all the strength he could muster. In his mind, it was his final audition for the Management Training Program. He intended to roll up his blue shirtsleeves and give it his best shot. Inside the canteen, he passed Faith Warden, who was the secretary of his boss Gavin Chance; striking in a pink jumper, she flashed him a warm smile.

Hart spotted a penny on the floor. It brought back memories of his father Pop saying, "A penny in the pocket beats two on a poker table," whenever they stumbled on a coin during one of their summer hikes through Fairmount Park. He picked up the copper coin. Then, Hart plucked the token in the air. It landed in his palm with the profile of Lincoln turned face up. He felt the image winked at him.

As he pocketed the change, he spied Foster Petty early for once, with a coffee mug on an otherwise empty green tray. Sporting a yellow leisure suit, the white worker smirked from the end of the checkout line. Their relationship had been strained ever since Chance had moved Hart from Bargains Menswear in the basement to Casuals off the concourse, where Petty held a sales position. It turned ugly when Hart told the associate he had forgotten to stamp the new markdown price on sweaters stacked in the storeroom. He imagined Petty would have welcomed the tip from his pal Max Morone in Appliances. Following the incident, Hart had overheard Petty, around Morone, express contempt for the store plan to hire more blacks in sales. Petty preferred the previous policy that had restricted nonwhites to jobs in food services, building maintenance, or shipping and handling. The white worker insisted black men lacked the necessities to manage financial transactions. All blacks could do, Petty alleged, was cost the business money.

The first black salesman in the Menswear Division, Hart strove to dispel stereotypes and encourage hiring blacks in sales. Hart tried to watch his steps. He worried that Petty saw him collect the change and might suspect he stayed broke because he had not saved a buck. Being between paychecks, Hart could see the white man thinking he was scrounging for dough. And so, Hart decided to skip the special on the menu and buy the Hungry Man platter to prove he had plenty of cash.

Waiting to pay, he surveyed the room. To his delight, Petty had disappeared. Hart spotted an empty table in the rear, where he hoped to eat alone in peace. Chance appeared, scratching his head and looking confused. The division manager shrugged, dumped the *City Examiner* on a chair, and headed for the exit. Interested in the newspaper, Hart aimed to read it, considering it another favor from the man who had advised him to apply for the Management Training Program.

Without warning, Petty's pal, Morone, draped in a gray flannel shirt, raised a ruckus. Boyd Holman, a black custodian in butternut trousers, was a quarter short for the daily special. Morone objected to an offer by Grace Temple, the black cashier in a cream smock, to let Holman pay later. "No preferential treatment," squawked Petty's pal. Hart stepped out of line and walked forward.

Born the middle of five boys, Hart had often settled

disputes between his brothers. He hated fights. Therefore, he settled the bill for the janitor. Afterward, Holman took his tray and went to the locker room. Morone slipped into a seat beside Kurt Carriage, a white guard in a black uniform.

Hart was enjoying an article in the *City Examiner* when a sudden announcement on the public address system silenced a surge of chatter in the cafeteria. He heeded the speaker: "Attention! An employee has lost a black leather wallet. Keep an eye out for it. Anyone who finds the item should bring it to the Personnel office. The owner offers a twenty-dollar reward for its return. Thank you."

An uproar ensued. Several remarks about the notice circulated the room. Groups wondered who had lost the wallet. Some wagered whether the loser would find it. Bunches prayed for the reward. Few sat indifferent. The majority dwelled on the matter until the chimes signaled the start of inventory. In response, people gathered themselves to punch their cards.

From the clock to his post, Hart dreamed of displaying his true colors and winning a chance to soar in the company. Pop struck him again. "It's not the deal," his father had preached in the park, "but the play that wins a hand." After Mom's death in a flood caused by a hurricane in Mississippi, Pop had carried the boys to Philadelphia on the flatbed of a Reading railroad truck with a hand from a Pullman porter with whom Pop had served in the Korean War. The Street Authority hired him to dump trash. Counting every penny, Pop worked hard to fill his sons with hope.

"You can trump any trick with your head," Pop taught his sons. He repeated it to Hart and his brothers during their annual jaunts to the park on Independence Day. The man loved to shed his blue overalls from his job and shower his sons with life lessons. Pop made the park outings favor shopping for a feast. In his footsteps, his boys bottled fresh water from a spring and bagged wild berries from a grove. They cooled off in the Winding Creek, before they fished for catfish in the Hidden River. After their day in the park, back at their row house on Race Street, Pop cooked their fish from the river on the stove along with some potatoes from the closet, and he baked a pie in the oven.

Pop ran their lives on a schedule. It was like boot camp. Every day, except Labor and Independence, started at six. Monday through Friday, the focus fell on work and school. Saturday went to errands and sports. On Sunday, they attended church services at White Rock.

The neighbors admired Pop. By precept and practice, he propelled his sons into sound pursuits. He intrigued them with words of wisdom and inspired them through devotion to duty. Hard work and honesty were holy to him. His maxims and manners moved Seth, the first born, and Samson, the second, to join the military. Samuel graduated from Conwell University, and Solomon, next to last in line, almost had his degree.

Hart stumbled out of high school after a steady boyhood. From twelve, he had delivered the *City Examiner*. Rain or shine, Hart rose daily at dawn to serve a route, which he built into the biggest around. His customers commended him. He possessed a sense of pride and purpose until he abandoned the newspaper business to attend Conwell. In college, he expected his life to become brighter, but the opposite occurred. Pop's back buckled from hauling trash and landed the man on disability. Money got tight, and Hart took a job at the Burger Bliss counter on Locust; it left him too little time to hit the books.

He dropped out of college. Anxious to aid his younger siblings, he bounced from one factory position to another for a while. Thank goodness, his brother Solomon heard about the Fair Placement Bureau. The agency got him placed at Thimbles. His eyes widened as soon as he stepped in the store. The sweep of the concourse running from the cosmetics counter to the fitting room looked wonderful. All of the staff seemed engaged in an exciting adventure. He longed for a stake in the action.

His inventory day assignment told him he stood on the road to success. Chance had picked him to count damaged goods. The Menswear Division manager chose the most trusted associates for the task. Chance had thought the world of Hart since the salesman had set the record for sales in Bargains during the Founder's Day Extravaganza. As long as he had Chance on his side, Hart felt sure of success.

He entered the storage area with a smile that faded once he saw Petty with Warden. The secretary, a blonde with dark roots, directed Chance's affairs. Advising Petty, she appeared weary. Warden shook her head at the man. She noticed Hart and crossed the room to greet him. Warden paused as Petty barked, "What's the quota for today?"

She returned, "What?"

"How much are we supposed to count?"

"The lot," she snapped.

Petty muttered a curse that Warden ignored and again turned her attention to Hart, who now sensed a long day ahead. Warden informed him that he was paired with Petty. Hart struggled to stay upbeat while she told him how to handle the damaged goods. After the instruction, she quizzed him. Once she was sure that Hart knew what to do, she left.

Hart bristled at an attempt by Petty to act like the boss. His reaction made Petty have a fit and stomp away. Hart was happy to see Petty go until he remembered Petty's relative. The white worker was a cousin to the executive director of Personnel, Noah Krone. Chance must have placed Petty in damaged goods at the request of the director. Hart guessed Krone wanted Petty trained for management.

Hart agonized over the possible consequences of the clash with his coworker. Krone headed the company committee slated to select the new candidates for the training program. The director could hold the dispute with Petty against Hart. It could kill his prospects. Hart thought he should find his coworker and apologize for offending him.

A half hour later, a voice behind him demanded, "Are you Sterling?" It was the security chief, Hardy Dolt. He wore a stern expression.

"Yes, I am."

"Come with me, please."

Hart followed the officer. They rode the elevator three floors to Personnel. The receptionist buzzed them in the suite. She picked up the phone to announce their arrival. Next, she ordered Hart to the inner office where Krone waited with Chance.

"We believe," Krone told Hart, "you found the lost wallet."

Hart blurted, "Me?"

"Yes," answered Krone, "you."

"No, not me."

"Witnesses saw you take it off the floor after Gavin dropped it in the cafeteria."

"That's right, Sterling," interjected Chance.

"Who saw me?"

"Foster Petty and Max Morone," asserted Krone.

"Return the wallet," said Chance, "and we'll forget the matter."

"They lied." Hart reached in his pocket for the penny that he had found. "Morone never saw me find anything." He exhibited the coin. "Look," he said, "this is what Petty saw me get off the floor. It's a penny!"

"I've never known Foster to lie," said Krone.

"I'm telling you the truth."

Krone continued, "Mr. Morone said you treated yourself and your buddy to a big breakfast."

"No. Boyd Holman needed a quarter. I let him have it."

Chance said, "Miss Temple saw you with my newspaper."

"You dumped it," said Hart. "It was trash."

Krone asked, "You picked up a paper and a penny that weren't yours, and you think we should trust you?"

"What do you mean? Who cares about a penny or an old paper? I never laid eyes on the wallet."

Krone had Dolt frisk Hart. Of course, the chief found nothing, but the result failed to appease the director. He speculated that Hart had stashed the wallet somewhere. Nevertheless, Krone deferred to Chance, who granted Hart the benefit of the doubt since Petty might have mistaken what he saw. Hence, the director let the salesman return to his post.

On the way back, Hart sensed word about the allegation against him had spread throughout the store. A cosmetics girl inside the elevator slinked to the rear and clutched her purse as he went to ride it. When he got off, he walked past workers who quit counting stock and clumped in corners where they whispered. He felt hit by slurs. His reputation seemed shot.

Resolved to avoid making matters worse, Hart bit his tongue when he faced Petty again in the storage area. He figured Petty had lied to shame him. Since Hart doubted challenging Petty would improve the odds for him in the long run, he resisted the urge to put his cards on the table. He thought it best for the time being to play them close to his chest.

Petty asked, "You still here, hotshot?"

Hart simmered.

"Weren't you canned?"

He balled his fists against his hips.

"Gave you a break, huh? I told everybody they would. Chance took your side, didn't he? The man's such a liberal. He worries the world to death about you people and your problems. He's the brainchild behind the new deal to have us bend over backward for you. And we're just supposed to take it."

An abrupt swing of events stifled an outcry from Hart. Warden appeared with good news. Holman had found the lost wallet in a bin outside the cafeteria when he went to dump the trash. Chance was going to pick up his property from Personnel. It looked like the janitor was going to reap the reward.

Hart heaved a sigh of relief. By chance, Holman had repaid his favor. Hart looked forward to repairing his reputation. He believed he was reborn to a bright future. His mind rested. Petty grew tolerable.

At lunchtime, though, the cafeteria crowd gave him the cold shoulder. He was hit hard by the thought: indictments capture the headlines; corrections come after the comics. The public address system had yet to announce the discovery of the lost wallet. As a result, Hart felt, he remained under suspicion in everyone's eyes. It was like the afternoon he had lost track of Pop in the park. He stayed uneasy.

Joining the checkout line with a baloney sandwich, he tried explaining everything to everyone whom he encountered. It was only a penny that he had picked up, he swore. With intense solicitude, Hart proclaimed himself innocent of wrongdoing. Besides, he offered, the wallet had been recovered. In turn, Hart received some broad smiles. His story however seemed not to change a single mind. Instead, behind his back, people continued to call him crooked.

Carriage elbowed him in the side and said, "Between you and me, bro, where'd you and your buddy stash the loot?"

Hart looked askance. "What buddy? What loot? Are you kidding? I only picked up a penny!"

With a wink, Carriage chuckled and strutted away.

Associates stepped ahead of Hart while the salesman stood in place and pleaded his case. In time, the line dwindled and disappeared. He ended up talking to himself. Consumed by hostility and humiliation, he drifted to the cashier. Hart prayed that Temple would take him at his word.

While in fact she sought to comfort him, before she made much progress, Warden arrived to deliver devastating news. Holman had turned in an empty wallet, she reported. An amount of two hundred dollars was missing. Rumor had it that Holman and Hart had split the money and hidden their shares. At the moment, the janitor was being interrogated by Krone. The Personnel receptionist had phoned the police. Dolt was going to search Holman's locker. Chance wanted to see Hart in his office.

The bell rang to signal the end of the lunch break. Hart knew he was innocent and doubted Holman was guilty. He maintained that it was unlike the janitor to cheat anyone. Holman had once chased a customer down a block of Bank Street to hand her a forgotten box of diamond earrings. Hart held him as honest as himself. Someone else must have taken the missing money.

He glanced at the spot where he had found the penny and wished that he had never picked the thing up. Casting his eyes toward the ceiling, he prayed to solve the problem that plagued him. Then, he spotted a security camera, prying above a side door to the cafeteria. Hope stirred in him. He swung his head from side to side. A video recorder hung over each of the four doors to the room. Had one of them caught the crook?

He shared the thought with Temple and Warden. They were intrigued. Yet Warden rued they would require permission from Krone in Personnel to review the video. She predicted a negative reply from the director. In light of the problem, Temple recommended the secretary solicit Chance to seek approval. It made sense to Warden.

The women put their heads together. They conceived a position for Warden to take. It involved reminding Chance of the fine job Hart had done in the past. The scheme worked. Chance agreed to discuss the matter with Krone. And he convinced the director to examine the surveillance video.

The cameras uncovered the truth. After Chance had eaten his meal, he had set aside the tray on which his wallet remained unattended. Petty had approached him and asked to use the tray since the manager was done with it. Engrossed by the *City Examiner*, Chance had allowed the thief to make off with his wallet. Based on the evidence, Dolt arrested Petty in the storage area. The chief found the missing cash, save one buck spent for a cup of coffee, stuffed in Petty's back pocket. Krone was beside himself.

Chance welcomed Hart to split the reward money with Holman and take the rest of the day off with pay. The manager promised Hart acceptance in the Management Training Program. He said, "We need more like you around here." Chance swore, as long as Hart continued to play his cards right, he would rise at Thimbles. "Sterling, you have it in you to make your people proud."

Roland Williams is a professor at Temple University, where he directs the undergraduate English program. He is the author of Black Male Frames, *in addition to poetry and fiction.* Smooth Operating and Other Social Acts *is his forthcoming book.*

Driving

Joshua Isard

Jack stopped halfway down his driveway and put the car back in park. He looked in the rearview mirror. His daughter was rolling her hands one over the other while shouting, "Wuh! Wuh!"

She wanted to hear "Wheels on the Bus".

Not quite at "wheel" yet.

He didn't have a long driveway, maybe four car lengths from the street to the garage, but it was long enough that he couldn't wait until he got to the street before putting on her music. Even that could cause a meltdown.

Not even close to worth the risk.

Once the car stopped he started the CD. His daughter giggled at hearing the song she liked and, Jack imagined, from having gotten him to do what she wanted.

He put the car back in reverse, pulled out, and got going to the playground. The good playground. There was one around the corner from their house, but the one in Malvern had her favorite slide, and since they had the whole day together it was worth a half hour in the car each way.

A woman sang "Wheels on the Bus", but Jack had no idea who she was. He knew she was British, because she let her accent slip, so he imagined her as older and beautiful and classy, like Elizabeth Taylor in her later years.

* * *

The CD Jack played for his daughter was the only one he still used.

He'd taken it out of the car disc changer once—knowing full well the danger of forgetting to return it before their next trip—and put it in his laptop to see if iTunes would recognize it and reveal the artist. No luck. He'd then downloaded a few apps that said they'd recognize any CD and provide track and musician info, but none got this one.

His friends' CDs, the ones they'd recorded in some guy's South Philly basement—they showed up on iTunes.

As he drove, he listened, both to the music and his toddler signing along. She kept asking him to look at her hand motions, and he kept telling her that he had to pay attention to the road, nicely as he could, because he did want to see them and also did not want her to break down in a fit. He thought maybe people should have to get retested for their driver's license after becoming a parent, driving the course with the DMV's examiner in the passenger seat and a whiny kid in the back seat, all while playing children's music.

* * *

His daughter had loved that CD since she was born. His mother gave it to them, a gift from one of her coworkers, copied from the original that this person's niece or nephew or grandchild or something also loved.

After "Wheels on the Bus" came "Ugly Duckling", sung by a man whose voice reminded Jack of a lecherous creep in one of those Very Special Episodes of '80s sitcoms.

He wished he could find the actual artists of these songs, just so he could stop thinking about what the singers might look like.

Music had always evoked visuals for Jack. Perhaps because he grew up in the golden age of music videos, perhaps because he spent his summers going to concerts. When "Stupid Girl" came on, he saw Shirley Manson in sepia tones, wearing eye shadow and a dress that'd fit in swinging London. When "Basket Case" played, he saw Billie Joe Armstrong on stage at the Camden Entertainment Center, giving some fan his guitar to play for a minute of the song, both small figures since back then Jack couldn't afford anything except lawn seats.

They hit construction in the left lane and Jack slowed the car as traffic bottlenecked. "Puff the Magic Dragon" came on, a duet between older Liz Taylor and creepy sitcom guy, so at least Jack could picture Peter, Paul, and Mary. He'd played the original song for his daughter, who shook her head no at the start of it and cried by the end of it. She wanted her version. A toddler does not know what is good, only what is familiar. This is what Jack told himself as he envisioned the famous folk trio on the sidelines, shaking their heads, listening to this terrible version of their classic.

* * *

When he'd been in the car alone before his daughter was born, he thought his mind wandered in a better way. He'd seen most famous bands at some festival at some point or knew their video or the cover art behind a scratched jewel case in his CD collection. Half the songs had been on some sex mix throughout his life, including the one he had made with his wife, the one they were probably listening to when they conceived their daughter.

But now: just the possibly beautiful woman singing with her possibly sinister partner. To children.

* * *

The construction added about ten minutes to the ride, but no big deal. They had nowhere else to be. When the left lane opened up, he went back to it and took the car toward seventy. "Hush Little Baby" came on. He thought that it was quite a leap from a mockingbird right to a diamond ring. Where do you go after that?

He got off at the Malvern exit and "Row Your Boat" came on. When his daughter sang along, she always said, "Whoa whoa whoa." Not quite at *r*'s yet.

But this time she didn't sing along. She always sang along.

He looked in the rearview mirror. She was asleep. It was a quarter to eleven, she couldn't be asleep. She napped at one. And he had not reached eighty-eight miles per hour.

Jack turned off the music and heard the light whistle as his daughter exhaled through her nose.

He knew his options: wake her up in a few minutes when they pull into the playground's parking lot, risking her then being unable to nap again for the rest of the day, resulting in fits of screaming over nothing all afternoon and evening until she falls asleep early and, as a consequence, wakes up early tomorrow, before his alarm. Or let her sleep while he plays with his phone.

No-brainer.

He pulled into the parking lot, one of five or six cars there, and slowly put the car in park. He'd woken her up a few times by sliding the gear shift too quickly, so now he put his foot on the brake and notched it up gear by gear: N, R, P. Then he reached to the side of his seat and reclined it one inch at a time.

He turned down the music and turned up the car's fan, which sounded enough like the white noise machine in her room to keep her asleep.

* * *

He picked up his phone. He did not have headphones with him and so could not listen to music in order to wash away those children's songs, so he first opened Twitter, then Facebook, then Instagram. Then the sports news. Then the national news. Then the local news, which was when he knew he was desperate to find anything at all interesting.

His phone had become mostly a tool for two things: storing pictures of his daughter and downloading apps to help kill time while she napped and he couldn't move. This wasn't the first time he'd been confined somewhere during a nap. He'd also been pinned underneath her on the couch and stuck with her in the stroller in a quiet part of the mall.

He never remembered to bring a book and reminded himself again to just keep one in the back of the car. He used to read books. Long ones. Novels like *The Secret History*, *American Pastoral*, and *Infinite Jest*. Walter Isaacson's biographies. During parenthood, when he saw a book longer than three hundred pages, he made a mental note to read it when the kid got older. Then forgot the name of the book.

He used to have lists in notebooks or, more recently, on his phone. He'd liked striking through names of books he'd wanted to read and gotten to. He had a similar list for movies. Albums. Restaurants he wanted to check out. Bourbons he wanted to try.

Jack never used to forget things. Let them slide. Pass by him. Used to.

He sat up a little and turned to look at his daughter. Her chin was on her chest, puffing up her already chubby cheeks a little more. Her lips were pushed out. She sighed. She often sighed in her sleep.

He opened the driver's side door and got out, then closed it behind him so it wouldn't click shut. He pulled the handle of the rear door and got it open without the kid even stirring. Jack moved some dolls from the floor and got in next to the car seat. He shut the door, again not enough that it clicked.

He leaned back as far as he could in that seat, closed his eyes, and listened for his daughter's breathing. This was instinct. If she wasn't standing up and running around, he checked that she was breathing. It had happened from the beginning. He'd wake up in a panic when she was an infant, roll off the side of the bed, and go to the Pack 'n Play. When he heard three breaths, he'd go back to sleep.

His wife said she did the same thing, though they never saw the other do so.

The seat he was in wouldn't be vacant for long. There would be another one. His wife wanted to name her Penelope, but that seemed too big a name to say all the time. Penny might be all right, though. He liked Mary. Two syllables. Worked well. Yelled well, with a snap to it.

He felt like he was about to start all over, that they'd blown up their whole life before, let it settle, and were about to do it once more. How very rock and roll of them, tearing everything down and trusting it'd all be okay, or not even thinking at all about whether it'd be okay.

His daughter sighed again. Jack leaned over and kissed her forehead, then fell back in the seat. She stirred, shifted—then settled into sleep again.

Jack fell asleep too. When he woke up, he didn't know how long he'd been out.

Joshua Isard was born and raised in Fort Washington, Pennsylvania; graduated from Temple University; and has taught at Temple, CCP, Drexel, and Arcadia University. He currently directs the MFA program in creative writing at Arcadia.

Cadillac

Chuck Corson

Brick stepped through the broken glass facade of a Wawa convenience store, shotgun in hand, looking for food. Beau Castles got the nickname Brick after starting off his amateur boxing career 9-0 with nine knockouts, a career that was abruptly ended by the war. When the attacks began, Brick's Philadelphia home was destroyed with the rest of the city. The militia was starving. Brick took this food-gathering mission on himself, not wanting to put any of the others at risk as he was the only one with enough strength left to fight.

Everything that could spoil had done so long ago; only canned goods and foods packaged and full of preservatives remained. Bottled water was a necessity; all fresh water was contaminated with anthrax or pathogens from the bodies.

The store was burned out and picked over. Carefully stepping around the shards of glass and overturned shelves, Brick scanned the ground like a hawk. A three-sided counter still stood in the middle of the store, a good foxhole should one be needed. Brick went behind it, where cashiers once stood, ringing up hoagies, iced tea, and Tastykakes.

The racks above the counter were empty, as were the first two cabinets beneath the counter. In the third and final cabinet, Brick saw something that brought him more joy than he had felt since the first Human Liberation Guerillas' bomb went off four years ago. One lonely carton of Newport cigarettes, still wrapped in cellophane, sat waiting to be found. The trademark seafoam green packaging reminded Brick of the satisfaction of having a smoke. Creature comforts were an exceedingly rare commodity, and the one that Brick cherished more than any other was before him, like a Christmas gift sitting under a tree with his name on the tag.

Brick snatched the carton and squatted down, hiding himself from any passersby. The Hu-Li-Gu's, as the militia took to calling them, patrolled this desolate area, and they were not in the habit of taking prisoners. Brick closed his eyes, held the carton up to his lips, and kissed it. He wanted to whisper sweet nothings into its ear, take it out for dinner, romance it, then bring it home and make love to it.

Snapping out of his fantasy, Brick looked about cautiously. He rose and inspected the countertop, the place where lighters were kept available for sale to unprepared smokers. Nothing. Anything that could start a fire was treasured, so Brick wasn't surprised. He would have to wait until he got to camp before he could consume the delicious menthol-flavored ecstasy.

When he'd started boxing, his trainer admonished him daily for his filthy habit. He would even go as far as taking Brick's clothes from his locker and throwing them out into the street, telling him that the smell of smoke was not welcome in the Joe Frazier Boxing Gym. Still, Brick could not give them up. He limited his cigarette intake as much as possible during the weeks leading up to a fight, but he could not leave them alone for good.

Two years had passed since Brick had his last smoke. The Hu-Li-Gu's destroyed tobacco products when they found them; their utopian vision didn't include addictive substances. A bunch of fucking wet blankets as far as Brick was concerned.

Seeing no one on the street, Brick made his way out of the store, leading with the barrel of his twelve-gauge. He crept along, staying close to the storefronts that lined East Erie Avenue. The bounty recovered from the Wawa was tucked in the waist of his pants, against the small of his back. Traveling during the day was dangerous, but it was impossible at night.

Having lived his life in the city, Brick had never seen absolute darkness until there was no electricity. Carrying a torch outside the camp was a death sentence.

Crunch. Brick stiffened. His head went up like a sleeping dog hearing a car door slam. *Crunch.* Someone was near, walking slowly, deliberately. This was bad. Any noise—a scream, a whistle, the explosion of a shotgun shell—and the Hu-Li-Gu's would be on him. Not being able to smoke at least one of the Cadillacs stuffed into his jeans would be a fate worse than death; he had to get moving fast.

Cadillacs was what Reece, his training buddy from the gym, called Newports. In prison, Reece told him, they called Newports Cadillacs because they were the best of the best and commanded the highest price. Reece was a smoker too; that was how he and Brick initially bonded. Walking home from the gym, Reece would always say, "Ayo, Brick, lemme get a 'Lac yo." Brick always told him to buy his own, then would hand him one. It was as routine as their training regimen.

Moving swiftly, Brick minded his surroundings, praying he didn't see someone. *For the love of Christ,* he thought. *Please just let me get back to camp. Allow me this so I can smoke these damn cigarettes, and I swear, if you want me dead tomorrow, you can take me. Just please let me have this one thing. I've earned it after all the miserable shit I've dealt with over the last four years. Don't you take this away from me, you motherfucker. Don't you dare.*

"Stop right there," the voice said evenly. "Drop the shotgun, put your hands over your head, and turn around slow, or I am gonna air you the fuck out."

Brick rolled his eyes. *Well played.*

"You got one second," the voice said.

Brick dropped the gun, raised his arms, and turned. He wasn't a Hu-Li-Gu. That was good, but he was holding a rifle.

"What you have?" the man asked.

"Nothing worth taking. Just the clothes I'm wearing and the gun I just put down."

"You sure about that? You didn't find nothin' in that Wawa? I saw you lurkin' around in there. What you got?"

"Does it look like I got anything? You think I was in there shoving cans of corn up my ass? I don't have shit."

"Bullshit. Take your shirt off."

"This ain't Chippendales, pal."

"Keep talking," the stranger said. "See what I do."

"What, you gonna shoot me? Go ahead, stupid. The terrorists will be on your ass before you cross the street."

Brick took a step toward the stranger, keeping eye contact, still holding his hands up over his head.

"Stop walking. Stop right now or I will shoot you. They wanna come, they can come. I might make it. Guarantee you won't."

Brick stood, no more than twenty feet away from this guy. He had the typical survivor look. Dirty mismatched clothes, overgrown beard, messy rat's nest of hair.

"Listen to me." Brick took another step forward. "I got no beef with you, and I got nothing for you to steal. You want my shotgun? Fine, be a thief and take it. I'm not going to chase you. You got the drop on me, so I guess that's your prerogative if you want it, but I ain't stripping for you, because I ain't hiding anything. And if you don't hurry this up, someone is going to see us out here and interrupt this little Mexican standoff with an RPG. So what do you want to do?"

The man appeared stunned. He stared, unresponsive.

"Didn't think this through, did you, bud?" Brick took another step forward. "Let me help you out. I'm not your enemy. You need a place to stay? I can take you somewhere." Another step. "I don't got much for you there. A little water. I can get you cleaned up. But, buddy, you gotta stop pointing that gun at me." Brick took another step forward.

"You just stop right there." He sounded unsure of himself. "You don't take another goddamn step, or I will shoot you. Now back up and take your fucking shirt off and show me that you ain't got nothin', or else I'm gonna—"

"Shoot me?" Brick stepped forward and hit the stranger on the jaw with lightning speed. The stranger's ass went back, and his top half crumpled forward, toward Brick, going down on top of his gun, which he pointed up and tried to hold onto while putting his hands straight out toward the ground to brace his fall. His right index finger stuck in the trigger guard, the butt of the rifle hit the ground, and the rifle went off with the barrel pointed under his chin, blowing his face off.

"Holy fuck!" Brick screamed, his heart literally feeling like it had skipped a beat. He turned without hesitation and ran, scooped up his shotgun, and took off down East Erie at a full sprint.

Motorcycles came speeding down the avenue toward the sound of the gunshot. Brick looked over his shoulder and could see them in the distance. He cut through the parking lot of the old Erie Lanes bowling alley. The wall had been blown out where the front entrance used to be. He dipped inside. Bowling balls were scattered around the floor, shook loose from their racks. Outside the reach of the sunlight coming through the missing entrance, it was pitch black.

Bikes pulled up, stopping in the street. Brick listened carefully as the Hu-Li-Gu's surveyed the strip mall parking lot where the faceless stranger lay dead. *Hopefully they didn't see me. People off themselves all the time. Maybe they will think he got tired of not finding food in bombed-out Wawas and decided to snack on a bullet.*

"Where is the other one?" one of them asked.

"How do you know there is another one?"

"Because you don't scream after you've been shot in the head. Someone else screamed, and I want him found now."

Well shit, Brick thought. *There goes that.*

Brick went down to his hands and knees and crawled through the bowling alley. He couldn't see his hand in front of his face, and rolling his ankle on a bowling ball guaranteed that he would be found. He could hear them getting closer to the entrance. Just as he felt the end of the rental counter to his left, he saw beams from flashlights enter the building.

He got behind the counter and took the Newports out of his pants, so he could sit with his back to the wall. He focused on keeping his breath to a minimum. Two Hu-Li-Gu's stepped inside, searching with flashlights that they had attached to their assault rifles.

"Hurry up," a voice yelled from outside.

Economy of energy, his boxing trainer Bernard had always said. Economy of energy, meaning save it when you don't need it, use it when you do. You don't need energy before a fight—panicking wastes it, nerves waste it. So don't worry, don't panic, don't even think if you don't have to. The fight was near, and it wouldn't end in a knockout.

Brick closed his eyes. He placed the carton of cigarettes on his lap, and as gently as possible, he peeled away the wrapper. He fingered open the cardboard box and slid out a pack. He traced the outline of the pack with his thumbs and pulled the cellophane from the top. He opened the pack and pulled away the foil, then brushed his thumb across the top of the filters. He pinched one, pulled it out, and placed it in his lips. Brick opened his eyes seeing the flashlights moving methodically in his direction.

The memory of his first cigarette, given to him by a sixteen-year-old girl in Love Park when he was thirteen, came to mind. Brick reached up, feeling around on a shelf under the counter. Between a metal canister and a rosin bag was an open box full of paper matchbooks. He took one and held it for a beat as the flashlight beams went across the countertop. He folded back the front flap and tore off a match. *Smoke 'em if ya got 'em*, he thought, striking the match, a wisp of sulfur stinging his nostrils. He put the flame to the cigarette hanging from his lips. The pop from lighting the match and the faint orange glow it gave off got the attention of the Hu-Li-Gu's. Brick racked his shotgun as he stood, inhaling smoke deep into his lungs.

Gunfire exploded everywhere.

The cherry of the cigarette extinguished as it touched the blood pooling up on Brick's chest. They continued shooting into Brick's body as he lay on a pile of old bowling shoes.

Chuck Corson is a state employee and author. He was born and raised in Lower Bucks County, graduated from Temple University, and lived in and began his career in Philadelphia. He still returns to the city often. Follow Chuck on Instagram @chuck.corson.

Hope Is Dawning for Peace in the Congo

Anndee Hochman

First Period: Math

We are stuck on fractions. Abe hunches at the dining room table, gripping his pencil, third-grade math book splayed in front of him. It's a Wednesday night, and his dilemma is existential: Which is greater, one-third or one-fourth?

"Look, Abe." And I start to draw a pie on the margin of today's newspaper.

"Yeah, yeah, I know," he says, before I've even finished my lopsided circle. He hops up, I hear the refrigerator door open, and Abe returns to the table with a pie—or, rather, a pie plate that appears to be filled with molten lava. He has a butter knife—he's eight, and I still don't let him touch the sharp ones—and he drags it through the blackened surface, carving the pie into four misshapen wedges.

"See, Dad, if you cut it into three pieces, that would be enough for you and me and Molly. But if you cut it in four, we could invite another person." And he looks hopefully at the remains of our dinner, a trio of smeared forks and crumpled napkins, the vacant spot at the table. "Four is more than three, right?"

I hear Molly's boots on the stairs, then a shriek from the kitchen. "Where's my pie?" She stomps to the table. Her brother is still holding the butter knife, guilty with blackened goo. "I can't believe you cut my pie. I made it for school. For Heritage Day."

Heritage Day? Molly is Connecticut Jewish on my side, western Pennsylvania Methodist on her mother's. Perhaps her pie is meant to be an ironic comment on our divorce, the burnt and craggy terrain of this last awful year. Or maybe it's something more innocent: a stained recipe card in my mother's impossible handwriting, with directions like, "two handfuls flour, or less, or more, pinch of salt, bake in hot oven till done." I'm hoping for the latter.

"What happened, honey, did it burn?"

"No, it's shoofly pie. It's supposed to be like that. It's southern."

The closest either of our families ever got to the South was a misguided trip to Disney World when the kids were six and two. A giant Goofy character stalked us through the park, and Molly threw up in Fantasyland. We should have seen it as an omen; instead, we blamed it on concession-stand pizza and the Mad Hatter's teacup ride.

"But we're not southern," I say. More and more, conversations with my children feel like a foreign film I entered late. I am always asking for translations.

"I know. But the Jewish kids will bring bagels—they always do—and all the recipes from Mom's side had mayonnaise or Jell-O."

"Well, let's try it," Abe says. He wields the butter knife, hacks off three shards of pie from one of the four demonstration pieces. He chews thoughtfully. I reach for my water glass, though I'm not sure the pie is water-soluble.

"This sucks," Molly pronounces. She grabs the plate and heads for the kitchen trash, stomps back through the dining room. "Who cares about heritage anyway? If you go back far enough, all our ancestors were paramecium. I have to study. There's a physics test tomorrow."

I still don't know what to tell Abe about fractions. He's a

smart kid—smart enough to know that if you take a family of four, subtract one mother, add a new apartment on the shabby side of town, divide the furniture, and double the toys, you still end up with less than you had at the start.

"Dad?" Abe says. "I think I've got it. If the thing you're dividing is a good thing, then one-third is more than one-fourth, because you'd want a bigger piece. But if it's bad, like Molly's pie, then less is more because each person only has to suffer a little."

"Abe, it's past your bedtime. We'll do more fractions in the morning." He gives me a half-hug and shuffles upstairs. I rake crumbs off the table into my hand. If it were possible, to spare my kids suffering, I would fish the seared pie from the garbage and fork down the whole thing, one bitter mouthful at a time.

Second Period: Language Arts

People tell you that divorce is a death and a rebirth. They tell you it's the end of the road and the beginning of the rest of your life. They tell you a lot of stuff that seems plagiarized from those inspirational posters shown in the in-flight catalogs on airplanes. Once in a while you get a nugget of good sense, from an old friend or a song on the radio, enough to nudge you into the next day.

But nobody tells you about pronouns. How you find yourself using them in places you never needed them before. You'd thought that everything—the marriage, the family, the milk in the refrigerator, the college fund, the hamsters—were there for everyone's delight and use, a little experiment in socialism. And then, one cold day, you hear yourself say to your kid, "Your mother will pick you up at six," where before you would have just said, "Mom," and he looks at you funny because he knows how much meaning that one pronoun packs—the inerasable blood tie and the undone marriage, the dumb fact that she will always be his mother but is no longer anything but your ex.

As it turned out, there were possessive pronouns inscribed everywhere—invisible in the sunny light of the good years but screaming out like ultraviolet when the mood turned black. *My* porcelain butter dish. *Your* Aretha albums. My Eames chair. Your framed Robert Frank photograph. My hamsters, because I was the one who gave in when Molly begged. Your fucking piano that I nearly slipped a disc hauling up the porch steps. My couch, because the check was made out to me even though it came in a Happy 10th Anniversary card, and notwithstanding the times we made love on it, breathing into the cushions so we wouldn't wake the kids.

The kids. My kids on Tuesdays, Wednesdays, Thursdays, the last weekend of every month, Jewish holidays, and the first two weeks of July. Yours on Fridays through Mondays except for the last weekend, even-numbered birthdays, Christmas, Easter, and the last two weeks of June. Mi casa no es su casa. Nunca, nunca, nunca. Never again.

The other night, Molly was doing Spanish homework at the table. "Listen to this," she said. "In English we'd say, 'I dropped the cup and broke it,' but in Spanish, you say, 'La taza se me cayó y se me rompió'—'the cup dropped and broke itself with respect to me.' Like the person had nothing to do with it."

I think of the agentless, blame-shifting language of politics—weapons were fired, homes were bulldozed, civilian casualties were incurred—and start to give Molly one of the little diatribes she calls "Dad's Unified Theory of Everything", about how language and power, authority and passivity, are all bound up in one nasty Gordian knot, and then I remember the helpless look on my father-in-law's face at his wife's funeral.

"Carl," he said, pulling on the sleeve of my suit coat like an anxious toddler. "I can't believe she up and died on me." I look at Molly's Spanish translations, her printing neat and spiky like her mother's. "The cup dropped itself, se me cayó." I didn't cause this catastrophe—at least, I didn't intend to cause it—but it will gnaw at me for the rest of my life.

People ask why Beth and I divorced. Nothing I can say—

faith lost or gained, the slow, then quick, collapse of trust, one too many disfigured spoons in the garbage disposal—even comes close to conjuring the swirl of bewilderment and responsibility I feel, even now, almost a year later. I remember my father-in-law shrugging toward the sky, palms open to all that is unknowable and sad.

El matrimonio se me rompió. The marriage broke itself with respect to me.

Third Period: Home Economics

When Abe was four, he said to me one morning, as I was stirring yellow—only yellow, never orange—cheese into his scrambled eggs, "Dad, can women cook?" It was one of those aha moments, the "clicks" feminists spoke of in the 1970s, when the true nature of our domestic arrangement suddenly snapped to consciousness. *Our* arrangement. I was still using the plural possessive back then.

"Of course women can cook," I said, pulling his toast from the toaster just as it reached the shade of light sand; one moment more and Abe would reject it as "too crunchy".

"Mom doesn't," he said.

"Mom does other things."

"Like what?"

"Well, you know about computers, right?" Abe rolled his eyes, impatient. "She works with computers. She, um, teaches them to think. She travels a lot. She has meetings and talks on the phone to very smart people in Japan and Israel." I wasn't just dumbing it down for Abe's benefit; that was truly the extent of what I knew about Beth's work.

She'd started at Microsoft back when no one had heard of the company. We moved to Seattle with our possessions in four boxes in the back of a 1988 Volvo. We wore GORE-TEX and Birkenstocks, went hiking in the rain and learned to order coffee drinks with adjectives formerly reserved for personal ads: tall, skinny, extra-hot.

When we had Molly, and then Abe, it made sense for me to work from home, get my MFA at night, start a graphic design business from the den. Beth worked twelve-hour days. I made the pediatrician appointments, drove on the preschool field trip to Pike Place Market, called the plumber when Molly flushed a sneaker down the toilet. At Beth's work parties, I hovered around the hummus and Perrier. Listening to the conversation was like turning on the radio in a foreign country—an excited, inscrutable babble occasionally punctuated by familiar phrases, "hard drive", maybe, or "market share".

And then there was the weekend—the kids were nine and five—when Beth found God at a work retreat in the Canadian Gulf Islands. I stayed home and sewed a three-piece suit for Abe's Barbie doll. It had been raining every day for two and a half months. "Don't you think she'll be cold in this?" Abe said, holding up the nylon scrap of lingerie that came with the Barbie. I had to agree that she would.

Beth came home late that Sunday night and told me she'd been born again. "Wasn't once enough?" I said, remembering the pulsing umbilicals and midnight screaming that accompanied Molly's and Abe's deliveries. Beth was serious, though. Farewell to the Church of Microsoft; hello to the New Covenant Community of Greater Washington. It took me another two years to understand that she really had been born again, that the Beth I'd loved and married wasn't just lurking under this latest ideological passion, ready to emerge next as a Wiccan priestess or a devotee of African dance. She was gone, it was over, the perfect incontrovertible past tense.

So here I am, at my Salvation Army dining table set for three, every Tuesday, Wednesday, and Thursday night, doing homework, trying to be of use. Already the kids are far ahead of me: Molly painstakingly balancing ions, acing physics, parsing the known world into elements, equations. And Abe, who could be a great philosopher if he ever passes third-grade math. There ought to be a law: No Parent Left Behind.

But it is the law of the universe, ever since the paramecium, that they will leave us, taking our blind spots and missteps and transmuting them, we hope, into something like a happy life. I hope they'll find a path between their mother's absolutes and their father's ambiguities. I hope they'll look back from whatever heights they reach and wave to their old dad.

Fourth Period: Mythology

Molly's class is studying myths from around the world. They've read about Sisyphus, doomed to roll that damned rock uphill until the end of time. They've discussed the first chapter of Genesis—this being a progressive school—and the ideal of the utopian past. "Mrs. Fenimore wanted us to list contemporary myths," Molly tells me. "Want to hear?"

And she reads: "The West was won. Good things come to those who wait. You deserve a break today. Sticks and stones may break my bones, but words will never hurt me. America is the land of freedom and opportunity. Peace is on the march. The truth will set you free. Just do it. It'll only hurt for a minute. Every vote counts. Your mother and I love each other very much. Love means never having to say you're sorry. And they lived happily ever after."

I feel as though a piece of Molly's pie were lodged in my throat. "I'm not sure those are the kind of myths Mrs. Fenimore had in mind."

"Really?" she says. "I turned it in last Tuesday. I got an A." She leaves her paper on the table and goes upstairs. In the end, there are really only two kinds of myths—the ones that say things used to be better than they are and the ones that assure, despite all evidence to the contrary, that the world can be made better than it is. Take your pick: nostalgia or idealism. Subscribe to the first, and you're stuck, wheels spinning backward toward some blinkered utopia. Believe in the second—well, it wouldn't fit Beth's requirements, but it's the closest thing to religion that I've ever found.

Fifth Period: Current Events

If the census taker arrived at my house on a typical Wednesday evening, here is what she would find: one self-described adolescent science geek wearing black lipstick, a midriff-baring T-shirt, and a small piece of navel jewelry; one eight-year-old boy who sleeps with a cross-dressing Barbie; one father still trying to make the scrambled eggs come out right. The dinner dishes are strewn across the table, and we're engaged in one of our favorite evening activities: reading parts of the newspaper out loud.

Certain sections are off-limits: we chuck the TV page and gossip columns. I had to say no to the obituaries, too, after I found Abe one night in bed, nearly in tears after reading the death notice of a Mary Rose Coyle, predeceased by her husband and survived by one daughter, three granddaughters, and two great-grandchildren. Molly says the only true parts of the paper are the comics and the weather report. I say I'm not so sure about the latter.

In the game, we each grab a page or a section and read bits aloud. The fun is in the juxtaposition, trying to follow one excerpt with another that connects in some surprising or funny or sad way. Not like a unified theory of everything—more a sense that these stories of blindness and greed, generosity and survival, are jostling around, bumping shoulders, rubbing off on one another whether we acknowledge it or not.

"The worst pollutant in the region yesterday was particulates, produced mainly by motor vehicles and power plants," Molly reads from the weather page. "Already behind, EI work may stop," Abe responds. "A desire to help others: the question is how?" I read from page A3. "Seventy-eight detainees die in Thai police trucks," counters Molly. As if that weren't enough, she continues, "Cheney hits back on lost weapons . . . Allawi blames coalition for massacre . . . Illness stirs talk of jurist's successor." She is on a roll. I up the ante with an item from the News in Brief column: "Rescuers have pulled more bodies from a coal mine in central China, raising the confirmed death toll to 122 in a gas explosion, with twenty-six miners still—"

"Wait, Dad, Molly, listen to this," Abe says. He is clutching page A17. His eyes shine like alleys after a hard rain. "Hope is dawning for peace in the Congo."

"Really?" I say.

"Really?" says Molly.

And we lean toward Abe, our heads nearly colliding over the paper, because that's how much we want to believe.

Anndee Hochman is a journalist, essayist, storyteller, and teaching artist in Philadelphia. Her column, The Parent Trip, appears weekly in the Philadelphia Inquirer, *and her work has also been published in* Poets & Writers, Moravian College Magazine, Broad Street Review, *and* Purple Clover. *Anndee teaches memoir and poetry to writers of all ages; she is currently at work on a young adult novel titled* My Plural Is People.

RELATIONSHIPS

Millie Floating

David Biddle

I was convinced by lunchtime on a very snowy November day that my wife, Deena, had murdered our dog. Millie had been urinating every few nights in the same approximate part of the dining room carpet for months. She was getting old. Her bladder muscles may have been weakened by a near-death experience a year earlier rooting through garbage sweetened with propylene glycol. Deena didn't exactly despise Millie; she had just gotten to the point, I think, where she didn't see that the benefits Millie brought to us outweighed the costs. Deena manages a data team with the Wharton Economic Systems Group.

For my part, I put up with Millie because I loved her desperate stupidity. She was a Weimaraner. The kids had wanted a Weimaraner because of those ridiculous *New Yorker* photos. Mary in particular, who was eight at the time, wanted a dog she could dress up in a business suit or tennis outfit. Adelaide, just four, went along with her sister but had, I'm afraid, the idea that the dog would be the size they were in the magazine. Twelve-year-old Mike, on the other hand, was simply happy to have unanimous support in his quest (a battle, really, from the age of six) to have a dog. By that time, he probably would have been just as satisfied with a Dachshund or a Chihuahua as a Weimaraner. So Millie came into our lives at those ages: four, eight, and twelve. Those are the right ages for a dog, and my children did a good job loving her. Millie left thirteen years later when only Addie resided in our nest.

As luck would have it, though, that snowy Tuesday morning before Thanksgiving, the whole family was home here in Philadelphia. At the same time, the room we were going to eat our turkey dinner in was scented with a bitter, rusty urine tang, and the thick ivory carpet was discolored and stained as if a large rodent had once been slaughtered there—a groundhog or raccoon maybe.

Thirteen is over ninety in dog years. Millie slept long, deep sleeps. My wife is strong and athletic. It wouldn't take much: one of our thick, white bath towels; sneak behind, wrap the towel around the sleeping face; grasp the head and neck firmly; straddle the dog; hold on for maybe two minutes. The struggle is more a dance with death than a fight to survive. Loyal dogs are like that. They do their family's bidding because they can't exist otherwise. Millie often slept during the early portion of the night in the back hall off the kitchen, guarding the rear entrance to our house.

I woke several times to hear the wind moaning against the northern face of the house. From the bedroom window, our backyard was sculpted smooth, glistening with shiny night-lit snow. It had to be close to well over a foot thick and still falling the first time I woke up. Deena had been in bed two of the times I came up from sleep. I remember, however, around four fifteen, waking suddenly and knowing immediately that her spot in the bed was empty. By the early morning hours, Millie had often moved into our room, sleeping on the floor under the window near the heating register. But one of her habits of enthusiasm was to follow anyone who was up with insomnia around the house. She was gone then, with Deena, wherever Deena was—or so I assumed.

Every few years, heavy November snowfalls in Philadelphia give a silent sort of promise to all of us, particularly in our Mt. Airy neighborhood, so close to the wilds of the suburbs north and west and what I think of as the canyons of the Wissahickon Creek. We wake on another planet, it seems. This other planet is perfect because it is so surreal. It has been rendered by artists. We have been here before, of course, on and off all of our lives.

I recalled other winters of the past in this old house made of creek schist and the surprising gift at being snowed in with my family, playing on the streets and hills around our house with all the kids and parents in our little spur of Mt. Airy just above the ruins of the old Buttercup mill and cottage. Millie would gamble and weave around us as we shoveled out our driveway. She had such impressive enthusiasm running through deep snow, such endless, daylong energy. It was equally as impressive the way she slept from dinner on into the night, exhausted and spent, her legs hilariously churning as she dreamt, we imagined, of still playing in the cold white drifts, floating through the neighborhood, possessed by nothing other than her simple-minded sense of belonging and being what she imagined was the center of attention on this new planet sculpted and turned into story and soundtrack by all of the artists, poets, and musicians who live out here in the northwest opened palm of Philly.

I smiled to myself in the half dark of our room with all of those memories and thoughts rolling through my head, the promise for the new day to come. The whole family was home, and we had another chance to live through a snow day together. I slid my hand to my wife's spot. It's true that I had no idea if she loved me anymore. Most people don't after nearly thirty years together. I lay there wondering where she was in the house, wanting to go back to our twenties when we couldn't keep our hands off each other and we walked three miles to work every day and three miles home, talking about the life we wanted together, making plans that would come true but forgetting to include what we felt in those days and how to make it grow.

Millie came along probably at the beginning of our shift away from love. She was one of those unfortunate pets with a low IQ but a simultaneous belief that she was the center of the universe. She stole food off kitchen counters, badgered guests to pet her, waited all morning to scare the mailwoman with violent barking, and felt it her right to go on any car ride in the offing. What Millie lacked in intelligence she made up for with enthusiasm. She'd been a strange form of glue for the family in our last decade or so as college and beyond undid the simple package that had been all of us.

* * *

I was drifting back into sleep when I heard Deena's body move through the doorway. As she slid into bed, it seemed like she was trying to sneak. I wanted to touch her, to smell her scalp, feel her warm shoulders, but I stayed in my place trying to breathe like I was sleeping.

Not knowing whether you still love someone after how many ever years is beyond pain. Wondering if they feel the same about you is the opening up of a chasm that you never knew could be there. Not knowing. It is one thing to fear driving down a strange highway on a moonless night or to walk in a dangerous neighborhood after sunset; it is quite a different thing to look a soft and familiar face in the eyes and not see that look. Why does that leave and how?

Deena was beside me breathing softly. The snow, I thought, made a sentient form of silence for the world. That kind of silence is not the absence of sound; it is a reflection of the emptiness hidden inside us. My wife and the snow were both inside of me. There was this emptiness. But there was as well the other, the promise of a special day walking from Allens Lane out to Germantown Avenue, life filling us up on our new, white planet. Everyone home. Almost Thanksgiving.

* * *

The smell of coffee, bacon, and frying butter woke me. I heard voices downstairs in the kitchen. I listened for Deena's but could only hear my children. The peels of laughter and excitement were gone now, as were the boisterous digs and insults. The cadence of voices coming up to me were mature and measured. I couldn't make out the words being spoken, but I could feel the intent of these three grown siblings. I heard surprise in the air and respect in the way sentences inflected up. All three were testing out their new relationships as adults. Gone was the mocking big brother and the competitive one-upping of just a few years earlier. I imagined Deena cooking and moving around the kitchen listening to the three of them, feeling the same sort of pride I was feeling.

When I got downstairs, the scene was more or less as I'd imagined: the three kids were sitting around the table while their mother cooked. They each had a piece of the Inquirer but moved randomly from what they were reading to cups of coffee and the confident conversation of long-lost friends.

"Good morning, Daddy," said Mary.

"Hey, Dad," Mike chimed. "Addie gets a snow day. We're going sledding at the Cricket Club golf course, sneaking in just like when we were young. Don't worry though, first we'll shovel the drive and walk."

"You get a snow day too," Adelaide said. "Your office called. The whole city is shut down. SEPTA trains are even canceled until they clear all the tracks."

I stood at the door. Deena was turning bacon. I waited for her to glance up. Just as I'd given up hope and could feel the contours of my face beginning to sag, her eyes darted up to me. There was the smile of recognition she always had, but then I noticed something just slightly different—a sort of resigned sadness maybe, or some kind of fear. I wondered reflexively, "Is she angry with me?"

"Good morning," she said. There was a faint catch to her voice.

"I slept in," I told her. "Is it really almost ten?"

"You heard Addie, it's a snow day for you, too. Everything's shut down except Wawa."

"No, it feels good to wake up like that. I didn't sleep that well anyway."

She stepped across the room to the coffeepot. "There's one cup left for you."

The kids went on talking as their mom poured me a cup. She had her arms spread wide with her back to all of us, her left hand clutching at the edge of the counter.

"You okay?" I asked.

"Private," she said quietly.

"What?"

"Dining room."

We left our grown children to their conversation and went through the laundry room, around the corner and into the dining room. Deena moved to close the swinging doors on both sides. A faint acidic bite of old urine flitted through the air. I glanced over at the stain, which I noted was near Deena's place at the table.

"What's up?" I asked as carefully as I could.

We stood at opposite ends of our dining room table. Deena crossed her arms as I took a sip of coffee. She said, "Millie's dead."

My first thought was that she was going to tell me it had been a mercy killing. We could hear the murmur of our children in the kitchen. I moved to the china cabinet, took out a painted ceramic coaster with a cork bottom that we'd bought at a craft fair in Chestnut Hill, went back to the table, put the coaster down and my coffee mug on top. She had delivered those words with little emotion. There might have been a slight challenge to them. I know now that she'd had a good piece of the night to contemplate Millie's passing and that the death of a family pet, especially a well-meaning goofball dog like our Millie, should strike the soul in its center. Counting Millie, I have had four dogs in my life. Deena had had three. And yet a basic, cold, untwisted truth came out of Deena's mouth—no remorse, no regret, no pain, no sorrow, not the slightest semblance of mourning.

The fact that she waited for me to say something led me further to believe that she had committed the murder. Images of my wife strangling Millie or smothering her with a pillow in the middle of the night gave me goose bumps. The conjured look on her face in the middle of this act frightened me. I balanced my weight on the table using my fingers.

"What do you mean?" I finally asked.

"The dog's dead."

"You found her?"

"Last night."

"Where?"

"In the living room. Right where she sleeps. I moved the body into the garage."

"She sleeps in our room next to the radiator."

"Not always. You know that. Sometimes she wanders into the living room, sometimes the kitchen. It all depends."

I searched her eyes for the truth. Something had to be there if she'd done what I suspected. But maybe Deena's a good liar. She plays poker well. How well do you really know someone you love if they're a good liar? No one knows what good liars really think.

Images of a happy Millie plowing into a tall, thick vanilla cake of snow in our backyard came to me, her dusty, shadow-colored body working hard to stay on the surface, ears flapping with every bounce. Millie, floating through our neighborhood, stupid but so deeply loved.

My wife was staring at me. "I can't figure out whether a dog has a personality," she said a bit oddly to me. "Or if they're just mirrors for our own feelings toward them."

"What's that got to do with anything? What are we going to tell the kids?"

"She was old. Dogs die. They know that."

I glanced down at the surface of my coffee. It didn't matter whether Millie had a personality or whether we'd just made one up for her. She'd been the dog of our children's youth in Philadelphia. I could still hear them out in the kitchen talking. We would need to go out and tell them. Their sloppy, foolish friend was gone. The one they'd dressed up for dinner when she was a puppy. The one who seemed desperate always for happiness between the three of them and for riding along in the car to go shopping at Weaver's Way, for traipsing out to do yard work, standing guard at the Germantown Friends playground. The actual end of their childhood. The actual end of that part of our life together.

"I woke up in the middle of the night," I finally managed. "And you weren't there."

"Probably that's when I found her."

"At four fifteen in the morning and you didn't wake me?"

"What point would there be to that? You needed to sleep. You never get enough sleep."

"But she was dead, Deena. I could have helped you. I could have done something."

"There was nothing to do."

"You dragged her out to the garage?"

"I carried her."

"My God!" I said.

She stared at me, waiting, it seemed, or trying to figure out what I knew.

"I guess you can replace the carpet in here now," I offered.

"Yes, I thought of that."

"Of course you did," I muttered.

"What was that?"

"Nothing."

"Nothing? Did you say what I think you did?"

"What? Of course you did?"

"Why would you say that?"

"I don't know, Deena. You tell me?"

She fixed stone-heavy eyes on my face. "I'm not happy about it," she said, "but you're right, the dog can't piss on the carpet anymore. And I'm relieved. Is that so bad? Do I need your permission to get on with our life?"

"You never liked her."

She shrugged.

"You despised her."

"In the end I despised what she was doing in here. Yes. We've got guests coming tomorrow. Thanksgiving dinner. It's sick what I have to put up with sometimes."

"Had to . . ."

She didn't reply to that.

We both stared at each other. I could have told her my thoughts. My fear? Instead, she said, "I need you to help deal with this now. I don't want the children—"

"The children loved her."

"They also love video games, rappers, and movie stars."

"No, Deena. They loved Millie like a member of the family. They loved playing with her at Pastorius Park and taking her for walks down at the Wissahickon. And they adored her companionship in the neighborhood on days like this."

"She was a dog."

"A good dog. And you . . ."

Yes. I stopped right there. So much about our life was not being said across a shining dining room table in the late morning of an early winter day. Nearly three decades of marriage and I wanted to accuse her of murdering our dog two days before Thanksgiving in a sad urine-scented dining room. Three decades of marriage and it seemed right then that she didn't care whether I knew or not.

Out the window was an endless white world that was somehow no longer our Mt. Airy neighborhood in Philadelphia.

I was hungry. The smells of breakfast were still in the air with the urine. I could hear my children laughing through the door. I loved Millie. I loved my children. I still wanted to love my wife. Deena's eyes are my eyes. Snow brings out the universal mind. We are all in this together, says the mind.

"I want to tell the kids," she said. "Can you please call the vet and see about the body?"

David Biddle is a mixed-race Quaker American author who lives in Philadelphia. His novel Old Music for New People *will be published in December 2021. You can track him down at www.davidbiddle.net.*

An Old-Fashioned Story

Andie Tursi

You are a terrible person for sneaking out in the middle of your father's sixtieth-birthday dinner to have a cigarette. You left your poor boyfriend back at the table with your entire family. You draw in the last drag and pause by a group of old men near the entrance. You linger in their cloud of cleansing cigar smoke, intruding on their ceremony to cover up the smell of Marlboro Lights.

A valet opens the door for you, and you step back into the restaurant's dark world of brown on brown. The Rackhouse is one of the oldest steakhouses in Philadelphia, the kind of place where powerful men eat dinner every night and men like your father come only on special occasions. It is a shrine to man's dominion over nature, animal hides tanned into leather seating, great trees felled into mahogany furniture. A perfect place if you enjoy eating steak under the gaze of a mounted moose.

You linger by the bar, not eager to get back to the table. It's not especially busy, but the man who tends it busies himself. He moves constantly, tasks flowing one into the other as if they are choreographed. He refills the olives. He dries a glass and hangs it up. He acknowledges an approaching customer with a nod.

"Yeah, gimme another one," the patron says without looking at the bartender. He wears his belly and expensive suit with equal pride. He seems like the type who appreciates the decor.

He is of the age that is attracted to the idea of immortality and the notion that power, or the illusion of it, can be preserved no matter how old and dusty you get.

The bartender flips a rocks glass over his wrist and tongs in a few cubes of unbleached sugar. He dashes them with bitters until they're soaked. You're thinking about how large his hands are as he grips his muddler. You're staring as he grinds it into the glass, creaming the sugar. It isn't long before you notice—this bartender is sexy. You think back on the handful of boyfriends you had during high school and college. Boys, all of them, including the one back at the table, but this full-bearded bartender in front of you is a *man*. You admire the back of him as he turns to take a bottle of bourbon down from the shelf, his arms as he jiggers some into the glass and adds ice. He gives the drink a quick and deliberate stir with a long metal swizzle, then he pulls out a thin knife.

He takes an orange from a bowl of citrus and cuts off a large swath of peel. It yields its fragrance, squirting a fine mist into the heavy air. You are biting your lip as he rubs the expressed oil slowly around the rim of the drink. You are practically drooling as he takes up the knife again and, this time, slices into a lemon. The twill of rind he hangs on the edge of the glass is impossibly pithless, so thin it's translucent. He lays out a cocktail napkin and sets his creation in front of the old man with an unceremonious nod. The old man practically flicks a twenty-dollar bill at him and walks away, drink in hand.

When you get back to the table, your mother gives you a dirty look. Everyone has already finished their first course. Your wedge salad is waiting, but your appetite has vanished.

Henry leans over and places his warm hand on your shoulder to welcome you.

"Everything okay?" he asks. "You're shaking."

"Of course," you say, "I'm just cold." You shrug off his touch.

You look down at the unmanageable chunk of lettuce dotted with flecks of blue cheese. Vegetables are not the specialty of the house. You look at Henry. He's the sweetest boyfriend in the world, but you know you'll never fuck him again.

Maybe a week later you break up with Henry. You've been together for two years and were beginning to make plans, but it's over for you. Some fundamental switch has been flipped.

"I wanted you to be a part of my family," he says when you break the news. But even while he's crying, you are thinking about the bartender, the way the wide straps of his apron crisscrossed his back, the bottle opener sticking out of his back pocket.

* * *

All your friends and family are pissed at you. They all loved Henry. "You'll never find a nice guy like that ever again," your girls say, which almost turns out to be true.

A few days later, you wear a sexy dress under a blazer to work, and at the end of the day you take off the blazer and take a cab to the old man's favorite steakhouse.

There is a different person behind the bar tonight, a woman, and you are relieved, but also disappointed. You are kicking yourself because you're practically broke, but you can't just walk out without ordering a drink. You ask for the first specialty cocktail on the list. It's brown, of course, boozy and bitter, but you manage to fight your way to the bottom of it with a straight face. You try your best to look comfortable, looking down at your watch every once in a while to indicate that you are waiting for someone, which you aren't. Even the trophies seem to know you don't belong there. They are only disembodied heads with glass eyes, but still they judge and seem to disapprove.

As soon as you get up to leave, a door opens on the side of the bar, and he appears, Mr. Professional. The female bartender takes away your empty glass, inquires if you'd like another. She seems to shake her head no, a warning so subtle it barely registers. You order the second cocktail on the list.

The night has taken a pleasant turn. The next drink is fruity and vodka based. The alcohol warms your face, and you get to watch your fantasy man at work. He is all business, but since his duties involve scanning the bar for seeking eyes, he finds yours more than once. By the third time it happens, he knows that it isn't because you need another drink.

He looks right at you as he makes his next cocktail, his biceps on full display pumping the shaker up and down in a rhythm that is almost perverse. He pours the contents into a highball glass with an unnecessary flourish. He is performing for your benefit, but you are too shy to react. He chuckles to himself as he dunks the shaker into soapy water and wipes it down with a white towel.

You down your drink, and finally, your courage finds you. You call him over by way of your empty glass.

He approaches, leaning far over the bar toward you. He smells musty, but maybe it is just the restaurant, the wood and cigars, the abundance of taxidermy. His eyes are deep and brown. They penetrate.

"Would you like anything?" he asks.

Your courage leaves you.

"Uh, just the tab," you say. You look down at the bar, pretend to study the knots in the wood.

"What's your name?" he presses.

You look right at him even though you're blushing hard.

You tell him. You smile your most flirtatious knowing grin, but he is not ready to end the game.

"I meant your last name," he says, "so I can find your credit card?"

You can barely squeak it out, but you give him your last name. You think about just leaving, abandoning your card so that you don't die of humiliation, but as soon as you stand up,

An Old-Fashioned Story

both drinks hit you hard. He comes back with your card, the receipt, and a pen. The balance on the bill is zero.

"Write down your number," he says, and his voice is deep and confident.

It is a command, not a request, but you don't really notice this until later, when it is already too late.

You talk on the phone a few times and then invite him over one night when your roommate isn't home. You imagine that you'll get acquainted over drinks, maybe go to the bar around the corner or out to dinner. But when he arrives, you feel overdressed. You're self-conscious as he's looking around your apartment, which suddenly doesn't seem very sophisticated. You offer him a beer because that is what men drink.

"Wow, I haven't had this since college," he says, and it's not the first time he has referred to the age gap between you. You aren't *that* young. You are no virgin. You've been out of the country twice, to Spain to study and Mexico to party. You have a degree and a full-time job, a couple of pieces of real furniture. Your car is a piece of shit, but you own it.

You sit down together on the couch. He takes one sip of the beer and puts it down on the coffee table.

"Come here," he says.

Henry was always polite. Gentle. You've led the way for every guy you've ever been with, but this man grabs you, practically picks you up and places you astride his lap. His beard scratches your face as he kisses you. You were never into beards before, but now you are, big time. It makes you wet. Everything about him makes you wet. His expert hands remove your shirt and bra. He cups your breast, and you're reminded of the bowl of citrus on the edge of the bar. His other hand palms the back of your head. He gathers most of your hair and tugs it—hard. You moan. You grind down into his lap. The jangling sound of his belt buckle is almost enough to make you come.

You reach down to rub him through his jeans, and the

gap between your thumb and forefinger widens as your hand slides down its length.

"Oh my God," you say, but you stop moving.

He is proud to take it out of his boxers for you, and even in your aroused state, this seems a little premature. You lean backward and away. His dick is huge. It stands between your bodies as if you share it.

"It's huge," you say.

But he knows this already.

"Do you want it?" he asks.

He squirms beneath you, places his hand around the base of this thing, and starts moving it upward. It's fun to watch, but you are thinking, no fucking way. You are thinking that no amount of sweet talk or lube could make you want this monster cock. You are thinking that two weeks ago, Henry was your future husband.

"Uh-uh," you say. "That's not happening."

"I know you want it," he says. And he is so confident, but he is so wrong, and this whole thing is so ridiculous. And so you laugh.

But then his face changes. Falls. He stops stroking himself.

"Is something funny?" he asks. "Are you laughing at me?"

The first chill of fear creeps up your spine.

"No . . . I'm just laughing because . . . wait . . . You're seriously angry right now?"

You begin your dismount, but he grabs your thigh and presses down on your shoulder. You gasp. He flips you. Now your back is against the couch and he is above you. He holds your wrists in one hand, pressing them together painfully above your head. You think about your first boyfriend, how easily his skinny body could pin you down on his parents' living room rug when you wrestled. He digs his knees into the fronts of your thighs, and you scream from the pain of his crushing weight. He slides them onto the couch, forcing your legs apart. You try to kick your heels into his back. You try to scream again, but he covers your mouth. Your arms are free to pound at his sides, but this has no effect. He drops his weight again, and you feel yourself tearing as he forces himself inside you.

Years later, the first time you give birth, this moment will come back to you. The rip. The tear. The burn. When they place your baby boy on your chest, wet and warm, before you think the word *Jonathan*, the name you have carried in your heart for nine months, you think first of this insignificant person who still manages to intrude on your most precious and private moments.

He must like the moment of giving up because that's what does it. As soon as your sobs turn to whimpers and your body goes limp, you feel him leave you and a warm spurt hit your thigh. The bartender stays still for a moment and then leans back on his heels. He looks at his hands as if they are foreign.

"I'm sorry," he says, when he sees your face. "Did I hurt you?"

You tuck your thumb along the bottom of your fist, throw it out level to your shoulder, aim with your first two knuckles. Bam! You get him right in the nose. The hardest you've ever hit anyone in your life. You wanted blood to spray, cartilage to crack, but nothing happens.

"What the fuck!" he yells. "You fuckin' bitch!"

Then he's up fixing his pants, grabbing his keys, walking out. He slams the door behind him, and you know you should get up and lock it, but you can't move. You try not to even breathe.

Okay. Okay. Okay. You tell yourself. You stand up like a robot and go directly to the door. You think of nothing else until it's bolted shut. For the first time in your life, you wish you had a weapon. For the first time in your life, you're angry enough to use one.

And then your eyes land on the beer you served him, and the shame hits and swells inside of you. Sweat beads on the bottle. The beer is still cold. This man had his way with you, and he was here and gone in less time than it takes for a beer to reach room temperature.

In a few days the soreness goes away, and in a few weeks you know that you are not pregnant. In a month you learn you are disease-free. You escape unscathed. You survived your first time with a "man". You never call it rape. Real rape victims are joggers who are attacked by strangers in the park. You wanted this guy. You invited him to your apartment. You had condoms in your bedside drawer.

You minimize it in your mind. You call it rough sex, and you convince yourself that you liked it. You masturbate while thinking about his rough hands on you, his deep voice, and the way he pulled your hair. You tell all your girls about it, except you leave out certain details. They will make a huge deal out of it, and that's the last thing you want. You're gonna tell a room full of cops how you stalked this guy where he works? That you had been drinking? That you dressed yourself up like a prostitute? Besides, it's possible you imagined the whole thing. Did you ever explicitly say no? Did he think you were playing around? Is that why he was so confused and pissed when you punched him in the face?

The girls are scandalized. They can't believe that you had sex with some older guy so soon after you broke up with Henry and that you have no plans to see him again. You play it like you are into some cool new lifestyle where you just don't give a fuck anymore, which turns out to be kind of true.

You begin chasing that feeling you got when you threw that punch. You start going to kickboxing. You say you're learning to defend yourself, but really you just want blood. You watch the guys in the ring destroy each other, sweat and spit flying, leather on flesh. You beat the shit out of the heavy bag, but it's never enough. You fuck every guy who trains you.

You buy a tactical keychain, a four-inch pepper spray baton with a swivel for your keys on top. You walk the city streets in wish-a-motherfucker-would mode, swinging your keys around, flicking the safety on and off. You take your uncle up on his offer to get you a handgun, and you keep it in the bedside drawer. Sometimes when you're reaching for your vibrator, your fingers close around the barrel.

For the next couple of years, you date your way through a parade of assholes—a liar and manipulator, a pair of narcissists, an alcoholic. The girls all stayed in touch with Henry, and you hear that he married some nice girl. They always emphasize her niceness. "She's really nice," they say, which implies that you aren't. Hell, you know you aren't, but at least you aren't boring. You picture Henry and the nice girl in some big house with a family portrait hanging over the fireplace, a couple of stupid kids, probably some dumb dog. You still don't miss Henry. You never did. You called him a few months after the breakup. You didn't want to get back together, but you wanted to apologize. He said his whole family always thought you were a bitch. He called you an evil slut. He said everything about you, including your handwriting, was ugly. And then he hung up.

Maybe if he had stayed on the line you would have told him what happened. Even if just to say, hey, if it makes you feel any better, at least I got what I deserved. I got treated like shit by someone, and it sucks. I'm sorry I did it to you. But you never get the chance.

Five years pass and your old man hits another milestone birthday. The big 6-5. He wants a dinner downtown with the whole family, and of course he wants to go to the Rackhouse.

At first you think you won't go. You'll fake sick or something. But then you think, why not? What's he gonna do to you in public? And in private, who knows? Maybe you will seduce him again. Bring him back to your new place, pull out your piece this time.

You're dressed to fucking kill it. Your kickboxing days are over, but you're consistently hitting the regular gym. Once you climbed out of the shit spiral that began on the night you broke up with Henry, you really did clean yourself up. You step out of the cab, your hand gripping the pepper spray stick that's hidden in your coat pocket. Just caressing the knurled aluminum calms you. You bring it to your mouth and lick the tip of the rod, mining the hole with your tongue until you feel the tingle and burn of expired capsaicin. You walk in and head straight for the bar. He probably doesn't even work here anymore.

Andie Tursi is a communications professional by day and fiction writer by night. Originally from Delaware County, she has lived in Philadelphia for most of her adult life and finds her inspiration in its people, streets, and sports teams.

Three Yellow Lights

Corianna Jackson

"I'm nervous," Jorja blurted out as she slammed the car door, leaving it idling to continue warming up. Something about Eli could have her admitting things she couldn't even admit to herself. Truthfully, he was the only person she wanted to talk to right now, even though the thought of running him down had crossed her mind when he'd appeared at the end of the driveway.

"And I'm black," Eli said, rolling his eyes and walking up to her.

She didn't bother giving his signature joke any of her usual praise. His hands played with the bracelet around his wrist—turquoise beads. They probably meant something. She tended to tune him out when he went off on colorful tangents about his jewelry, something about divine crystals and spirituality.

Nonsense.

"And here," she noted. Her voice was strained. She let her eyes flicker over his tall frame for the hundredth time since he'd reappeared. Summer still lingered on him, bringing out the red tones in his dark skin and turning his brown eyes into a stew of gold and bronze. His hair was different though, now in five neat cornrows that met in a topknot.

He sighed in response, shifting his gaze toward the pavement and slumping his body up against the driver-side door. The car jolted at the contact, and the radio continued to play faintly, singing what was left unspoken and teasing with what could've been. Jorja knew he hated this song. Too many memories.

"You shouldn't be nervous," he said.

"And you shouldn't be here."

He winced.

"Besides," she huffed. "I already told my mom about what you did. There's no turning back now." Her curls bounced as she shook her head. Despite wanting to be nowhere near him, her feet carried her next to him. Their arms brushed against each other as she pressed her back up against her car's cool metal exterior. Her mother knew all about their convertible conferences and their magical midnight drives into nowhere. She knew about the dreams that lived in the glovebox and the secrets that were embedded in the stained seats. She knew about the songs sung and the tears shed. But above all else, she knew about the radio silence, his sudden disappearance, and his new girlfriend, who stalked Jorja on Instagram from time to time.

Eli laughed. It was short and fake, nothing like the deep howl she was used to hearing. "I'm sorry for letting her down."

"You should be. She's really disappointed."

He nodded, his expression falling. They listened to the loud hum of her car over the radio, waiting for the engine to calm and the sound to smooth out. Bella, who was pulling off a more modest look for the fall season by keeping her ragtop up, always revved too high at first. Eli taught Jorja to have patience with Bella, to rub her hands along the wheel and truly listen. "Where are you going? Can I come?" he asked.

"It's getting late."

"We've been out later."

The sky was pink and fluffy, reminding her of cotton candy and summer carnivals. Her thoughts always wandered back to the summer. It was his fault.

She looked over at him once again, taking in the way he was shaking his leg and popping the bracelet on his wrist. With a roll of her eyes and a nod, she gave in, grabbing the door handle of the driver's side as a gesture for him to move. A part of her hated seeing Eli as anything other than his overconfident, easygoing self.

Eli shot her a grateful smile and walked around to the other side. He groaned once he fell into the seat, scrunching his face as he turned to look at her. His knees were pressed up against his chest, and his body was leaned forward.

"Lots of other people have been in your seat," she said, shrugging as she smoothed her hands along the wheel and watched the dials on her dashboard slowly level out. That was a lie, of course. She had recently gotten her car washed, and the workers left the seat pulled forward. Usually, the seat was pulled back and at an obtuse angle, making room for Eli's long legs and laid-back aesthetic.

Eli fiddled with the levers on the side of his seat and ignored her comment. Once content with his seating arrangement, he rested an arm on the center console and looked back at her. She was much more rigid, her seat only a few inches from the wheel to compensate for her lack of height. Jorja insisted on sitting up at a ninety-degree angle, her body on constant edge to stay alert. Eli allowed himself a smile at the familiar image, but it quickly disappeared once she reciprocated his gaze with furrowed eyebrows.

"Are you going to tell me why you're here?" She stole a glance at herself in the rearview mirror before he could answer and cursed herself for not making more of an effort to look her best before leaving the house. Her hair was matted down, spruced up with an old headband just to keep the tangled mess of curls out of her face—which was currently breaking out.

"Oh, sweet Jorja, you know that's not how our car talks work," he said. There was the Eli she had come to know. Some days she felt as if she had made the summer's events up. She'd made up all the intimacy and the longing glances and the silly games they'd played just to revel in how unearthly their connection felt. Looking back, games weren't the only thing Eli was good at playing.

Nevertheless, she nodded and put the car in reverse. Three yellow lights. She had to run through three yellow lights to earn Eli's first confession.

"I have to get a few more materials for my final piece. I have to show some important people my portfolio tomorrow," she said, answering his question from earlier without sparing him another glance. She pulled out of the driveway, took a deep breath, and set off down the block. Everything stood still in her hometown. Not even the leaves from the trees rustled in the subtle fall breeze. Home was a picture she could spend hours painting perfectly, down to the cracks in the sidewalk. It didn't matter if she could flawlessly recreate her surroundings in oils with one swift, calculating glance. Her fancy art professor would still critique her harshly, even if it was spot on. "You're too detached. More emotion," he'd spit.

Nonsense.

Eli rolled his eyes and grabbed the aux cord. "You probably need nothing else for your project. You're just pulling a Jorja."

Her hands clenched the wheel. "So?" There was no point in denying things around Eli.

"I've always enjoyed your paintings." He hummed as his fingers scrolled through his vast music library, which housed songs like secrets, poetry only whispered between him and his artists. "Especially that one you did of me."

"Of course you did," she grumbled, shifting around in her seat. That painting, full of swirly lines and vivid, unfamiliar colors, was the only piece her professor ever praised. Lately, she'd been working in black-and-white—and dreaming in greyscale.

"I can't believe you got me to sit still for that long."

"Trust me, I can't either."

They approached an intersection. Jorja narrowed her eyes and floored it, the light turning red just as she flew through it. "Two more."

Eli settled on a song and grinned. There was a time when Jorja would have jerked the car to a stop before the light even turned red. Eli had constantly teased her about all the risks she refused to take, but Eli was the biggest risk she ever took—and what did that get her? A broken heart, songs she couldn't play anymore without wanting to burst into tears, and a car that still managed to smell like his cologne despite several desperate car washes.

His phone rang, causing the music to fade out. Jorja tried to mind her business, but she couldn't help but take a glance at the display as it lit up. Her face fell. The girlfriend. The girlfriend that sort of looked like her, though she had a feeling that it was the other way around. Jorja was the distraction, the closest copy of what he couldn't have at the time. Jorja was Eli's second choice.

She eased up on the gas and bit her lip, watching as the cotton candy sky turned into an orange and raspberry sorbet. Eli declined the call. He was a lot of things, but not stupid. His fingers created a symphony of clicks and clacks instead, filling the silence in the car until a new song came on: "Blessed" by Daniel Caesar.

"What did you tell her?" The question flew out of her mouth before she could stop herself.

"The usual," he said, and waved off the question. When Jorja frowned, he sighed. "She's just always asking where I am and who I'm with."

There was obviously a reason for her insanity.

She wondered whether Eli ever mentioned their escapades to her, or whether he and his girlfriend had the same ones. Sometimes it felt like the moments she spent with Eli couldn't be replicated, that the sun would never be in that exact same angle the way it had been that one day when the bass in her car hit a little too hard and Eli's soul roared right along with it. But the sun would always exist, the bass would always boom, and there would always be another girl.

She ran through the second light without knowing it, surprising herself.

"Have you been practicing or something?"

"Maybe."

They passed the diner they used to stumble into on their Friday three a.m. drives. Delilah's skillet chocolate chip cookies were heaven in cast iron. They passed the Guitar Center they used to spend hours freeloading in, pretending they could play all of the instruments that shaped their favorite songs. They passed their preferred bodega, the thrift store that defined Eli's taste, and the best pizzeria in the universe. She didn't blow through the final warning light until the sun had officially gone down, and the shadows washed away the town Eli had gotten her to fall in love with in three measly months despite having lived there all her life.

"I miss you," he breathed out, playing by the rules. He reached over to turn down the music as Jorja turned onto their secret highway. It was a curious, vacant road that went on for a few miles yet only featured two exits and looped back around in a wide circle. It wasn't very well lit, but Jorja hadn't known that due to long summer days and Eli's tendency to ward off darkness. "I shouldn't have stopped talking to you suddenly. I'm trying to work on being a better friend."

Nonsense.

"I did exactly what you were afraid of. I know, and I'm so sorry," he continued.

Bullshit.

"You just seem so happy at art school, and maybe that's because I'm not around anymore. And I know it's my fault that the only glimpses I can get of you are from your Snapchat—"

Jorja sped up, letting the trees fall away in a blur along with his words. Sixty mph . . . The only thing that had really changed was the seasons. Seventy mph . . . Perhaps there's a time limit for righting wrongs. Eighty mph . . . Speed felt faster in the driver's seat, with control.

"Jorja?" His voice cracked, but he showed no signs of fear. Not even as they reached the end of the highway—where the white lines decorated the pavement at an attempt to slow drivers down before they reached the bend—or even when she showed no signs of stopping. He placed his hand on top of hers, and she jumped, suddenly aware.

She stomped down on the brakes. The tires screeched. Eli held his breath, and Jorja struggled to find hers. Her hands shook around the wheel, and her leg locked into place. Her heart was pounding and aching and stuttering. Eli put the car in park.

"I loved you!" she shouted, overcome with all of the emotion she'd been trying to repress for months now. "Don't dumb this down to a friendship gone wrong!"

Eli blinked. He opened his mouth but closed it shortly after.

Jorja squeezed her eyes shut and slammed her head into the steering wheel. The horn pierced the air, drawn out and off key. "I loved you, and I thought you loved me too," she choked out. She could barely string together the words. Her throat felt tight, and tears pricked at her eyes. Heartbreak had turned into anger, and now all that was left was humiliation, the inescapable shame that came with being another victim of love unrequited, of being another cliché, of being just another expendable girl to Eli.

Eli still refused to speak, gifting her the same silence she'd grown used to.

"Nonsense." She was so tired of being all of those things.

"Huh?"

Jorja didn't bother to give him an answer this time. Instead, she chuckled in disbelief, her giggles turning into a crescendo of breathy gasps and bellowing laughter. She laughed through the tears and the pain, her racing heartbeat and her trembling fingers. She laughed until her stomach hurt and her vision went blurry.

The ride back home was smooth and somber. The roads proved empty, emerald lights guiding them through a ghost town of passion. Jorja didn't say anything as she dropped Eli off. Nothing else needed to be said.

Her canvas took the brunt of her emotions. The 30" × 45" depiction of a rainy, gray London alleyway didn't even flinch at

Jorja's confident yellow splatters. She made them purposeful, rubbing the vibrancy back into her art until it seemed as if the darkness was glowing with warmth.

Without regret, she let her piece dry and climbed into bed, exhaustion taking over. Her phone lay neglected for a couple of hours; white numbers and a few notifications greeted her as she checked on it to say good night. There was a text from Eli, the first one she had received from him in months.

I think I might've felt the same way too.

With one last laugh, she blocked his number and rolled over.

Nonsense.

Corianna Jackson is a Black female writer who attends Temple University as a journalism student. After one short-lived year in Philadelphia, she can proudly say this city is way better than Long Island, New York. This story is based on one of many failed love attempts, or whatever love is to a nineteen-year-old living in a digital hook-up age.

I Was Always a Mad Comet, but You Have Fixed Me

Stephanie King

The trouble with widowers is they tend to cry after sex. It can be alarming but also something of a compliment, the way a springtime rain feels refreshing rather than cause for an umbrella, the lightness of the drops a benediction.

I hadn't meant to make it A Thing. Larry was older but within the highest end of my specified range, and he seemed as mildly uncomfortable with it as I did. He and Caroline had been married for twenty-four years, right out of high school, and the youngest child had just left for college. Still, he dressed nicely and enjoyed foreign films, and we had pleasant conversation across several dates before he shyly asked me if I might like to take it to another level.

I wasn't a widow. I was a newly divorced mom of one, and Jake took Elisabeth every other week, leaving me a wide window of opportunity to date. She was eleven and had recently decided she needed to be called her full name instead of Betsy, which we nicknamed her as a baby. She was moving away from us more every day, even as we moved farther away from each other. I had grown a bit more curvy and more tired with every year of marriage, while Jake's grad students had not. Maryam was twenty-seven and bright and inquisitive, and I wished her well with him.

Larry was the first, and the crying alarmed me. "I'm

sorry," he sputtered. "I haven't been with anyone since . . ." He never finished the sentence. Since she died? Since 2007? Who knew? I consoled him as best I could, an awkward hug, a whispered "there, there", and when I stopped seeing him after a few more times, it wasn't because of the tears.

When I started picking widowers, it wasn't because I particularly wanted one. I went on a few first dates with divorced guys, and their ex-wives were all, coincidentally, total bitches. Some of them had kids and some of them didn't, but I didn't want to inevitably have an awkward introduction to another woman. I liked the way Larry had never spoken ill of his lost love. Single men my age seemed to be divorced or damaged, unless . . .

Jim was enjoying playing the field but cried anyway. I later found out he was seeing two other women at the same time and wondered if he cried on all of us.

Mark denied he ever cried; he seemed almost mad at Ariana for having left him, as if leukemia had offered her a choice. Their children were still young, and he worked in the building trades, all rough calloused hands and bulging biceps, different from anything I'd been used to. He sniffled in the dark like I had given him allergies.

Will didn't say that his spouse had died, but by then, I knew the telltale signs. The "just getting back into dating" without the mention of divorce. The pictures carefully cropped or else clearly smiling at a certain someone who had been behind the camera but was no longer. What he *did* say was that he was interested in "everyone", and I thought about it for a minute before I matched with him: Did I care? My primary criteria was the lost beloved, not the gender of the beloved.

It could've been awkward but it wasn't. Instead it allowed us to ask each other, "What was your husband like?" in the same even tone, a crisp conversational volley like a pleasant tennis match. Seven months had passed and his friends had started encouraging him to "get out there".

Will was the "cool" teacher, letting students scan rap lyrics for alliteration and enjambment for their poetry papers, but self-aware enough not to be a culture vulture about it and present their work at a conference or, worse, write a book. His students called him "oldhead" as an endearment.

Adrian had been a nurse, looking cute in scrubs, his hazel eyes sparkling above his mask in the pictures I unabashedly looked up on Facebook. They'd wanted to adopt or have a baby with a surrogate, but their salaries had never seemed enough and they thought they had time.

After a respectable number of dates, one night we ate Ethiopian food, and instead of heading to the bar upstairs, I suggested a walk because it was a lovely evening, purple piled on top of pink across the West Philly sky. We held hands and at some point stopped in front of a rowhouse no different than the others on the block, until I said, "This is my house." Will looked up at the bay window so warily that I added, "We can keep walking," before he broke out into a wide smile.

Will cried too, but not right away. "I hope I did okay," was the first thing he said afterward. "It's been awhile since I've been with a woman." He had been alternatingly brilliant and uneven; clearly at some point he had known his way around a woman's body, even if it wasn't like riding a bicycle.

I had thought he might want something weird but he didn't, or maybe my definition of "weird" was a bit weirder than most straight women. Jake and I had been married for twelve years and our sex life had been like a roller coaster, peaks of lust and experimentation that dipped into valleys of despondency when we had Betsy or had long stretches of fighting or being sick of each other. Also like a roller coaster, the peaks had gotten shallower as we came to the end of the ride.

I held Will in the dark, almost drifting off to sleep before I heard the unmistakable sound. I asked if he was okay and he said, "I'm sorry," which they always did, and then, "I'm just a little sad," which they usually did not. He wiped his face and then settled in against my shoulder, the slight graze of his now eleven-o'clock shadow a reassurance.

I enjoyed him several times before Will said it was too soon, disappearing, either deleting or deactivating the app. I assumed he'd matched with someone he liked better, whether man or woman I couldn't guess, and figured it served me right for being a widowfucker. I felt sorry for myself as I scrolled stalkerishly back, back, back through his pictures, from the year before when Will and Adrian found a stray kitten under their front step, all the way back to Adrian's graduation from nursing school. Will looked impossibly young and happy in all of them.

Then, two months later, a tentative text unfurling, Will asking how I had been. Watered with the slightest sprinkling of encouragement, it quickly blossomed into an invitation to dinner. He was sorry; it had truly been too soon but now it wasn't.

Not long after, I was spending my weeks off from motherhood fully in the swing of dating, once even making out with him on my front stoop on a Wednesday when I couldn't wait the whole week to see him again, while Elisabeth slept upstairs. What would I have said if she had woken up and wandered downstairs, looking for a glass of water? "This is Will, he's been a little sad since his husband died"? I hadn't introduced anyone to her in my year of being back into dating.

Not long after, we had to put our ancient cat named Percy Jackson to sleep, after adopting him as an adult with health needs from the cat café and giving him a good life in his last years. I cried, Elisabeth cried, even Jake looked a little misty when I told him. Elisabeth asked if now, finally, we could get a kitten, and I said it was too soon. Really, I was thinking of Will and his Barnabas, now no longer a kitten, and would he get along with another cat? In the interstitial hour between sending Elisabeth with Jake and waiting for Will to arrive, looking at my paused profile, my thumb slid lazily over the settings wheel, ultimately drifting down to "confirm delete".

Stephanie King lives, works, and teaches in Philadelphia. Her stories have won the Quarterly West Novella Prize and the Lilith Short Fiction Prize, while her education writing has appeared in the Philadelphia Inquirer *and* Billy Penn. *She received her MFA from Bennington and serves on the board of the Philadelphia Writers' Conference.*

Chill

Amy Beth Sisson

Jane removed her sheepskin mittens and sat on the pew next to Matt, her date, if that's what he was. He took her chalky white fingers and stroked each one until the blood began to flow with a burn. On his wrist was a tattoo of a dog tag with the word *sacrifice* inked in gothic font. They were in an overheated church, waiting for a folk concert. The steam radiators hissed like a chorus of asthmatic cats. One of her hands was trapped in his; the other was clutching her parka and purse to keep them out of the puddle of salty snow melt on the wood floor. No one had held her hand since she took the Trailways from Boston three weeks earlier. In fact, no one had touched her at all for months before that. Her husband had been sleeping on the couch ever since she yelled at him for spending a thousand dollars of student loan money to buy a 1927 edition of Joyce's *Dubliners* in Russian—a language he did not read.

The band played adequate Dylan covers. The soprano sang with an un-Dylan like purity. Her plaint to the jack of hearts was convincing enough, but her rendition of "Just like a Woman" wouldn't fool anyone.

After the applause for the last song died down, Matt put on his tan cap and desert camo jacket. He was the most beautiful man. She wanted to put her arms around his strong shoulders but shuffled behind him out of the church with the crowd.

Jane's feet slid out from under her on the wet step. The handrail was too thick to grip with her bulky mitten, and she landed on her butt. Matt reached for her elbow and lifted her to her feet.

"You're okay, right?"

"Yep, okay," she said, rubbing the sharp pain in her tailbone.

Matt led Jane down the block to a pub that occupied the first floor of a Victorian house. In the front yard, patio chairs were tipped on their sides, and tables dripped with stalactites of ice. The room was warm, but there wasn't any place to put coats, so she left hers on. All the tables were occupied. They crowded up to the bar. He ordered two Dogfish IPAs and handed one to her. Bitter wasn't what she wanted, but she sipped the beer anyway, wishing she could get some food. Even one beer on an empty stomach hit her hard. He downed his, then ordered a second right away and drank it just as quickly.

The Eagles' "Hotel California" blared. Matt said something, but the bar was noisy and she wasn't sure what he was asking.

"Right, I work at the college."

"I asked if you liked this old music, but that's nice," he shouted. "I got my BA there, but I still work construction."

"What was your major?"

"Communications."

The conversation died. They just couldn't hear each other.

"My place is close. I'll make you some cocoa." He spoke loudly into her ear. Without waiting for her answer, he led her out the door and away from a couple scraping ice from their windshield in the parking lot. Matt smoked a cigarette as they walked down the hill past the general store. On the short walk, her hands and feet went from overheated to icicles.

His apartment was on the second floor of a house with peeling paint. At the top of the stairs there was a rag rug covered with dog fur and crusted footprints of mud and dried salt. She wondered where he kept the dog but didn't stop to ask, even though she was phobic.

She heard a growl behind Matt's apartment door. Matt leaned in to kiss her so heavily that she had to shift her weight against the wall to balance. Her cold hands made her self-conscious, and she didn't embrace him.

"Let's get you inside and warmed up." Matt unlocked the door and walked into the kitchen. "This is Brandy." The dog was big, with long red hair. "Sit," he ordered. The dog whimpered and sat down. Jane inched around Matt, making sure he stood between her and Brandy.

"Not a dog lover then?" He grabbed the dog's collar.

"Sit," he said, looking at Jane.

She almost protested, but his eyes crinkled at the edges, his expression inviting.

"I need to take her out, but it won't take long. She hates the cold."

Jane lowered herself gently into the metal and vinyl chair, her tailbone still aching from her earlier fall. This wasn't her plan, going to the apartment of some guy she'd met at a food co-op. They'd worked their volunteer shift in the storeroom, a dim space in the back of the store that smelled of cinnamon, incense, and cheese. His muscular arm looked impressive slicing through a giant wheel of cheddar with a large knife. Her job was to wrap each oily wedge in plastic, weigh it, and write out the price on a sticker. They got into a contest to see who could guess the weight, and he won every time. This wasn't his first shift weighing cheeses. And he made some bad cheese-cutting jokes in his thick Vermont accent. Laughter rose like an uncomfortable bubble in her chest. She hadn't laughed in months. Her husband was more likely to give a lecture on the fart joke in Joyce's *A Portrait of the Artist* than to find humor in what he called "our human corporeality". When the shift ended, Matt said, "Hey, there's a singer at the church this evening. She's pretty good. Want to stop in?" He peeled off his latex gloves and carried the knife over to the sink.

"Maybe? If it won't run too late. I have work tomorrow." She knew she needed to meet people in town. Make friends. The other staff at the college development office were all her mother's age. Dim light from the window in the back of the co-op lit him from behind. His hair and beard looked like a red halo; his face was in shadow. The only things she knew about him were that he made her laugh and—judging from his accent—he was a local. He knew too much about her already. She'd spent the afternoon spilling her story about leaving her husband.

Howie was probably in their apartment in East Cambridge. His last text to her had a crying emoji. To be honest, she didn't believe he was crying at all. The days of believing him were over after she found him one evening in a Starbucks playing mahjong on his phone. It was weird that this game, which her grandmother played at the senior center, click-clacking tiles with her friends, was now popular as an iPhone app. Howie always bragged he'd never go to Starbucks because they overroasted the beans. For weeks he had lied to her saying he was working every evening with classmates on a team project. The next week she found out he had dropped out of school altogether, which meant his loans would come due and they'd lose his student health insurance.

The sound of Matt and the dog bounding up the stairs brought her back to the present. She fiddled with her shirt making sure the V-neck was centered.

"Just a sec, I'll put her in the utility room." Matt shoved the water dish and dog food behind a door off the kitchen. Brandy followed, wagging her tail.

Matt got out two mugs, filled them with water from the sink, and tapped powder from packets of hot chocolate into them. Then he stuck them in the microwave. They came out with drips of chocolate down the sides and undissolved lumps floating on the surface. He topped off each mug with a large shot of rum. She took one sip, then put it down on the red Formica table.

He tapped a pack of cigarettes and slid out two. He put both in his mouth and lit them. Then he placed one between her lips.

She put it, still lit, into the old pie tin sitting on the table full of butts.

"I don't smoke," she said.

"Yeah, you do."

"What makes you say that?"

He took her hand. "The smell on your jacket."

"Must be from you." She left her hand in his. "I quit a year ago. My husband hated it."

He grinned. "Well, tonight you're going to unquit."

"Maybe just one," she said. She slid her hand from his and put the cigarette back between her lips, drew in the smoke, and coughed. Her eyes watered. Matt leaned back in his chair and chuckled.

Then, she took a long smooth draw and exhaled a perfect smoke ring.

"Neat trick." He grinned and answered with a ring of his own. They sat drinking the cocoa and blowing smoke rings across the table, trying to pass one ring through the other, but the air currents didn't work out. She giggled at each failed attempt. After he took his last sip, he reached over and took the cigarette from her hand and stubbed it out. Then he led her by the wrist toward the bedroom. Her head was spinning from the rum, which was stronger than she realized.

It was hard for her to know if the warm feeling in her pelvis was want or fear. Let go, she thought. Enjoy. She let herself embrace him. His kisses tasted of smoke.

But then she remembered that she wasn't prepared. "I don't have protection. We can't do this."

He smirked. "Me neither. But it's okay, we can do all the other things." He led her toward the bed. The sheets weren't particularly fresh, but it was cozy under the quilt. She peeled off everything except her socks and lay down. He nudged his muscular legs between hers and balanced his weight over her. Soon he had one of her hands in his, pinned to the mattress, and his other hand between her legs, stroking. He studied her face and smiled as she flushed and squirmed. Then he shifted his weight and kissed her ear.

"Too loud." She laughed to show she was enjoying it and to make sure he didn't think she was criticizing his kiss. He took her other hand and pinned that to the bed as well. She felt something prodding between her legs and realized his fingers weren't down there.

"Wait, get off." She wrenched her hands from his grip and rolled out from under him.

He put his hands up in a gesture of surrender and laughed. "We can slow down."

She gathered up her clothes, ran out the door into the hall, and dressed on the rag rug, fumbling with buttons and zippers, hoping no one would see her on the landing. Brandy's barks echoed in the hallway.

He yelled from the bedroom, "Wait. Aren't you gonna kiss me good night?"

As she ran down the steps, she heard him yell, "Cunt."

The sidewalks were slippery, and she was too dizzy to walk, so she stumbled away as fast as she could. Her chest expanded with relief each time she looked back and he wasn't there. A few blocks away, her legs folded under her. She collapsed onto the sidewalk and shivered, not feeling the cold.

Amy Beth Sisson is sheltering in a small town outside of Philly. Her poetry has appeared in Cleaver Magazine *and* The Night Heron Barks. *Her fiction has appeared in* Enchanted Conversation *and* Sweet Tree Review. *Her nonfiction for children has appeared in* Highlight's High Five *and* Fun for Kidz *magazines.*

How to Walk across the Beach: A Simple 66-Step Guide

Nicholas Puntel

1. Smuggle some clear vodka in oversized water bottles in the trunk of your friend's car.
    a. Warning: do not proceed unless under twenty-one years of age.
2. Bubble with envy that he's cool enough to drive across NJ alone with vodka in his car.
3. Feel stupid.
4. Laugh at yourself, maybe.
5. Enjoy the sound of his tires crunching the pebble bed of the driveway when he arrives.
6. Ask to see the vodka.
7. Watch him open the trunk to show you, like it's contraband.
    a. Technically, it *is* contraband.
8. Invite him inside, awkwardly.
9. Eat doughy spaghetti lathered in cheese with him and your family.
10. Watch him make awkward conversation with your family.
11. Wonder how you will talk to *your* kids' friends when *you* have kids.
12. Debate having kids, briefly.
13. Have kids (in a decade or two).
14. Realize having kids might be extra complicated for you.

15. Have kids anyway, moron.
16. Feel your stomach stretch around all the food.
    a. Like a snake that swallowed a squirrel.
17. Leave at five thirty with your friend.
18. Drive in his car to the empty parking lot of Carnival Pizza.
19. Retrieve the vodka.
20. Fumble with the heavy bottles like a moron.
21. Spill some on the pavement and briefly panic.
22. Watch for cops.
    a. As though the cops give a shit about you.
23. Drink.
24. Drive to the boardwalk.
    a. Too many people. People suck. You hate crowds.
25. Drink.
26. Climb up the big wooden ramp.
27. Smell the sand, even though it's cliché.
    a. Is it cliché?
    b. Why are you always wondering if things are cliché?
28. Wander the boards.
29. Drink.
30. Smell some decadent salt-soaked boardwalk french fries.
31. Crave those french fries, even though your stomach is already caked with pasta.
32. Buy pizza instead.
    a. No, not from Carnival Pizza.
33. Realize the pizza slice is larger than your face.
    a. Warning: the pizza slice *must* be larger than your face.
34. Find a pavilion and nibble at the pizza.
35. Wash it down with vodka.
36. Watch the sun slide under the horizon.
37. Discuss your first year of college.

     a. He says he's not a virgin anymore.
38. Bubble with envy.
39. Drink.
40. Discuss sex.
41. Wonder if you should come out to him.
42. Don't. Not yet.
43. Drink.
44. Wander out onto the sand.
45. Discuss porn.
46. Discuss sex.
47. Drink.
48. Wonder if you should come out to him.
49. Don't. Does it even matter?
     a. Probably.
50. Find a lifeguard station and sit on the bench together.
51. Realize the bench is tougher than marble.
     a. The bench is tougher than granite.
     b. The bench is tougher than stoichiometry.
     c. The bench is tougher than coming out.
     d. Well, maybe not.
52. Watch the winds shuffle the sand.
53. Watch the moon.
54. Discuss porn again.
     a. The most fucked-up thing he's watched is "brother-sister stuff".
55. Want to share your own fucked-up thing, but you don't understand your own gayness yet.
     a. And besides, you haven't come out to him yet.
56. Wonder if you should come out to him.
57. Come out to him.
     a. He doesn't expect it.
     b. Well, you're not very obvious about things.
58. Listen to him support your gayness.
     a. What a strange phenomenon.
59. Feel your nerves unwind from around your throat.
     a. He's supportive!

      b. I mean, are you surprised? He's a college student.
      c. No, but . . .
60. Feel strange and happy in equal quantities.
      a. Your stomach bubbles.
      b. You can never go back. Now you're officially a gay.
      c. He will now always know that you're a gay.
      d. The gay genie is out of the gay bottle.
61. Listen to him ask about your parents.
62. Tell him that you've not come out to them yet.
63. Listen to him worry if they'll be accepting.
      a. Of course, they will be. They live in a blue county.
64. Nonetheless, bubble with fear at the prospect.
65. Get up.
66. Walk across the beach.

Nicholas Puntel is a graduate student of creative writing at Temple University, working toward an MFA. He was born and raised in greater Philadelphia, where he still lives with his family and, more importantly, his two dogs.

The Wingman: A Philadelphia Story

Melissa Strong

The bouncer waved me through as I entered, even as I reached for my ID beneath the "WE CARD EVERYONE!" sign. My symmetrical haircut and lack of tattoos made me look conspicuous—and old. This crusty hipster bar seemed to attract seekers of a specific South Street experience, with its loud music and vegan cheese fries. It could be authentic, or a parody of itself. Like hipsters. Like South Street.

I chose an empty seat among the laughers and the drinkers I hoped would give me a chance. As I shrugged off the bulk of my coat, an enthusiastic discussion began to escalate at the end of the bar. One debater had receding dyed-blue hair. The other's button-covered hoodie betrayed office-worthy attire.

"Jesus was a douchebag!" cried the one with dyed hair.

His friend played along. There were accusations aplenty, if few audible rationales. Could walking on water constitute a desperate grab for attention?

Meanwhile, I sat by myself, the only one drinking alone. There were couples to my left and at tables nearby and groups of three with Jenga and nachos, all talking to each other over the music. Funny how this transforms solitude from the familiar ease of a fleece pullover into a too-tight pair of jeans. Yet there is something like home in the discomfort of not belonging. I moved to Philadelphia from a college town in the homogeneous middle South, a place I didn't want to be. The feeling was mutual.

But I had brought a secret weapon to that South Street bar: my tarot deck. Tarot, I hoped, would be my blue hair and my wingman of sorts. Arranging the cards atop the bar would start conversation, I reasoned. I also imagined I could exchange tarot readings for drinks. This was the South Street experience I sought, a dare to myself. I shuffled the cards, formed the cross and the ladder, turned their faces up, willing it to happen.

I waited, reading my own cards again and again.

The bartender noticed. First, he gravitated toward the increasingly loud heresy, interrupting its potential disturbance to offer another round. The subsequent appearance of two full glasses turned down the debate's volume. Next, the bartender materialized before me.

"Are those tarot cards? Can you read them?" He wore small, round turquoise studs in both ears, and he looked me in the eye. "Will you read mine? I'll buy you a drink."

Before I could, a man and a woman entered together. She plumped into the seat beside me, carrying a stack of fliers. I could smell her perfume, softer than her looks.

"Are you the manager?" she asked the bartender. "What's your name?"

"Adrian."

"Yo, Adrian!" she exclaimed.

"Never heard that one before," he deadpanned, setting a martini before her.

She spoke with Adrian, animated, while her date leaned uncertainly on the chair beside her. Adrian took one of her fliers. Fascinated, I tried to watch with my eyes on the cards.

The woman turned to me. Her top was cut low. Silvery glitter sparkled on her bare skin. The man hovered nearby in a baseball hat and jeans.

"Tarot! You have to read my cards! His too! But mine first!"

Her name was Lisa. His was Kevin. I let her tell me about their Bumble date. They had met just a few hours ago. Lisa was gregarious and loud. Kevin was not. And I am soft-spoken. They both struggled to hear me over the Deftones. I asked questions, something I do so well it can become a game. A game of the appearance of conversation, for one player, to see how long others will speak until they realize they should ask a question in return. Often the conversation ends first.

Lisa was an entrepreneur. Kevin worked in remodeling. Neither lived in the city. Watching first dates unfold is a singular entertainment, and a touching one. Kevin seemed both game for and bewildered by his date with Lisa, and I recognized the performative nature of her sociable persona, fragility hovering just below. Here were two people searching, hoping. Did they know what they were looking for? Sometimes I believe most of us don't.

With my tarot deck, I offered a mode of connection between Kevin and Lisa, mediating between the virtual possibilities of a dating app and the reality of two strangers together at the bar on a Sunday evening. I was a buffer, with an amusing activity. The cards drew the couple to me, drawing me out of solitude. Maybe the cards could bring them closer together.

I shuffled and explained how it works: Ask the cards a question, one you can share with me. The question cannot have a yes or no answer. Lisa wanted to ask a yes-or-no question. I helped her rephrase it, shuffled again, and showed her how to select from the deck the cards that would answer. My jacket, practically the size of another person, kept slipping off the back of my seat. Kevin reached down to pick it up every time. Anyone could tell what Lisa wanted to hear. I crafted a reassuring narrative from the symbols and archetypes, the Seven of Cups pouring out possibilities in work and love. She cheered and snapped a photo of the cards.

Kevin was next. I shuffled again and asked him about his job. He was a little sheepish but matter-of-fact. A family business. His ex's family. I recognized the candor of trauma and survival, wondering if Lisa was a survivor too or just surviving. I thought of the Three of Swords and its trio of daggers piercing a heart, waiting for the storm to break.

"You'll never guess what I do," I said to Kevin.

He tried. "Accountant?"

I might have winced. I told him that I am a professor at Community College of Philadelphia. I did not tell him that this job has given me superpowers. Besides grading essays faster than a speeding bullet, I divine what others want to say when they can't find the words and diffuse tensions with pirate jokes. Now Kevin had joined my experiment to test these powers beyond 17th and Spring Garden.

We were startled by a thudding sound behind us. Heads turned. Someone had tripped on the stairs. Heads turned away. I glanced down at the cards, certain I could keep it up at this bar as long as I wanted. Instead, I looked back to the stairs. A dispute unfolded between the bouncer and a younger man. The young man's date had fallen on the steep stairs. She had not stood up. Shouting ensued. If the shaken young woman truly was unhurt, she could not remain on the landing. The bouncer, doing his job to squelch disruption, wanted to preserve the authority necessary for his position. What did the boyfriend want? What upset him? I saw this clearly.

I raced over, darting between the boyfriend and the bouncer to crouch beside the young woman on the landing. I gathered her purse and her phone, brushed the hair out of her face. She and her date immediately relaxed. It was like an eye-rolling icebreaker in an eight a.m. class, one of those questions students love, or love to hate: What is your theme song? Where would you travel in time? If you had a superpower, what would it be? The girl on the stairs needed a kind hand. The boy simply wished someone would help him help his date.

A switch flipped. The shouting ceased; the bouncer stepped away. The young couple left quietly.

I returned to my seat at the bar, remembering the story of a UArts professor who hugged a student looking for a fight. I could never do that, I thought. And yet I just had. I saw now that the hug takes all the fight out, at least some of the time. Tonight, I was not a third wheel but an intermediary, bringing people together or pulling them apart as they needed. A new kind of wingman.

Lisa expressed her astonishment at my intervention, swift and effective. "You look so meek!"

Like an accountant? A singular advantage in preventing a fight. A table opened up, and Lisa claimed it. She invited me to join her and Kevin, but he wanted to be alone with her now. I pulled on my puffy coat and walked the six blocks and three flights of stairs back to my apartment.

A week later, I described these events to my oldest friend over dinner in Manhattan. I had read her cards. She knew why I had brought the deck, the reasons I wrote stories like this one, telling and retelling to craft narrative and find meaning. But despite knowing me nearly thirty years, she had not expected my tarot-reading bar scheme.

"Do you believe in it?" asked a former student, when I shared my wingman story over falafel sandwiches on Market Street during spring break. I had read tarot cards at the bar while my students worked and slept, while my colleagues stayed home with sick children.

"Believe in what?"

"Tarot."

"It isn't something to believe in," I explained. "It's a tool. You can use tarot to uncover what you already know but don't see."

You can use what you learn to find the story. To build

bridges. To soothe disputes about grades, Jesus, bar security. To challenge preconceptions. To persuade people to give you a chance, no matter the differences between. To make a space for yourself. To make human connections in this gritty city.

Melissa Strong (she/her) is an English professor at Community College of Philadelphia and the author of American Lit Remixed: Music in Twenty-First-Century American Literature. *She writes about dance for* Broad Street Review *and about film for* Moviejawn. *She lives in Center City.*

Lilith and Adam

Kathleen Murphey

In the beginning, God created heaven and earth, light, the separation of the land from the water, vegetation, the stars, the birds, the creatures of the earth, and the fish and sea creatures. Then God made humankind in God's own image, female and male, and God gave them dominion over the earth and all vegetation and its fruits, all the creatures of the air, of the land, and of the seas. God was pleased with God's creations. God blessed them and said that God's creation of them was good. God bade them to be fruitful and multiply; it was the end of the sixth day.

    Left alone, she turned to him and asked, "What do we call each other?"

    "Do you want me to name you?" he asked.

    "No, I think we should name ourselves." She hesitated and looked herself over. She ran sounds around in her mind; she mouthed some to herself, testing how they sounded to herself. "I am Lilith," she said finally.

    "Lilith?" he said, testing it out himself. "It sounds pretty. What do you think of Adam?" he asked. Plainly he had been exploring possibilities himself.

    "Adam?" she said. She smiled at him. "I like it." He smiled back.

    "What do we do now?" he asked.

    "It's getting dark. Most of the animals have quieted. Perhaps we should too," she said.

He held out his hand to her in invitation, and she clasped her hand around his. They walked around considering resting spots. They found a stand of pine trees with a bed of pine needles beneath them. They lay down together and snuggled together. Lilith ran her hands over his body, and Adam ran his over hers. They hadn't really understood what God had meant when God said be fruitful and multiply, but suddenly they did. Fully joined they could produce life.

Their mouths met in exploration and desire. Their hands continued to course over each other. Her breasts were so different from his, so full and round and perfect. Her nipples seemed as sensitive as his, turning hard and erect under his touch or tongue, like his did at her touch. Her hips moved, echoing a response he wanted to make himself, but they called to him, and he moved his hand between her legs and touched her, gently at first, and then she urged him further. He touched her—her nipple and her clitoris. She urged him on; her moaning caused desire to course through him. Some part of him wanted to ram her with his throbbing penis, but he knew that would be base and could hurt her. She cried out in pleasure, and he thought he might climax himself as her body convulsed in the wake of her pleasure.

She pulled him over her, and happily, he moved over her, holding himself above her. She helped him move his penis into her. She gasped as he touched her there. "Am I hurting you?" he asked, pulling back.

"No," she whispered, "it is just so sensitive after. Slowly," she murmured.

It was excruciatingly painful and yet the most natural command in the world. He entered her slowly. She braced herself—assuring him it didn't hurt but was just still so sensitive. When he was fully inside her and she was used to the feel of him, she rocked her hips and kissed him.

"It is okay now," she whispered into his ear, and he thrust himself into her, softly at first but then with building momentum. She wrapped her legs around him and touched his nipples, and he spurted into her. He lay over her for a moment, savoring their joining. He moved off her and lay down on his back, and she fitted herself against him—her head nestling his shoulder, her one arm stroking his chest, her one leg draping over his. "It was good, very good," he thought abstractedly, and then he thought no more but drifted off to sleep in her arms.

They woke in the morning urgent to relieve themselves. The sound of the river called them, and they went. They did their business in the water and then turned to each other. He kissed and stroked her, and she kissed and stroked him. Somehow he realized that the water changed things for their joining, and she seemed to understand, too. He brought her to orgasm in the shallow water, but then she pulled them into the deeper water and wrapped her arms around his neck and her legs around his waist. She was so light in the water. The lips of her vagina were as swollen as they were the first time, but the slippery wetness from her orgasm was lost in the water. She helped guide his penis, but it took a lot longer to get inside her comfortably. Once he was though, it was great, like before but different. It was so easy to move her up and down, and she moved too. He came quickly, crying out, and she relaxed against him. Her legs slid down his, and she stood in the water in front of him, resting her head against his chest. They were still joined, but his penis was contracting, and he slipped out of her. The nice part about making love in the water was that the water washed away the aftersex—not that it was bad, but it was sticky.

They left the river and looked around them. Lilith pointed out that birds and squirrels were eating the fruit that had fallen on the ground by a small tree. The fruit was a golden yellow color, full and round at the bottom and narrower at the top where the fruits attached to the tree. They picked some fruit from the tree. Some were hard and rather tasteless, but the softer fruits were fragrant and juicy and sweet. Pears would be a good name for them they decided. Their bellies full of pears, they sat watching the world around them. They watched fascinated as two squirrels chased each other. The one mounted the other, and Lilith and Adam realized that they were making love to each other. It was so different from what they had done, so fast and fleeting, the minimum of contact. Lilith seemed to find it distasteful, but Adam was curious.

"I am glad we don't do it like that," she said. "I like touching you and you touching me." She ran her hand over his chest and leaned over to kiss him. He kissed her back but kept his thoughts to himself.

They explored more of the world around them. They found another fruit tree. Adam liked the name peach for the round, cleft fruits. "They remind me of something," he teased her, running his hand lightly over the cleft between her buttocks.

"No, more like yours," she teased right back, "fuzzy," and she ran her hand over his left buttock.

They started kissing and touching and exploring. "Can we try something?" she asked breathlessly in his ear.

"Yes," he answered back, part of his mind thinking that he had some moves he wanted to try as well. To his surprise, she pushed him flat on his back and straddled him. He laughed and reached for her nipples. She moaned as he touched her. She moved her hips, and he pulled her down a little, so he could pleasure her with his tongue. She came—he could feel it build, her orgasm, and then radiate out, her body shuddering and convulsing with the power of it. When it was over, she moved down his body and helped guide his penis into her. Slowly, she moved over him, overcoming the hypersensitivity of her vagina and accustoming herself to his being fully inside her.

"Help me," she said quietly, and he grabbed her hips with his hands and helped rock her back and forth over him. He came quickly. When he cried out and released himself into her, she stilled and then moved off him and snuggled into his side. They dozed and woke sometime later to the squawking of a pair of geese making love. The male, bigger and more colorful, was mounted on top of the female, who was smaller and less colorful.

"I want to try it like that, next time," he said when he realized that she was awake, stroking her face lightly. She frowned but didn't say anything. They explored the world around them more and found a sheltered place to sleep as dusk came.

In the morning, they went to the river again to wash and relieve themselves. They kissed in the water, but then Adam led her out of the water. They lay down in a patch of soft grass, and Adam kissed her and touched her until he made her come. Then he pulled her up to her knees and went behind her on his knees as well. He pushed her down so that she was on her hands and knees, and then he pressed against her, his penis finding its way into her from the different angle. He was slow and careful at first, but once he was fully inside her, he found that the position allowed him to thrust into her in a way that he had not been able to do before. The power of it surprised him; he liked the feeling it gave him. It wasn't tender or gentle; their flesh slapped against each other. It was different than before. The non-face-to-faceness of it allowed him to concentrate on his pleasure only, and he came spurting into her. She pulled herself away from him, and he lowered himself onto the grass. She lay beside him, but she didn't touch him or snuggle against him. He looked at her; she was looking at him in a funny way.

"I liked it," he said, finally.

"I didn't," she answered back. "I like it better when we touch." She reached out her hand and touched his chest to emphasize the point.

"We *were* touching," he said testily.

"You know what I mean, Adam. I like looking at you and having you look at me. I like feeling your chest against mine." She paused, struggling to articulate what she was feeling. "It is more tender, more human," she added.

"The animals all seem to do it that way. Maybe that's the way all creatures are supposed to do it," he said defensively.

"We haven't seen all the animals yet, and I am not an animal. I am a human being who was made in the image of God, in the image of the divine. I will make love like a human being."

He was filled with a sudden anger. "You are *mine*," he said, grabbing her wrist, "and if I want to make love like that, we will," he said savagely.

She ripped her wrist out of his grasp and sat up. "I am not yours. I am my own person. God made both of us at the same time and in God's own image. We are equals and partners, Adam. Surely, you see that, don't you?" she asked.

He wouldn't meet her gaze. He realized that he could make her. He was stronger than she was. He could make her do anything he wanted, but then what would that do to relations between them? If he hurt her, would she hate him? Would she ever let him touch her again?

"Adam?" she called. He looked at her then and saw the wary expression on her face.

"Yes," he said to placate her, "partners. Let's look for some food." They found a tree with round, shiny red fruits that Lilith called apples. They ate their fill, and as evening came, they found shelter and made love. He made her come and then rose over her to find his own release. If she wasn't on her knees, then at least he was on top, he thought to himself. After he climaxed, they drifted to sleep wrapped in each other's arms.

The next morning, they went to the river as usual. After their assorted toiletries, they went to the soft grassy patch again, and he was filled with the desire to make love to her the same way as the day before.

"I want to do it again like we did yesterday," he whispered, kissing her neck and stroking her body.

He felt her body stiffen, and she pulled away from him slightly, looking at him and saying, "I don't."

"I can make you," he said.

"You wouldn't," she said, pulling completely away from him.

The look on her face of complete horror made him hesitate. But the male animals all compelled the females into sex—why should they be any different? He grabbed her wrists. "Kneel," he commanded.

She struggled against him, but he was stronger. She

wouldn't kneel, so he pushed her down on her back in the grass. He tried to kiss her, but she bit him. He forced her legs apart with his. She begged him to stop, struggling against him the whole time. He let go of her wrist for a moment to slap her in an attempt to get her to stop struggling. She started crying but continued to struggle against him. She begged him to stop. He hadn't meant it to be like this at all, but there could be no tenderness now. She wouldn't let him touch her; there would be no pleasure for her in this act, he realized. He held her immobile as he pushed his penis into her.

"You're hurting me. Please, Adam, stop. Don't do this," she cried over and over, but he didn't stop. Her tears angered him. He climaxed and was stupid enough to relax against her. She bit his cheek savagely. He jerked away from her. The blood ran from his cheek to her breast. He slapped her again.

She whimpered for a moment and then said, "Get off of me, you filthy beast, you demon," in a voice that chilled him to the bone. He still had her pinned beneath him. He looked at her and could see nothing but anger and hatred in her eyes and in the cold expression on her face. What had he done? He was filled with apprehension. If he let go of her, she might try to hurt him. He wondered suddenly how badly he had hurt her.

"You're *mine*," he said again in some illogical way that tried to justify what he had done to her and to himself.

She glared at him. "I have never been less yours, you brute. I hate you."

"There is no one else. You're stuck with me, Lilith, mine," he hissed at her.

"Let me go," she hissed back. "I wish to wash the stain of you from me."

He was shocked by the words and tone of them; for her, his seed had turned from something good to something polluting, foul, and dirty. He felt a deep sense of shame. He moved off of her and then released her. He left her alone and wandered to the pear tree and collected some of the fruit. At first, he waited for her to join him. But she didn't, so he ate alone. When she still didn't appear, he went looking for her, but he couldn't find her. At dusk, she still hadn't appeared, and he spent a fitful night worried about what had happened to her.

In the morning, there was still no sign of Lilith. He searched everywhere they had ever gone, but there was no trace of her. After days, he was forced to conclude that she had chosen to leave him—that what he had done to her was so unforgivable that she would rather live and die alone than be subject to his brutality. "Beast", "demon", and "brute" she had called him; she had asked him to make love to her as a human being, and instead of rising to that higher nature, he had descended to the crudest form of joining possible, his pleasure the only measure of the act, and so he had lost her forever. He felt the most devastating sense of loss for both of them; they would never be whole again, and he wept for their loss.

Kathleen Murphey is an associate professor of English at Community College of Philadelphia. She has been a full-time faculty member there since 2002 and taught part-time at CCP for several years before that. She has had a play performed in Philadelphia and artwork displayed at City Hall.

Red Flags

Jamila Beale

Reading Suzanne Collins's *Catching Fire* isn't as interesting as watching the clock.

Hass, a college friend, messaged me on Facebook a couple of days ago saying he was in Philly and wanted to hang out. I was so happy. I immediately said, "Yeah." The last time a guy asked me out was months ago.

We had been among a handful of other blacks entering the Behavioral and Sciences College. He was the partier type—he'd show up hours late for a study session but somehow still managed to get a decent grade.

Now he's late for our date. Is he even coming?

I check my phone for the fifth time in the last ten minutes—still no calls or text messages. His last text said, "I'll be late," and that was sent three hours ago. I got tired of pacing back and forth from my living room to the front window, so I retreated to my room. Part of me is hopeful he will still show up. I'm so confused.

We've been talking on the phone over these past couple of days, and he's even hinted at wanting more than just friendship. We have so much in common. We graduated from Penn State, we both pledged a black Greek letter organization, and we majored in the medical field. Still, we've never hung out alone before. I've only known him to be the funny guy, especially among friends or large groups. Maybe Hass is the one? So far, it's not looking good.

Being single is the worst, especially when all your besties have boyfriends. Everyone has plans on Friday night except you. It's just sad when date night becomes watching Netflix on the couch with your parents. I've been praying for God to send me a loyal, ambitious man who can hold a decent conversation.

I hear my phone buzz. It's a message from Hass. "On my way." Instantly, my heart beats faster.

Hass lives in Cincinnati. The last time we saw each other was three years ago. Earlier in the evening, I narrowed it down to three SZA-inspired outfits and finally settled on some high-waist tribal shorts and a tight black T-shirt for our date. I'm sure these chocolate legs will keep his eyes on me. Plus, I spent eight hours in a chair yesterday getting these Senegalese braids and my nails done. I hope he appreciates the effort.

Finally he's outside my house. Through the window, I watch him squeeze out of a purple car. He's gained a considerable amount of weight. Think "freshman forty". And what in the hell does he have on? He has taken casual wear to another level. A striped long-sleeved flannel shirt with floral-printed Bermuda shorts! And are those brown . . . penny loafers?! We're going to Six Flags, not a church.

"Fee! Fee!" Fee, short for Felicia, he calls me when I open the door. "I'm so happy to see you!"

I'm so happy he's finally arrived. I smile tightly and invite him inside.

"You're late. And what do you have on?" I ask while lacing my boots.

"My fault. My aunt wanted me to meet with some of her friends this morning." He sits down on the love seat. "These are the only chill clothes I packed."

I put my Coach bag across my body and grab a sweater.

"Let's go. We're already late."

Before getting on the road, we make a pit stop at the mini-mart. I suggest Hass purchase a white T-shirt, so he won't be hot in the park. He does as he's told, and as long as you're not looking at his feet or his ashy ankles, he looks a heck of a lot better.

I offer to drive after he says he's tired. He takes me up on it. I am hoping we'll spend the time catching up on the last three years. Ten minutes into the car ride, he falls asleep like a big baby.

We arrive at Six Flags Great Adventure four hours behind schedule, and he still hasn't said much. Perhaps he's nervous?

"I come to Six Flags at least two times a year. Do you like roller coasters?" I ask.

"I like you," he says, swallowing my hand in his.

When was the last time a man held my hand? Darnell, the ring bearer. We held hands at my cousin's wedding. Darnell's hands were soft and kind. *What happened to him?* Hass's hand is firm, like he is leading me through a dense jungle, instead of the parking lot, and doesn't want us to get separated. I like it. What does he like about me?

I can think of a hundred questions to ask Hass right now, but apparently he can't think of one. He hasn't even said anything about my hair.

As we near the park gates, I ask, "Do you like the med schools in Philly?"

"The schools are cool, but they're all in the ghetto."

What an ass. "The ghetto" is a code word for "black", and there is nothing wrong with living and learning among black people.

Before I can check his ignorance, though, Hass freezes like a statue right in front of the park gates. He closes his eyes and moves his head. George Clinton's "Atomic Dog" is blasting on the park's loudspeakers. "Atomic Dog" is Hass's fraternity song. Back when it was played at one of their parties in college, all the members started dancing.

"Bow wow wow yippee yo yippee yay . . . Bow wow yippee yo yippee yay."

I let go of his hand and step out from under his six-foot frame, so he can clearly see my glaring eyes. "Not now!" I tell him. "We have to purchase our tickets."

He sways his arms and strolls in a circle. His loafers make it sound like he is tap-dancing as he jumps, spins, and clasps his hands under his legs. When he turns into a dog, I draw the line. Crawling on the ground, sticking out his tongue, and wagging his "tail" is absolutely unacceptable. I leave and wait in the shade.

I doubt he even knows I left. Visitors are stopping. I would be curious too if I saw a large black man pretending to be a dog at an amusement park. I'm not embarrassed. I'm more annoyed at his lack of interest in me. Suddenly I see the two red flags waving: first, he was late; now his immaturity is showing.

It feels like an eternity before the song ends. Hass gets off the ground and howls toward the sun like a beagle. A few people clap. He then realizes I'm still here.

"What? You ready to go inside?" he says, out of breath, with sweat dripping from his face.

"Hasson, are you ready? Because dogs are not allowed."

"Bye, Felicia."

My eyes roll so hard I feel them reach the back of my head, and I walk past him toward the ticket line.

Hass is following behind me, apologizing. I decide to forgive him. I will be a good friend and show him my favorite amusement park, but that last comment has landed him permanently in the "friend zone". I pay for my ticket, he pays for his, and we enter the park.

"First stop, Movie Town," I tell him.

Feeling the wind whip my face on the Batman roller coaster makes me feel fearless, like I can tackle anything, even this slow date. We take pictures, making silly faces along Gotham City with Batman and the Joker. I shut down Hass's attempt to hold my hand again.

After bumper cars and burgers in Frontier Alley, we head to the boardwalk for carnival games. Hass doesn't want to play any games. He wants to whine about me not holding his hand.

There is one particular game I play every time I visit Six Flags: the ring toss. It's hard to land a ring on the neck of those bottles, but the prizes are the best. And there's no disappointment today, with a large Pikachu on display. I spend ten dollars on a bucket of thirty rings. Hass claims he's won this game before, but he loses over half of my rings! I lose too.

We are now waiting inside the train car to ride the best wooden roller coaster in the world, El Toro. There is one problem—the car bar won't lock down on our seat because of Hass's colossal frame. No matter how hard we push the bar down, it will not lock. I decide I can ride by myself, just as one of the ride operators arrives to assist us.

But he can't lower the restraint bar either. The operator calls for backup. Should we even be riding if it takes two operators to secure us in a ride? Hass isn't concerned.

"On the count of three, we'll push down really hard, and you suck in your stomach," the first operator says to Hass.

"One, two, three!"

At the count of three, the bar clicks—and Hass lets out a huge, loud fart! I'm sure the people waiting on the platform heard it as well. I'm so disgusted I can't even laugh.

"Thanks!" he says.

No "excuse me", no acknowledgment, nothing at all from him. Even after the operators leave without a word. There's nothing but silence. I scoot as far away as possible from him and tilt my head outside the car to breathe because the odor is so bad. It smells like hot greens and ass. I'm ready to go home.

After El Toro, we head for my car. Hass wants to go out for drinks, but there will be no after party.

"Sorry, I already made plans," I tell him.

"With who?" His first real question of the day.

"Suzanne Collins."

For ten years, Jamila Beale has worked as a program manager and aerospace, electrical, and computer engineer for the Department of Defense. Her great passion is writing and sharing stories that are both real, interesting, and inspiring. She believes that life is a great teaching moment. She was born and raised in West Philadelphia, and all her stories include a piece of her African American culture and upbringing.

Bliss

Merry Jones

Snip. Snip. Snipsnipsnip snip.

Stan was clipping his toenails. Of course he was, even here. Even now. No one clipped toenails more often than Stan.

I lay back on the ornate comforter, my jaws tightening with each clack of the clipper. *Snip snip.* I grabbed the remote, turned on the large flat-screen TV to drown the sound, not caring what the program was.

Snip. I scratched my arms. Wanted to fly out of my skin. To escape. *Clackclackclack.* Oh God. Eight more nails to go. No one but Stan clipped so much—at least seven clips per toenail. Why? Why couldn't he just clip off the whole nail at once? Why was he so damned ineffective? Inefficient even at positioning toenail clippers. I covered my ears to smother the sound, but I could feel it, vibrating the too thin walls. *Clack. Clack.* Christ. I pushed a down pillow against my ears. Closed my eyes. Began counting. One Mississippi, two Mississippi.

At forty, I stopped. Cautiously removed the pillow. Listened. Waited.

Thank God. No more clipping. But now, the water was running.

Which meant he was about to gargle.

There was no way to escape Stan's noises and habits. Over the last ten years, they'd penetrated my mind. Hell, they'd entered my skin, my bones, and viscera. I knew Stan's routines, predictable, unshakable, unvaried, and maddening.

Not just in the bathroom. Anywhere. Stan didn't deviate. Ever. Chewing with his mouth open. Bouncing his knee when he sat. Jingling coins as he waited. Even breathing too loud. Whistling "Zip-a-Dee-Doo-Dah" when he was cheerful. Stan was achingly paralyzingly numbingly predictable. And he would be. Forever.

But maybe I was being too harsh. After all, the man was making an effort, bringing me to this extravagant hotel, surprising me. Even though he'd made the plans only after our fight, just to prove me wrong.

"Predictable?" His nostrils had flared. As always after dinner, the kitchen table had vibrated with the bouncing of his leg. "You think I'm predictable?"

"I don't think it. You are." I'd braced myself for the wet squeak of air sucking through his front teeth. Stan's habit when he was annoyed.

"What are you saying, Claire?" He'd sucked air. "I'm not exciting enough for you?"

"I didn't say you were unexciting. I said you were predictable. Please stop bouncing your leg."

"Really? After ten years, what would you like?" Air suck. Foot bounce. "What would be unpredictable enough for you?" Suck.

"For God's sake. Stop sucking air through your teeth."

"What?" He'd stopped, midsuck.

He'd stood, shoved his chair away from the table. Oh Lord, he was going to start pacing.

"Predictable, huh?" He'd paced in a circle. "So should I get my nipples pierced? Take up sky-diving—"

"Don't be ridiculous—"

He stopped pacing. "Ridiculous?" Air suck. "Now I'm not just predictable. I'm also ridiculous?"

Finally, I'd told him to forget I'd said anything.

But then, the very next day, he'd surprised me: For our anniversary, he was taking me to the Drake Hotel, where we'd been married, to stay in the very same suite. And to dinner at the restaurant of my dreams at the top of the Stock Exchange building.

I'd been astonished. Stan was normally frugal. "Can we afford this?"

Stan had formed an uncharacteristically wide grin. "It's our tenth anniversary, Claire. We should let go. Do something . . . unpredictable?"

And so, there we were. In Chicago. At the Drake. Spending a wad. Celebrating.

Or in Stan's case, gargling.

My fists pressed into my belly. I should be grateful. Stan made a decent living selling insurance. He was devoted to our son. And he'd made all the plans for this getaway to the very hotel where we'd had our wedding. I sat on the bed, trying to remember. Had he clipped his nails that night? Or gargled? Had sex been better then? Or just newer.

Miraculously, the gargling stopped. Next would be shaving, which, thank God, was silent. But, on TV, *Wheel of Fortune* was starting. Our dinner reservation was in half an hour.

"Stan!" I shouted. "I've got to shower, too. Hurry up!"

"Be right out, honey."

No, he wouldn't. He still had to gel his receding hair. And then, he'd flex. So help me. The man was short, paunchy, forty, and balding, but after every shower, Stan posed in various body builder stances, asking the same question, verbatim: "Not bad for an old guy, right, Claire?"

Ten years. Ten endless, predictable, monotonous years with the most unimaginative, predictable, monotonous man on earth.

Finally, the water was off. The door swung open. Stan stepped out butt naked, adopting a pose. Biceps flexed, head lowered, knees bent. "Not bad for an old guy, right, Claire?"

I pushed past him. If I didn't hurry, we'd lose our dinner reservation. But at last, the bathroom was mine. And the shower was strong. I stood, savoring the solitude, eyes closed, hot water streaming over me, tension easing from my shoulders. I imagined having my own bathroom all the time, being free of coin jingling, flexing, nail clipping. I'd just have to divorce Stan—

When he touched my face, I yelped and reflexively covered my breasts. I hadn't heard him come into the bathroom, let alone the shower. Why—What had happened? Was Junior okay?

"Stan?" I began, but he put a finger on my lips, hushing me, and a kiss—ever so gently on my lips. Water poured over our heads, coating our faces.

His thick wet body pressed against me. Stan's kisses traveled from my lips to my neck to my breasts. He moved slowly, undaunted by the water ruining his hair as his head moved lower and lower.

"Stan—"

"Shhh." His head moved down my belly.

In ten years of marriage, Stan had never done anything like what he was doing then in that shower. He knelt, his arms around my legs, his face buried between my thighs. Oh my. I let out a moan, grabbed Stan's head, and closed my eyes, losing myself in the moment. And then Stan grabbed my knees and stood, pulling my legs up high and out from under me. I fell backward, slammed my head against the rim of the tub. Heard a crack.

"What was that?" I demanded.

He glared at me. "I'm predictable, huh? Was that unpredictable enough for you, Claire? Fat nagging bitch—"

"Fat? You called me fat?"

"Ten years, Claire. Ten years I put up with your nonstop complaining. Nothing—not one thing I ever did was right. Well, I didn't fuck up this time, did I, you ungrateful cow?"

Cow? Really? "You're calling me a cow, you . . . you hairy little orangutan?"

He didn't reply, just got out of the shower.

"Wait! Stan—help me up!"

He didn't. He dried off, hung his towel up.

I was livid. "Stan? Apologize."

But Stan wasn't listening, was busy gargling again.

Sputtering, I struggled to get up. The shower was still running, splashing my face.

Why was it so hard to pull myself up? Was I hurt? Oh God, maybe my neck was broken. Was I paralyzed? "Stan!"

Stan flexed a few times. Then, before he left the bathroom, he turned and winked at me. "Not bad for an old guy, right, Claire?"

"Fuck you," I snarled. Alone, I planned to get even with him. I'd lace his mouthwash with rat poison. I'd put acid in his hair gel. I'd spend every nickel he'd saved. I'd make Stan pay.

But first, I had to sit up. I pulled my way to an upright position from which I assessed my body. My toes wiggled on command. Fingers, too. No broken bones.

Stan was going to be less fortunate. This fat nagging cow was going to cause him serious damage. Carefully, I climbed out of the tub and followed Stan to the bedroom.

"Bastard!" I flew at him, fist aimed at his nose. Stan didn't even flinch when I landed my punch. I didn't get it. I'd hit him so hard that my knuckles reverberated. But he reached for the remote, channel surfing, oblivious.

I slapped him as hard as I could, right across his shiny smooth-shaven face.

No reaction. Nothing.

Absently, Stan whistled "Zip-a-Dee-Doo-Dah".

I'd just assaulted him. His cheek wasn't even red where I'd hit it. And he was happy.

Okay. Something was off.

Someone knocked at the door. "Room service."

Room service? Had to be a mistake. We were going out for dinner. Stan had made reservations.

Stan got up and opened the door. Suddenly I remembered

that—oh God, I'd just come from the shower. I was standing there naked. I ducked back into the bathroom, heard someone ask Stan where to set up dinner.

Stan shushed him. Lowered his voice to explain that dinner was a surprise for "the missus", who was in the shower. In fact, come to think of it, she'd been in there quite a while. Maybe he'd just check on her. Stan's head poked into the bathroom, almost rammed me.

"Room service, Stan? What about our dinner reservations—"

But he didn't look at me.

"Darling? Claire, are you almost—"

Stan stopped midsentence, opened his mouth, and let out a shocking soprano howl. "Claire!" He ran to the shower, reached in. Repeated my name. Whimpered, "Oh God."

I stood immobile. Confused.

What was he doing? I stood beside the sink, watching. "Stan? What's going on?"

He groaned, low and long.

A young man in a hotel uniform raced in and stood behind Stan, gawking. I wrapped my arms around myself, trying to hide my nudity. But the guy didn't even glance at me. He reached into the shower and turned off the water, staring into the tub. Stan crouched there, soaked, rocking back and forth. Hugging a large naked woman.

Who looked just like me.

It couldn't be. And yet, there she was. Stan clung to the sopping thing, its hair all matted and drenched. Its stretch marks and breasts exposed. Everything exposed.

He shouted into its ear, "Claire, Claire! What happened? Did you slip?" He looked at the gaping hotel guy. "The shower floor must be too slippery. She slid and hit her head. Look—back here. It's crushed!"

I felt my head, found a soft spot in the back.

"She was fine, ten minutes ago," Stan blithered on, and finally I understood.

I was dead.

Stan had fucking killed me.

I looked in the mirror. Saw dripping wet brown hair. The dimples in my cheeks, the mole on my neck. I touched my face, felt soft flesh just like always. I looked and felt real. But apparently nobody else saw me.

I flew at Stan, shrieking and clawing.

Stan didn't notice.

The hotel man stammered. "I'll go call . . ."

Stan hovered over the corpse as hotel managers, police, and emergency medical people arrived. When the coroner's people wanted to take the body, he held on tight, squeezing as if he couldn't let go. "It's our anniversary," he cried. "I ordered filet mignon. And Champagne."

"Aha! Liar! You didn't make dinner reservations," I shouted.

Somebody covered Stan's shoulders with a blanket. "I'm so sorry, sir."

Someone else muttered, "What a tragedy. Poor man."

Poor man? What about his poor murdered wife? I wandered through the suite, listening to strangers. "Did you know they got married here? He brought her back for their tenth anniversary."

"How romantic. Sweet guy."

"Tragic. You just never know."

"No. You never do."

Certainly, I never had. I'd never suspected that Stan would lie to me about dinner. Much less have the balls to kill me.

But there it was. Stan wept, honked as he blew his nose, snorted when he sniffed. People coddled him. Gave him whiskey. A doctor was called in case he was in shock.

If anyone was in shock, though, it wasn't Stan. Shocked to the core, I watched my body get zipped into a coroner's bag and rolled out of the room.

So what was I? A ghost? Stan had turned me into a ghost?

I cursed. I fumed.

And finally, I understood about the room service dinner.

Sam had ordered it for the sole purpose of having a witness present when he discovered my body. The trip to Chicago had never been about our wedding anniversary. Stan had planned it just to kill me.

"Coward," I shrieked. "Murderer!"

Stan sipped whiskey, feigning grief. I sat beside him, hissing.

Eventually, the room became silent and dark. No managers. No police. No Stan. No me. My body was gone. Maids came and cleaned, changing the linens. Restocking the minibar. Vacuuming. And then I was alone.

In days that followed, I mostly spent my time thinking up ways to get back at Stan. But everything required skills. I learned to turn on the television, change channels, to work the light switches and the faucet.

But there was one skill I couldn't master. When guests opened the door, I tried to leave with them. But each time, a gust sucked me back as if the room were a vacuum cleaner and I was lint.

Time passed. Seasons changed. But within my suite, all that changed were linens. Everything else remained constant, especially my fury. Stan was free, living his life, raising Junior to clip, gargle, and flex, while I was a prisoner, hungering for revenge, losing hope.

Until one day, the staff brought in flowers and Champagne on ice.

Maids chattered about newlyweds. I remembered me and Stan, how this had been our bridal suite, too.

"It's creepy." Clara dusted the dressers.

"But he stays for free."

"Still, if I were him, you couldn't pay me to come back."

"Especially when he could stay anywhere. After that lawsuit." Katrina tested the remote.

"And the life insurance—"

"Doubled because of some clause."

"Vacuum up those petals—the GM wants everything perfect."

"Fuck the GM." Clara turned on the vacuum.

I dreaded spending the night with newlyweds, so once again, I tried to escape. When she left, I clung to Clara, but at the doorway, I bounced back as if I'd hit a trampoline. Trapped and frustrated, I was plucking petals off flowers when the door swung open.

A radiant blond bride in a lavish gown burst over the threshold.

In the arms of Stan.

That's right. Stan. My Stan. Stan the liar, Stan the killer. With his new wife, a young thing of maybe twenty-five.

She giggled as he dumped her onto the bed in her lavish lace and pearl dress. Giggled as he plopped beside her.

Why was I surprised that he'd bring her here? Hadn't the maids just said Stan could stay free? They'd also said that, between life insurance and a lawsuit against the hotel, my death had made him rich.

I stood, gawking. The bride had implants, blue eye shadow, nails with acrylic tips. And on her left hand, my rings.

I looked at my hand, saw the same exact set. Stan the apparently new millionaire had scrimped, reusing his dead wife's square-cut diamond. They kissed, canoodled. Made chirping sounds. In sex, Stan was as predictable as ever. I stood at the foot of the bed and sucked air through my teeth.

Finally, Stan got up and went into the bathroom, whistling "Zip-a-Dee-Doo-Dah". I jolted back to my senses. Stan was here, within my reach. This was my chance.

I followed him, waiting as he did his after-sex gargling. Finally, he stepped into the shower. Locking the bathroom door, I stepped in beside him.

Stan lathered up, water cascading over his shoulders. I planted a kiss on his mouth. It twitched as if something tickled. I copied his pattern, planting kisses along his neck, his chest, his belly. His hand followed my mouth, scratching away the tingle of a dead woman's lips.

Finally, I squatted. My mouth closed in, hooked on, and confused him. Stan stopped whistling and looked down, must have wondered why his privates were standing up, dancing. But before he could react, I centered my energy, grabbed him behind the knees, and stood, yanking them high.

Stan fell backward. His skull made a sharp cracking sound as it slammed the rim of the tub. His eyes remained open as water streamed into them. His jaw hung limp.

Stan was dead.

I'd done it! I'd taken my revenge. I felt delirious. Giddy. I laughed out loud. I chortled and hooted. "Yahoo! Not bad for a dead woman, eh, Stan?"

I got out of the tub and danced a triumphant jig. I sang "Zip-a-Dee-Doo-Dah", celebrating my revenge as steam coated the mirrors and mist filled the air. Finally, I turned back to the shower, gloating and breathless.

Stan lay sprawled in the tub, water still pouring into his open eyes. "Claire!" He sucked air through his teeth as he tried to sit up.

Oh dear.

Stan lifted his head, peeling away from his body, looking back at himself, gaping at his corpse.

I stood motionless, dumb.

"Stannie?" The bride jiggled the doorknob. "Honeycake, room service is here."

Her voice jarred me to action. I unlocked the bathroom door, and as she swung it open, I bolted. Stan propelled himself out of the tub, roaring, coming after me.

"Claire! Come back here!"

I sped past the bride, dodged the busboy and his cart, felt Stan's energy grabbing at me as, with the full force of my raging spirit, I charged the open door to the hall, desperate to break free.

I had one leg out the door before the vacuum-like force took hold and sent me flying backward. I soared helplessly across the suite, landed limbs akimbo on an easy chair just a moment before Stan crash-landed on top of me, cursing. For an endless moment, we sat that way, glaring at each other, dazed and unable to move.

But then, in the bathroom, a woman screamed.

Merry Jones is the author of fifteen suspense novels as well as two nonfiction and five humor books. She taught college writing for a dozen years, cohosts the Liars Club Oddcast podcast, and leads a monthly Writers' Coffeehouse. Jones lives in Philadelphia, where, when not writing, she's an avid sculler.

Acknowledgments

A sincere thank you goes out to a group of people without whom this book would just be an idea: our interns! An incredibly big thank you to Claudia Langella (lead intern), Ail Goodwin-Dancy, Becca Koestler, and Grace Tinneny for their tremendous efforts.

We are especially grateful for our readers—Kate Carey, Peter Henry, Brandyce Ingram, Dynas Johnson, Christy Lee, Ben Saff, Dixon Speaker, and Doris Zheku—and for the readers who really went beyond what was asked: Gray Caston, Tatham Dilks, Pietra Dunmore, Ginny Parfitt, Nancy Rasmussen, and Susan Schwartz.

A very warm thank you to Alexandra Marie Morehead and Michael Angelo Smith for their stunning photography.

We must extend a special thanks to our guest editor, Quinn D. Eli. His care, compassion, and attention shines throughout this book. Thank you as well to our editorial assistant, Ana Mitchell, for all of her help, big and small.

We are grateful for all the writers who took a chance on both us and this project by submitting their work. We wish we could have published all of you. Thank you doubly to those whose pieces were selected. Without your trust and generosity, we would have nothing to publish.

Finally, thank you, reader. We hope you enjoyed this literary journey. It took us a year to get here. Thank you for your support. Please learn more about us (and stay in touch) through our website: tohopub.com.

Made in the USA
Middletown, DE
23 May 2021